THE QUADRA STORY

JEANETTE TAYLOR

THE QUADRA STORY

A History of Quadra Island

HARBOUR PUBLISHING

Harbour Publishing Co. Ltd.
P.O. Box 219, Madeira Park, BC, V0N 2H0
www.harbourpublishing.com

Cover: Cape Mudge Lighthouse photo by Bill Sturrock; author photo by Gary Dobbs; Title page: Alfred Joyce and children; photo may be by John Hood and is courtesy Elsie (Joyce) Wargon, Museum at Campbell River (MCR) 9274
Edited by Pamela Robertson
Cover design by Anna Comfort
Printed and bound in Canada

Harbour Publishing acknowledges financial support from the Government of Canada through the Book Publishing Industry Development Program and the Canada Council for the Arts, and from the Province of British Columbia through the BC Arts Council and the Book Publishing Tax Credit.

Library and Archives Canada Cataloguing in Publication (hardcover edition)

Taylor, Jeanette, 1953–
    The Quadra story : a history of Quadra Island / by Jeanette Taylor.

Includes index.
ISBN 978-1-55017-488-5

    1. Quadra Island (B.C.)—History. 2. Quadra Island (B.C.)—Biography.
I. Title.

FC3845.Q26T39 2009   971.1'2   C2009-904036-0

This book is dedicated to my sister Leona Taylor,
who found a treasure trove of stories about the
Discovery Islands in Victoria's Colonist *newspaper.*

Contents

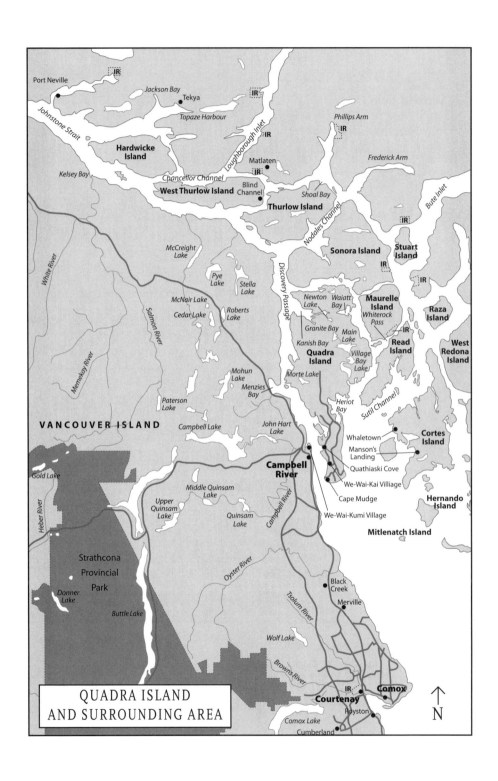

QUADRA ISLAND
AND SURROUNDING AREA

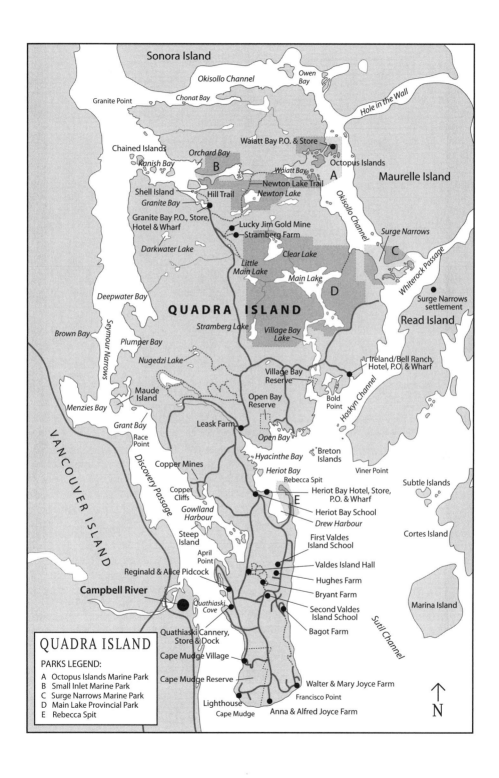

Sonora Island

Okisollo Channel

Owen Bay

Granite Point

Chonat Bay

Hole in the Wall

Chained Islands

Orchard Bay

Waiatt Bay P.O. & Store

Kanish Bay

B

Waiatt Bay

Octopus Islands

A

Maurelle Island

Shell Island

Newton Lake Trail

Hill Trail

Newton Lake

Granite Bay

Granite Bay P.O., Store, Hotel & Wharf

Lucky Jim Gold Mine

Stramberg Farm

Surge Narrows

Okisollo Channel

C

Darkwater Lake

Clear Lake

Little Main Lake

Main Lake

D

Whiterock Passage

Deepwater Bay

Surge Narrows settlement

QUADRA ISLAND

Read Island

Stramberg Lake

Village Bay Lake

Brown Bay

Plumper Bay

Seymour Narrows

Nugedzi Lake

Ireland/Bell Ranch, Hotel, P.O. & Wharf

Village Bay Reserve

Maude Island

Open Bay Reserve

Bold Point

Hoskyn Channel

Menzies Bay

Grant Bay

Leask Farm

Race Point

Open Bay

VANCOUVER ISLAND

Discovery Passage

Copper Mines

Hyacinthe Bay

Breton Islands

Heriot Bay

Viner Point

Subtle Islands

Copper Cliffs

Rebecca Spit

Heriot Bay Hotel, Store, P.O. & Wharf

E

Gowlland Harbour

Heriot Bay School

Drew Harbour

Cortes Island

Steep Island

First Valdes Island School

April Point

Reginald & Alice Pidcock

Valdes Island Hall

Hughes Farm

Campbell River

Bryant Farm

Marina Island

Quathiaski Cove

Second Valdes Island School

Quathiaski Cannery, Store & Dock

Bagot Farm

Sutil Channel

Cape Mudge Village

Cape Mudge Reserve

Walter & Mary Joyce Farm

Lighthouse

Francisco Point

Cape Mudge

Anna & Alfred Joyce Farm

QUADRA ISLAND

PARKS LEGEND:

A Octopus Islands Marine Park
B Small Inlet Marine Park
C Surge Narrows Marine Park
D Main Lake Provincial Park
E Rebecca Spit

N

Introduction

There were only about 1,300 people on Quadra Island when I joined the throng of back-to-the-landers who converged on the island in the 1970s. Billy Assu, the powerful We Wai Kai leader, had died about a decade prior, and his children, along with those of the first non-Native settlers, were in their senior years. Their tales of rapid tides, immense trees, barroom brawls and impossible feats of endurance and fortitude enthralled us city kids. We had been raised with TV, health care plans and convenience food—but we wanted to turn back the clock.

I left a job transcribing taped interviews at the BC Archives in Victoria to move to Quadra Island on a youthful whim. That job led to work at the Museum at Campbell River, where archivist Irene Ross and I shared a cramped office tucked behind the exhibitions. We would shove our paperwork aside at the sound of Bill Hall's laboured breath as he shuffled through the gallery to our office. We recognized the rapid step of Ruth (Pidcock) Barnett too, with family documents or letters from Katie (Walker) Clarke, who grew up on the island in the 1890s. Bill (Quocksister) Roberts, Chief Wamish's grandson, was an occasional visitor, as were Tommy Hall and Harry Assu, both of whom worked for Quathiaski Cannery before World War I. It was a privilege to know these people from a generation now passed.

I've drawn upon their recollections for this book, plus those of many others. I've also used archaeological records, letters, diaries, photographs, newspapers and books to bring Quadra Island's past to life.

As the largest of the Discovery Islands, Quadra has its own book, written as a companion piece to *Tidal Passages: A History of the Discovery Islands*. As in that book, *The Quadra Story* focuses upon the years before World War II, with a fast-paced glance at the decades that followed.

What unfolds is a narrative packed with drama and characters like We Wai Kai chiefs Wamish and Sewis, who lived through the smallpox epidemic of 1862 to face the first wave of Euro-Canadian settlement. In later decades, larger-than-life woodsmen like Moses Cross Ireland and Mike King made the island their home. Their industry spawned communities at Quathiaski Cove, Heriot Bay, Granite Bay and Bold Point, each with its own distinct personality.

Islanders of the 1890s came from around the globe. A night in the bar at the Heriot Bay Hotel in the 1890s rang with every possible accent, from the guffaws of thick-necked Scandinavian loggers to the dulcet tones of a recitation by Lord Bacon or the Celtic lilt of soft-spoken Orkney Islander "Skookum" Tom Leask.

Though Billy Assu's people, the We Wai Kai, were said to be a "vanishing race" by 1900 they survived many harsh tests to become a pivotal force in the island's current economy and culture. Their resident population reached about three hundred by the twenty-first century, and they are joined by about 3,200 non-Natives today. Many of the latter are newcomers, with sometimes divergent views, but all are united by their love for the island's seascape and its engaged community. They're also united by a thirst to know the island's secrets, from the We Wai Kai people's roots as a warrior nation to the old rivalry between Quathiaski Cove and Heriot Bay. This book and its predecessor, Doris Andersen's *Evergreen Islands*, fill that need and will no doubt tease forth many more stories to be enjoyed by future generations.

In addition to the long-time residents already named, I cherish memories of the late Stan and Joan Beech, Eve (Willson) Eade, Peggy Yeatman, Jimmy Templeton, Tommy Hall and Grace (Willson) McPherson. This is their book and they were in my thoughts throughout the writing.

Gerry, Elise and Etienne Côté, my family, provided critiques and enthusiasm. Others who read and commented upon the manuscript include We Wai Kai Band chief councillor Ralph Dick, Bill Assu, Don Assu, archaeologist Don Mitchell, James Foort, Bill Nutting, Ruby (Hovell) Wilson, Joy (Walker) Huntley and Museum at Campbell River curator Linda Hogarth. Anthropologist Joy Inglis, co-author of *Assu of Cape Mudge*, critiqued the early chapters, as did Peter Macnair. Both provided valued insights. French anthropologist Marie Mauzé, who wrote the definitive text on the Laich-Kwil-Tach people, also read and commented on the early chapters. Lisa Chason's unpublished history of the Leask family was an inspiration, as was Candy-Lea Chickite's genealogy work. Sandra Parrish, with her grace and skill, made it a pleasure to use the Museum at Campbell River Archives. The staff at the Vancouver Island Regional Library and at the BC Archives were always helpful, aided by their comprehensive websites.

The members of my writers' group—Annette Yourk, Jocelyn Reekie, Heather Kellerhals-Stewart, Ian Douglas and Mike Redican—are my writing mentors, along with my long-time friend Sue Donaldson. The Haig-Brown Writers in Residence program in Campbell River, initiated by Trevor and Ruth McMonagle, is a boon to writers of our region. I owe a huge thanks to residency writers Myrna Kostash, Don McKay, Margery Doyle, Brian Brett and David Carpenter.

Howard White and his hard-working staff at Harbour Publishing have captured the essence of BC culture with their many books and deserve our applause. I also thank editor Pam Robertson for her skillful finessing and attention to detail. And finally I give thanks to my sister Leona Taylor for the hundreds of stories she unearthed from the pages of Victoria's *Colonist* newspaper and for her tireless assistance with research at the BC Archives.

CHAPTER ONE

A Man's World

A few stragglers sprint down to the ferry landing from Rudder Road, where they've parked their cars on a steep side hill to avoid the two-dollar fee in the lot below. It's not so much the money that's at stake. It's the principle of the thing. No one wanted the parking lot paved and metered.

In front of me, on this dash for the 8:00 a.m. ferry to Campbell River, is Pat Field. He pushes against the wind, his coat zipped tight to hold off the driving rain. His jeans will be soaked before he hits the ferry ramp but he'll change into his lawyer duds once he gets to his Campbell River office.

Brad Assu, with the closing gate in hand, greets us with an amused grin as we dash onto the boat. He seems oblivious to its drunken roll as the wind pitches the boat against the dock. His people, the Laich-Kwil-Tach, have worked this tricky stretch of water for hundreds of years.

Pat and I take seats among the other adults on the passenger deck, surrounded by a throng of 150 teenagers. It's a noisy run. In all, including those in their cars, there are about 250 people aboard, headed for work and school. The two previous runs this morning were busy too, with labourers, teachers and forest workers off to an early start.

There are school kids jammed together on the benches and others on the floor, amid a jumble of backpacks. Occasional wads of paper and snacks fly past our heads. Otherwise the kids seem a bit subdued this

MLA Claire Trevena discusses ferry rate increases with Randy Mellanby aboard the *Tachek*, 2008. PHOTO COURTESY CLAIRE TREVENA

morning, surely a reaction to the ferry as it shudders with each hit of a broadside wave.

I glance across to the big lifejacket box near the exit. If it gets much worse in mid-passage I'll go sit on it and wonder why I didn't stay home. Just as I'm about to, Captain Esther Allen, a third-generation islander who is no doubt enjoying the challenge of this storm, announces that there's a pod of whales off the starboard. Everyone, no matter their adolescent cool, crowds against the windows. Some of the kids push out onto the outer deck where the wind plasters back their hair. It's a large pod, spread across the passage in little groups of twos and threes. They leap straight out of the crests of huge waves, then glide through the swells that follow. Each time a whale surfaces near the ferry there are collective oohs and ahs. Gone are any thoughts of impending doom.

Captain George Vancouver could not have imagined such a scene—played out just over two hundred years after he sailed through Discovery Passage in 1792—and especially not a woman at the helm of a vessel much larger than his. To start with, in Vancouver's mind this part of the coast was scarcely habitable, with mountains on two skylines and trees crowding down the hillsides to the water's edge. "An awful silence pervaded the gloomy forests," wrote Vancouver during his fortnight's stay near Desolation Sound, "whilst animated nature seemed to have deserted the neighbouring country."

Rainy weather and no place to walk onshore formed part of Vancouver's negative impression, but his gloom was also due to a malady now thought to have been Addison's disease.[1] He suffered extreme bouts of lassitude and irascibility that sometimes kept him from accompanying his survey parties as they explored and charted the coast in the ship's boats. He did, however, keep meticulous journals of both his own and his officers' observations, which formed the basis of his book *Voyage of Discovery to the North Pacific Ocean and Round the World, 1791–1795*.

Vancouver's mission was to explore the coast of the Pacific Northwest in search of the fabled Northwest Passage. The inner coast, between the mainland and what came to be called Vancouver's Island, was of particular interest because it had not yet been fully charted. The British hoped the Strait of Georgia might lead into a passage across the continent, providing a shorter route for silk and spice trade with Asia. He was also commissioned to negotiate a resolution to a dispute with the Spanish over possession of the northwest coast.

In 1792 eighteen-year-old master's mate John Sykes stayed aboard the *Discovery* while the officers went ashore to see a village on the bluffs at Cape Mudge, next to the current Tsa-Kwa-Luten Lodge. Sykes sketched the village of about 350 people from aboard the ship. MCR 18089

Spain sent Cayetano Valdés y Flores and Dionisio Alcalá Galiano on a similar mission in the summer of 1792. The two exploration parties met near what's now Vancouver and agreed to work together, travelling in tandem to Desolation Sound. But when they noted the tides from the north and south met off southern Quadra Island, which told them the land mass to the west was a large island, they split up and the British headed for the larger channels along the shores of Vancouver Island.

It was a clear July day when the thirty-metre (hundred-foot) *Discovery* captained by Vancouver set sail into a westerly breeze to cross the top end of the Strait of Georgia and enter Discovery Passage. The consort ship, the *Chatham*, followed later, after extricating a tangled anchor:

> Numberless whales enjoying the season were playing about the ship in every direction, as were also several seals. The scene now before us was more congenial to our minds, not only from the different aspect of the shores, but from the attention of the friendly Indians, who, as we were crossing the gulf, visited us in several canoes, with young birds, mostly sea fowl, fish and some berries, to barter for our trinkets and other commodities.

It was just after midday when the explorers anchored the *Discovery* off Cape Mudge at the southwestern tip of Quadra Island, within sight of a village on a sandy cliff. Eighteen canoes surrounded Captain Vancouver and several officers as they rowed ashore:

> On landing at the village . . . we were received by a man who appeared to be the chief of the party. He approached us alone, seemingly with a degree of formality, though with the utmost confidence of his own security, whilst the rest of the society, apparently numerous, were arranged and seated in the most peaceable manner before their houses. I made him such presents as seemed not only to please him excessively, but to confirm him in the good opinion with which he was prepossessed; and he immediately conducted us up to the village by a very

narrow path winding diagonally up the cliff, estimated by us to be about an hundred feet in height. Close to the edge of this precipice stood the village, the houses of which were built after the fashion of Nootka, though smaller, not exceeding ten or twelve feet in height, nearly close together in rows, separated by a narrow passage sufficiently wide only for one person. On the beach, at the foot of the cliff, were about seventy canoes of small dimensions, though amongst them were some that would carry at least fifteen persons with great convenience.

Archibald Menzies, a botanist and physician on Vancouver's expedition, was commissioned by Sir Joseph Banks to collect plants for the Royal Botanical Gardens and gather ethnographic data. Menzies wrote about the Cape Mudge people in some detail.[2] They were slender-bodied and of middling height. The women were "decently" covered with wool or cedar bark garments but many of the men "went entirely naked without giving the least offence to the other Sex or shewing any apparent shame at their situation," wrote Menzies. Some people were adorned with copper and shell ornaments pierced through their ears and the septa of their noses. Others had their hair puffed over with eagle down and their faces painted with red ochre and black glimmer "that helped not a little to heighten their ferocious appearance."

Physician and botanist Archibald Menzies was with Captain George Vancouver's expedition, which charted the Quadra Island area in 1792. Menzies was commissioned to collect plants and ethnographic data for the Royal Botanical Society of London. Menzies and Vancouver were sometimes at odds as Menzies's large glass terrarium on the deck of the *Discovery* took up valuable space and required a servant to tend it. BC ARCHIVES A-01509

Menzies counted about twelve houses at Cape Mudge, all made from large planks and decorated with painted designs. Some were big enough to accommodate several families. From his count of canoes on the beach Menzies guessed the village comprised about 350 inhabitants.

The British ended their visit with an evening stroll along the flat benchland to the north of the village. They passed several grave houses built from two-metre (seven-foot) planks. "A few of the Indians attended us in our walk," wrote Vancouver, "picking the berries from the trees as we passed, and with much civility presenting them to us on green leaves."

At 3:00 a.m. the next morning the *Discovery* and the *Chatham* set sail again to take advantage of an ebb tide and the continuing westerly breeze. Their next anchorage was at Menzies Bay, where they planned to rendezvous with men Vancouver had sent ahead in the ships' boats to explore areas to the north. From this vantage point Vancouver watched the tide race through Seymour Narrows. "The tide . . . rushes with such immense impetuosity as to produce the appearance of falls considerably high," wrote Vancouver.

Archibald Menzies passed his time at the bay that Vancouver named after him with a shore walk at Nymph Cove. "We visited two Huts in a small Cove," wrote Menzies, "close to our landing place, containing several Families to the Amount of about thirty people." Menzies asked the people to count their numerals and found they spoke the same language as the people to the south along the Strait of Georgia.

Later, when the British reached Johnstone Strait, well above Seymour Narrows, Menzies noted the people spoke an entirely different language and Vancouver said they were "more variously painted than any of the natives our gentlemen had before seen. In these respects they evidently approached nearer to the character of the people of Nootka, than of any other we had yet seen . . ." While Vancouver was sure his men were the first Europeans the Salish met, these people to the north were well armed with muskets and spoke "smatterings" of English.

Based upon these accounts, anthropologists suggest that in 1792 the northern boundary of Salish territory ran from above Kelsey Bay in Johnstone Strait and across to Port Neville on the mainland, where

Salish place names are still known. There were at least two distinct Salish groups: the Island Comox controlled Discovery Passage and north to Kelsey Bay, while the Mainland Comox had villages from the Sunshine Coast to Bute Inlet. To the north of them were the Laich-Kwil-Tach (Lekwiltok), whose language and customs were akin to the Kwakwaka'wakw (Kwakiutl) of northern Vancouver Island, the Broughton Archipelago and adjacent mainland inlets.

While the charts Vancouver created on his voyage were remarkably accurate and remained in use for decades, he missed the narrow channels that separate Quadra, Sonora, Maurelle and Read Islands. As a result he named what he thought was one large island Valdes, in honour of the Spanish captain who also explored the coast in the summer of 1792. (It was not until the 1860s that Read Island was found to be separate, and yet another decade before British surveyors identified the other three islands as distinct.)

Though the British only mentioned one village on Quadra the many archaeological sites on the island provide evidence of widespread

An ancient village site in Kanish Bay, near the north entrance to Small Inlet, with its three-metre (ten-foot) bank of shell midden is one of the largest archaeological sites in the region. PHOTO BY JEANETTE TAYLOR

occupation. The depths of the middens (refuse piles) in places like Heriot Bay and Waiatt Bay indicate they were winter villages in use for thousands of years. A site in Kanish Bay, at the northwestern entrance to Small Inlet, has a midden well over three metres (ten feet) deep.

Information about the island's distant past is limited as there has only been one comprehensive archaeological dig on Quadra, plus the chance find of a partial skeleton at Cape Mudge Village. The skeletal remains, found when a waterline was installed in 1986, were of an adult male and were carbon dated at two thousand years old.[3]

The 1966 excavation at Rebecca Spit, by Donald Mitchell, was on a rise at the first treeless opening and gave a keyhole view into the lives of people in the seventeenth century,[4] when the spot was last used. It was a place of refuge during times of war, with three or four small houses protected by a trench 1.3 metres (4 feet) deep and a partial palisade.

The dig provided clues about the people's diet. Rockfish predominated, but they ate salmon and dogfish too, along with mammals such as deer, harbour seal and raccoon. And among the stone tools excavated were spear points, ground slate knives and mortars. There were also wedges, harpoon valves and awls made from bone and antler, and a large clamshell bowl that still contained red ochre—powdered earth that was combined with oily substances like salmon roe to create paint.

The people who made these tools lived within an economy and social structure that dated back eight thousand years or more.[5] Every aspect of their lives reflected a deep understanding of the plants, animals and cycles of the coast. At the first hint of spring, when the long whistle of the varied thrush echoed in the forest, the large groups that congregated for winter divided into extended family groups. They fished for herring on northern Quadra Island and tended clam beds at Waiatt Bay. In mid-spring, when the sap flowed in the trees, they collected cedar bark and marked blue camas beds on Mitlenatch Island to dig in the fall. They harpooned seals off the Breton Islands and in late summer they prepared their fish weirs and traps on the streams at Quathiaski Cove, Hyacinthe Bay, Village Bay and Granite Bay. At Village Bay, with its chain of lakes, they harvested cedar trees to make canoes that were later floated down a creek to the ocean.[6]

In the late fall, with the harvest complete, canoes were rafted together with house planks between them to transport smoked salmon, dried berry and seaweed cakes, roots and clams to winter villages. Winter was the time to mark deaths or other life events.

"No one could raise a house or grave post," wrote anthropologist Homer Barnett in 1955, "or be married, or name his child, and expect the matter to be taken seriously if he did not 'call the people' as witnesses." Guests were invited from outside the extended family to what was called a potlatch in the Chinook trade jargon, to

Many Salish groups trace their history to the arrival of a magic ancestor at a specific locale. Andy Everson of the Comox Band, an artist who holds an MA in anthropology, suggests this petroglyph below Tsa-Kwa-Luten Lodge may depict a xwa'yxway. In the 1930s an Island Comox elder told anthropologist Homer Barnett that the xwa'yxway dropped down near Cape Mudge and the rights to the ritual spread from there. The ritual includes a dance mask with protruding eyes, an extended tongue and a fringe of feathers around the face. PHOTO BY JEANETTE TAYLOR

acknowledge the family's claims. And each guest received gifts of property and food, paid for through a complex financial system tied to the potlatch.[7]

Homer Barnett, who interviewed Native people in this region in the 1930s, was impressed by the number of rituals the Salish people attached to life cycles.[8] When a young man's voice began to change he lived on his own in the forest for "as long as he could bear," wrote Barnett. It was also a time to seek the aid of a spirit helper, supernatural being or animals that could bestow enhanced skills. These experiences, sometimes repeated many times, developed courage and self-control.

It was considered easier to access the spirit world at puberty than later in life. After a young person became sexually active, wrote Barnett, "he was not clean and the animals could smell him." But even so, he would bathe repeatedly to remove his human scent. He also fasted. "He had to dream of his spirit and receive its assurances a number of times before he knew it was his and before he dared to put faith in it," wrote Barnett. "Every spirit bestowed a song as a token of the help it promised to give. It also conferred the cry of the animal . . . or left a feather or a scale."

Salish girls also undertook ritual preparation for adulthood. With the onset of menstruation they were secluded in a partitioned area on the sleeping platform of the communal house. A girl's power in this state was considerable and could be malignant. "The sight of her drove fish and game away," wrote Barnett. "A drop of her blood would quell the most powerful spirit and drive it out of its owner for good."

Marriages were arranged for young people to bring social and political status to the families involved. The more important and wealthy the participants, the more elaborate the dowry exchange. If the marriage was not successful, the bride could return to her birth family four years later, four being the sequence observed in rituals, from the number of times a dancer circled the big house to the sequencing of events in legends.

It was also important for young people to learn about their lineage and history, dating back to the time of their magic ancestors. Island Comox elder George Mitchell told Barnett that at his family's beginning a young man on a spirit quest stole a ball away from a bear named Komokwe. He took the ball home and found it contained a "copper" (a shield of great value) and many blankets. The young man used his new-found wealth to hold a huge potlatch and his clan adopted the name Komokwe, meaning wealthy ones, from which the name Comox derives.[9]

Drawing upon the memories of his Island Comox mother Et-hol-mat,[10] who was from Salmon River, Mitchell told Barnett there were once ten distinct groups among his mother's people. The five highest ranking of these belonged to the "whale house" and wintered together where Cape Mudge Village is today. At the beginning of the world, said Mitchell, these five groups lived in the whale house and represented five "fires": two at the head, two at the tail and one in the centre.

"Once each year about twenty young men from the five superior groups used to enter a buoyant shell representing a whale," Mitchell told Barnett. "It was controlled by secret tow lines and, as it bobbed up and down in the water of the bay, it was made to spout feathers." The people of this clan also painted a whale in the gable of their house.

The five groups, said Mitchell, had their own seasonal sites. In spring the Sasitla went to Salmon River, at Kelsey Bay. The Yayaqwiltah went to Quathiaski Cove, where there was a stream for the ritual purification of corpses. The SaLaLt shifted to the point at Cape Mudge (likely where Captain Vancouver landed), the KatKaduL went to Rock Bay and the Komokwe went to Menzies Bay. These were the five "highest tribes"—the "real Comox," said Mitchell.

Most of the rich complexity of these people's lives was lost on Captain George Vancouver and his men, but they recognized that the people of the Strait of Georgia were in the throes of profound change. When the British reached the more populated Broughton Islands region, where they were surrounded by canoes and saw several large villages, Vancouver wondered if the Strait of Georgia had somehow been depopulated. He speculated the causes to be seasonal migration, disease or warfare.

While some of the Strait's people would have been away at seasonal fishing and food-gathering camps in July, historical geographer Cole

Harris suggests the major cause for depopulation was a smallpox pandemic that spread from Mexico via Native trade routes a decade prior to Vancouver's exploration.[11] He based this theory on oral history and various written records, including Vancouver's report that his men saw people with smallpox scars in the San Juan Islands.[12] Harris estimated that up to ninety percent of the indigenous population died.

Vancouver's observation that warfare was also an issue for the Salish people of the Strait of Georgia was prophetic. Although it's unlikely war was a major cause for depopulation in 1792, attacks from northern groups would annihilate the Salish of Discovery Passage within a few decades of Vancouver's visit at Cape Mudge. The story of the southward movement of the Laich-Kwil-Tach people from the Thurlow Islands region to Quadra Island is recalled in oral history accounts and early documents. It's a complex tale, loaded with drama and intrigue.

There are over fifty petroglyphs (carvings in stone) on the beach below Tsa-Kwa-Luten Lodge at Cape Mudge. Many of them were created so long ago they're now below the rising high tide line. Some have intriguing abstract images of animals or humans and others are simply circular "peck holes." The meanings behind these petroglyphs are no longer known. PHOTO BY JEANETTE TAYLOR

CHAPTER TWO

The Laich-Kwil-Tach

Vancouver and his men had to tack back and forth across Johnstone Strait to manage the summer winds that funnel down the channel. Beyond the strait, at the Nimpkish River, they anchored off a Kwakwa̱ka'wakw village of over five hundred people. Unlike the Salish to the south, who had no muskets and few manufactured goods, these people were adept bargainers and scorned the trinkets that were acceptable to the Salish. What they wanted were more muskets and shot, but when the British refused them firearms they settled for blue woollen cloth and copper sheeting in exchange for sea otter pelts.

The sea otter trade had become an important part of the Kwakwa̱ka'wakw economy by 1792. These pelts, destined for China, were exchanged for goods that were routed through a trading centre at Nootka Sound on the west coast of Vancouver Island and carried along a foot trail to Nimpkish Lake. Twenty-one American and European ships traded at Nootka in the summer of 1792.[1]

Not all Kwakwa̱ka'wakw groups, however, had sea otters. To the south and east of the Nimpkish River, in the warmer inner-coast waters, there were few otters, if any. To gain access to European trade goods the Laich-Kwil-Tach people, who lived on the southern boundary at the interface with the Salish, intensified their trade in slaves, which they exchanged for muskets, metal and cloth.[2]

The Laich-Kwil-Tach were frequently mentioned by Hudson's Bay

Company traders, who opened a post at Fort Langley on the Fraser River in 1827. They said the Laich-Kwil-Tach lived to the north of Texada Island. Their warriors travelled as far south as Puget Sound, where they captured Salish women and children as slaves to be ransomed back to their families or traded on northern Vancouver Island. The price of a musket, according to anthropologist and photographer Edward Curtis, could be as high as four slaves.[3]

War was their profession, says French anthropologist Marie Mauzé, who wrote her doctoral thesis on the Laich-Kwil-Tach.[4] The fact that other Natives and Europeans almost always referred to the Laich-Kwil-Tach by their group name, though their confederacy included seven tribes who occupied a wide region, suggests an organized and unified front. And they were equipped to travel long distances to fight, paddling by night. One of their signature moves was to send several canoes into the midst of their enemy's force to begin the attack, while the remainder swarmed both flanks.

The Kwantlen people of the Fort Langley area lived in terror of the Laich-Kwil-Tach. "At the very risk of Starving they will not appear in the main river in any Shape when the Yewkaltas are reported to be near, & that is not Seldom," wrote chief trader Archibald McDonald. When McDonald's men worked outside the fort they were on high alert for this "enemy," as there were rumours the Laich-Kwil-Tach planned to destroy the fort. These threats escalated in 1829, when a Laich-Kwil-Tach woman married to a Kwantlen man the HBC men called "The Doctor" was murdered. She was killed by her husband's people when her attempts to negotiate the release of some Kwantlen slaves met with only partial success.

Some months later, on March 21, 1829, 240 Laich-Kwil-Tach paddled into the mouth of the Fraser River in canoes that held up to thirty men apiece. They were repulsed by twelve HBC men who happened to be on the river and who quickly got ashore, from where they fired at the Laich-Kwil-Tach with muskets and blunderbusses. When the Kwantlens learned of this skirmish they were amazed the "invincible Yewklatus" turned back, but in fact the warriors had been repulsed after the loss of a number of men, including a "celebrated chief" who took a "Ball thro' the

Eye." Moreover, the HBC men were not their primary target. About a month later they returned with an even greater force and "butchered the poor Doctor and two Cawaitchins" at the mouth of the Fraser River.[5]

Father Bolduc, an early missionary stationed at Fort Langley, also wrote about the Laich-Kwil-Tach. He was impressed by their nervy courage and found the danger they posed exciting. "They put the fear of God in even the better armed ships. These savages breathe blood and carnage." Another priest called them the "Vikings of the Pacific."[6]

The Salish people of the lower mainland and the Cowichan on Vancouver Island joined forces in about 1830 to send five hundred warriors north into Laich-Kwil-Tach territory to retaliate. Upon their return, the survivors reported that about a hundred of their men were left stranded on an island, where presumably they were killed or starved to death.

The Lekwammen people of Victoria were also targets of slave raids. A Lekwammen boy named Katephset and a few other children were alone in their village in about 1830 when Laich-Kwil-Tach warriors attacked. The adults were away fishing at the time, as Katephset recalled in an 1895 interview for Victoria's *Colonist* newspaper. Katephset didn't run for cover fast enough and was grabbed by a large man covered in war paint. He was taken north, sold several times over and eventually wound up in Alaska. As an old man, Katephset escaped and returned to Victoria, where a few people still remembered him, though he could no longer speak much of his own language.[7]

The Island Comox and Mainland Comox took the brunt of Laich-Kwil-Tach slave raids. The late chief Billy Mitchell of the Klahoose of Toba Inlet and Cortes Island said his grandmother had deep scars on her back, the result of her attempt to keep her son from being carried off.[8] When Hudson's Bay Company trader John McLoughlin visited Bute Inlet in 1839 he reported that "not a single Indian was found, the population having been destroyed to a man by the murderous 'You-cul-taws,' who are deservedly the terror of the surrounding tribes."[9] (Fortunately he was wrong. There were Xwemalhkwu—Homalco—survivors.)

The Laich-Kwil-Tach were expanding their territories southward during these years. Their village at galdəd̕ulis, near the Nimpkish River, appears to have been transitional, but it was there that stories emerged

The Dick and Chickite families trace their descent through Sewis back to their powerful ancestor We-Kai. This family portrait taken in Nanaimo in about 1892 includes, from lower right: John Dick Sr. with his wife Louisa behind him and their sons John Dick Jr. (seated) and Major Dick standing. On the lower left is Jim Chickite. The three women in the rear, from the left, may be John and Jim's sisters, two of whom were Agnes Chickite and Mary Ann Chickite. PHOTO COURTESY JUNE JOHNSTON

of the powerful Laich-Kwil-Tach ancestor We-Kai.[10]

The tale of the theft of We-Kai's copper has been recounted by several different groups. Copper, a symbol of great wealth, was prized in its raw state, so Native people traded for sheets of it from Europeans to form into shields called "coppers," which then served as currency.

Billy Assu, a Laich-Kwil-Tach leader born in the 1860s, told one story of We-Kai's copper[11] to anthropologist Philip Drucker. He said We-Kai married a woman from Gilford Island named qehwuqʔanux. Her father, crippled by a cyst on his back, dreamed that if he stayed up all night he would find a cure. In his vigil the man saw a light on the beach and lay upon it. Not only was he cured, but he found some melted copper in his basket and made it into five coppers. He sent one copper to his son-in-law We-Kai, in a box so heavy it could not be lifted, not even by two men together.

The n̓əm̓ǧis people, who lived up the Nimpkish River from We-Kai's village, heard about this fabulous copper and wanted it. They sent many men to try to lift the box but none could. It was two strangers, with their faces disguised by hair that hung in front of their eyes, who finally lifted the chest and took it away.[12]

Mungo Martin, a n̓əm̓ǧis elder from Fort Rupert on northern Vancouver Island, recounted a slightly different version of this story. He said We-Kai's crippled father-in-law had a recurring vision of something that popped out of the sand at low tide in the early morning. He crawled down to it and dug up what turned out to be a clam covered by a film of copper. He scraped the copper from the clam, covered himself in it and was thereby cured. Then he formed it into a shield that grew every time it was used. The man had such tremendous wealth he gave some coppers in a large chest to his son-in-law We-Kai. As in the other tale, the box was later taken by two men in disguise.

The late Harry Assu of Cape Mudge, in an autobiography written with anthropologist Joy Inglis, said his people fought the ṅəmǧis for this chest of coppers and many people died.[13] "I don't know," said Assu, "but it could be the reason why our We Wai Kai band began moving south from there into the Strait of Georgia."

Mungo Martin, however, had a different story about We-Kai's departure from the Nimpkish River area. He said We-Kai attacked his father-in-law's village in a dispute over a dowry.[14] One young woman survived and as she sat on the beach near the decapitated heads of her relatives, a stranger appeared and told her to stop crying. "I'll give you power," he said. She wiped her tears down into her mouth and when she spat on some gulls on the beach she discovered that her spit could kill. Then she attacked We-Kai's people, but the chief escaped and fled far to the southeast to re-establish his clan at Tekya ("soil") at Topaze Harbour (sometimes referred to as Jackson Bay), on the mainland.[15]

Tekya is the place of cultural origin for two Laich-Kwil-Tach groups, the We Wai Kai (now of Cape Mudge) and We Wai Kum (now of Campbell River). Both are named for their great ancestor.[16] It was there, says a legend of the Walas clan of the We Wai Kum, that the first man, named Yakayālitnuħl, descended. Edward Curtis recorded the story of Yakayālitnuħl, who saw a very large bird covered in soft down "of dazzling whiteness" sitting on a rock near Tekya. He cried out to it, "Whatever you are I claim your special powers." At this the bird threw back the feathers and skin from its head, revealing the head of a man, and spoke: "I am kolus, yet I am a man. My name is Toqātlasaqiāq ['born to be admired']. His face was steaming with heat, because of the thick covering of feathers. Soon the entire coat fell away and he stood forth with the full figure of a man." Yakayālitnuḥl founded the Walas clan, said Curtis, whose members are easily thrown into perspiration.

The late Bill (Quocksister) Roberts of the Campbell River Band said We-Kai had a powerful ally in the Thunderbird. We-Kai was building a big house, said Roberts, but one of the beams was so large he couldn't lift it into place. At this critical point a stranger appeared and offered to help. "I am from above," the stranger told We-Kai. "I will protect you, and cry with you in your sorrows." The stranger left but reappeared in his Thunderbird form to pick up the big log and drop it into place. Thereafter the Thunderbird came to We-Kai many times, to bring fire, to keep dangers away and to tell of the passing of chiefs.[17]

It was at Tekya, in Topaze Harbour, that We-Kai predicted a great flood. This seminal tale has also been recounted in many variations. "A lot of people didn't believe him," said Harry Assu, but We-Kai wove a cedar rope and tied it to canoes that were anchored to a rock atop Mount Tlakustan, behind the village. When the flood waters rose We-Kai's followers got into these canoes and were saved, but one canoe broke loose and drifted north to Kitimat, where the people speak a similar language.[18]

James Martin Smith, a Laich-Kwil-Tach elder born in 1895, also wrote about the flood.[19] In his telling the mountain grew with the rising waters. One of the canoes tied to We-Kai's rope broke and the people drifted north to Smith Inlet. In other accounts, one of We-Kai's canoes went south to the Olympic Peninsula, where the people also speak a similar language.

The We Wai Kai and We Wai Kum forged links with groups near Tekya, both on Vancouver Island and on the mainland. They included the Walitsma and Hahamatsees (Salmon River/Kelsey Bay), the Kweeha (Port Neville and Phillips Arm), the Tlaaluis (Phillips Lake) and the Komenox (Loughborough Inlet). Cultural and territorial shifts were in process for these peoples too, as some are thought to have had Salish origins.[20] According to records compiled by the Hudson's Bay Company, the combined population of the Laich-Kwil-Tach was four to ten thousand people in the mid-nineteenth century.[21]

Edward Curtis said the name Laich-Kwil-Tach came from a

sea worm that cannot be killed. When cut apart, each piece gains new life.[22] Curtis's contemporary, Franz Boas, however, who studied the Kwakwala language, translated it as "people of the fire in the house."

From their base at Tekya the Laich-Kwil-Tach claimed an Island Comox site on the Salmon River sometime before 1829, when Aemelius Smith of the HBC visited. Some years later they took over Whiterock Pass, between Maurelle and Read Islands. The We Wai Kum split off and lived for a time at Waiatt Bay, on northeastern Quadra, and later still a number of Laich-Kwil-Tach groups lived together at Kanish Bay. After decades of both inter-marriage and warfare with Island Comox groups, the end result was an intermixing of cultures, legends and hereditary rights between the Island Comox and Laich-Kwil-Tach peoples.

In May 1840, HBC Chief Factor James Douglas came to Discovery Passage on a trading voyage. He anchored off Cape Mudge, at what he said was Island Comox territory, near their "three most populous towns, one of which was fortified with a stockade." The

According to the *Courier* of February 23, 1949, We-Kai's son Lalakutze created the crests for the family, seen on this totem pole: We-Kai is represented by a supernatural bird at the top of the pole. It descended from the heavens at Topaze Harbour and transformed into a man. The next figure is an orca that came to Lalakutze as he lay sick upon the beach and spat out a spring salmon that cured him. Next is a Huxwhukw, a bird with a powerful beak that Lalakutze saw near his village. Below this is We-Kai holding what descendant Ralph Dick says is a musket. At the bottom is a grizzly bear, which Lalakutze brought to We-Kai to defend the family.[23] PHOTO COURTESY PAT TALBOT, MCR 9157

The Comox reserve c. 1866–1870. Some Laich-Kwil-Tach families fished on the Courtenay River for herring in the spring and for salmon in the fall, though the territory belonged to several Salish groups. They were poised to take over the area in the mid-1860s, according to anthropologist Marie Mauzé, but British navy gunboats drove them off. BC ARCHIVES C-09265

other two were of a temporary nature, with moveable huts.[24] On his return that fall Douglas met several "strong camps of "Neekultaws" along Johnstone Strait, north of Discovery Passage.

The next fall, in October 1841, Douglas was again in the northern part of the Strait of Georgia, where he met a Laich-Kwil-Tach chief in a canoe with his men and slaves near Texada Island. Chief Nick-ayazi,[25] wrote Douglas, was a striking man with a mild expression. He had high cheekbones and his hair was swept back to reveal face paint that covered his forehead down to his eyelids. Nick-ayazi said he was the chief of the strongest of the Laich-Kwil-Tach groups.[26]

Nick-ayazi may have been a relative of a young man named Wamish ("people going to dry fish on a beach by the river"). Wamish, who would have been about fourteen at the time of this meeting with Douglas,[27] later owned a name that sounds similar, Nugedzi, and was also a noteworthy "war chief."[28] Another young Laich-Kwil-Tach man of a similar age to Wamish was Sewis ("noted man"), a direct descendant of We-Kai. Both would become important leaders decades later, when the Laich-Kwil-Tach people faced the most difficult era in their history.

By the mid-1840s the We Wai Kai and We Wai Kum bands had taken control of Discovery Passage.[29] Harry Assu said it was the excellent fishing that attracted his people. Marie Mauzé, however, contends their move was strategically planned to give the Laich-Kwil-Tach control of the trade that moved through Discovery Passage after a Hudson's Bay Company fort opened in Victoria in 1843. Within a few years the HBC built forts in Nanaimo and Fort Rupert as well. The Laich-Kwil-Tach are said to have kept a twenty-four-hour watch at Seymour Narrows in northern Discovery Passage, where they exacted a toll at the main transit point through the Discovery Islands.[30] Groups associated with the Laich-Kwil-Tach called out that they were "cut from We-Kai's rope" to gain safe passage.[31] The Laich-Kwil-Tach also had a village at the mouth of Bute Inlet, near another principal route through the islands at Yuculta Rapids.[32]

There are various recorded accounts of the Laich-Kwil-Tach's move into Discovery Passage. According to an 1892 story in the Comox Valley's *Weekly News*, the Island Comox people were forced to take refuge from the Laich-Kwil-Tach in about 1840 at a fortified site on a sheer rock bluff in Gowlland Harbour, on the west side of Quadra. "After two days stealthy marching through the forest," said the article, "the Ucaltaws attacked them in the rear, slaughtering about ninety, and scattering the remainder, who sought safety in hiding but finally concluded to join the Puntledge tribe [in Comox Harbour]."[33]

Edward Curtis, who interviewed Laich-Kwil-Tach people in the early twentieth century, recorded a story with similar elements.[34] In his telling, the Island Comox were at ǧʷiǧʷakulis,[35] a fortified village on a steep, rocky island "to the north of Quathiaski Cove." The Laich-Kwil-Tach landed at night in a bay near the fort. "During the night it rained," wrote Curtis, "and just before dawn they crept up to the breastwork of logs that protected houses on the two accessible sides." They showed no mercy. The only ones spared were Hekwutun, a man of Laich-Kwil-Tach and Island Comox descent, and a Laich-Kwil-Tach woman who was married to an Island Comox man. (She hid her husband in a food storage basket and he escaped as well.) These few survivors went to Kawitsn, near Maude Island, and then moved south to Comox Harbour to join with the Puntledge.[36]

The We Wai Kai and We Wai Kum lived together for a time at Campbell River and then established their winter village at Cape Mudge, on its current site. A few decades later the We Wai Kum relocated to Campbell River, where they were joined by the Kweeha in the late 1890s.

In spring We Wai Kai families fished the streams on Quadra Island. They also went south in large numbers to Denman Island and the Courtenay and Qualicum Rivers,[37] where they had an uneasy truce based upon marriage ties with the Island Comox.

During these years of territorial expansion, the Laich-Kwil-Tach continued to take slaves far to the south, but around 1840 they suffered a major defeat at the hands of the Cowichan and their allies. The Cowichan had heard about the approach of Laich-Kwil-Tach warriors and set up a decoy to lure them into Maple Bay, near Duncan. When the Laich-Kwil-Tach saw what they thought was a canoe full of women setting off from the beach for the day, they attacked—and were ambushed by a flotilla of Salish warriors. All but a few of the Laich-Kwil-Tach on this mission were killed. The survivors made their way back on foot to Discovery Passage.[38]

Intertribal warfare began to subside in the years that followed, but what finally stopped it was the smallpox epidemic of 1862–64, which took an estimated fifteen thousand Native people's lives in BC. The disease broke out in Victoria, brought there by an infected gold seeker, and it spread like wildfire through the camps of aboriginal people in Victoria for trade and work. With James Douglas, now the colonial governor, away, officials in charge broke up these camps and ordered the sick and dying people to return to their home villages. The editor of Victoria's *Colonist* newspaper railed against this inhumanity in June 1862. "The Native people are proceeding northward, bearing with them the seeds of loathsome disease that will take root and bring [them] a plentiful crop of ruin."

The Laich-Kwil-Tach of Cape Mudge contracted smallpox when

they attacked a group of Haida headed north. "This late powerful and warlike tribe," reported the *Colonist* on July 1, 1862, "are dying from smallpox in the scores." A survivor among the neighbouring Mainland Comox of Toba Inlet said the afflicted dragged themselves to the ocean to quell the awful fever of smallpox, and many died on the beaches. Gone were leaders and specialists both, leaving many Native groups rudderless and in despair. To make matters worse, those who survived had a decreased fertility rate. The impact of this epidemic has reverberated through many generations.

The arrival of Euro-Canadian settlers to this region coincided with the smallpox epidemic. A farm community of disaffected gold miners was established at Comox in 1862. Many of the newcomers feared the Laich-Kwil-Tach, who fished in the Courtenay River area for herring in spring and for salmon in fall. As a result the Laich-Kwil-Tach were driven off by Royal Navy gunboats over the next few years. But they persisted. In October 1865 the We Wai Kai and Hahamatsees people of Salmon River arrived in Courtenay in greater than usual numbers due to flooding on their rivers to the north. The We Wai Kai camped far upriver, beyond the reach of gunboats. Lay missionary Jordayne Cave Brown Cave demanded they leave but the chief of the We Wai Kai, Clalick,[39] refused. He told Cave his people had been driven off before but this time they were prepared to fight. "He then held open his blanket and danced on the beach in a defiant manner," reported Cave. "They said they would not go away till they had been there two months and had got all the salmon they require."

Cave sought gunboat protection and three ships arrived, including one carrying Rear Admiral Joseph Denman, who had thirty guns and a crew of five hundred men aboard the *Sutlej*. Denman was surprised to learn upon arrival that many of the settlers wanted the Native people to stay. Much of their fall crop had been ruined by heavy rains and they needed the help of the Laich-Kwil-Tach to harvest what remained.

"They benefit the settlement by cheapening Indian labor, by selling venison, fish, etc, cheaper . . ." wrote an anonymous correspondent to the *Colonist*. Laich-Kwil-Tach men were paid three buckets of potatoes for a day's labour and the women got two buckets. "Let it be understood that this was the middle of the fishing season, that none of the fish were dry, and removal in such a state would spoil them; that numbers had not fished much, being employed by the settlers in potato digging, etc, and that no crime was laid to their charge." The Laich-Kwil-Tach also contributed to the farm settlement, added the writer, through their purchase of potatoes during their lengthy stay.

"On my arrival," reported Joseph Denman to the colonial governor, "they hastily pulled down their houses and sent them in Canoes with their Women and Slaves down the River on their way to Cape Mudge." Denman arrested Chief Clalick and put him in irons overnight, on a charge of resisting arrest the year prior. When the rest of the chiefs consented to come aboard, Denman told them they had to leave and could not return in future unless they got the colonial governor's permission. Most left then, but a few We Wai Kai families remained, in quiet defiance. The next year they returned as usual, with only a few rumbles of dissent. Their labour was needed for the harvest of a bumper crop.

Marie Mauzé suggests the Laich-Kwil-Tach were poised for a complete takeover of the Courtenay area at this point. And while gunboat threats and a decreased population slowed the process of assimilation, it continued over the decades that followed, through marriage alliances and the territorial privileges those alliances brought.

In addition to providing farm labour, Laich-Kwil-Tach men and women worked in canneries that opened in various locations on the coast. From the 1860s on, some families also went to Nanaimo for trade and to work as stevedores for the coal mines. They established a camp in a gully on Departure Bay Road, about two kilometres (a mile) north of downtown, in the Newcastle townsite,[40] as well as on Newcastle Island.[41] The temptations of the city and removal from their traditional life and lands were ruinous for some. Alcohol abuse was often reported in the *Nanaimo Free Press*, with jail terms or fines handed out. A Laich-Kwil-Tach man named Galiquem, or Johnny Kalakuma, was a repeat offender. Each time he was released his mother distributed calico and other fabric among her people to clear the taint of jail from her son's name.[42]

The Laich-Kwil-Tach came in contact with many introduced

diseases during these years. They had no immunity to mumps, measles, diphtheria, tuberculosis or influenza, which all claimed lives. Syphilis also took a toll. In addition, the racist views of most Euro-Canadians weighed heavily upon the Laich-Kwil-Tach, who had begun to lose control of their lands and economy.

Whereas the combined Laich-Kwil-Tach population numbered in the thousands in the 1840s, by 1872–73 there were just an estimated 1,500 people left.[43] Several bands still maintained their primary villages in the Port Neville–Loughborough Inlet area, at the mouth of Bute Inlet and in Whiterock Pass, but Tekya in Topaze Harbour may have seen only sporadic use by this time. Tekya, however, remained the heartland for the Wei Wai Kai and the We Wai Kum. A Laich-Kwil-Tach man described a near-death experience to Edward Curtis in the early 1900s. He said his soul travelled on a ghost canoe through Seymour Narrows to the land of the dead at his old home at Tekya. "He saw all the familiar places he had known. He had forgotten none," wrote Curtis. There were still many houses at Tekya in his dream, all inhabited by the dead.

CHAPTER THREE

A New Wave of Settlement

In 1864 Robert Brown explored the Comox Valley region on behalf of the colonial government, in search of minerals and settlement land. "Here as everywhere else the Indians are growling about payment for their land," wrote Brown. "When traveling or sitting round the camp fire with them they always appeal to me on that subject & I assure you that it is no easy matter to answer the question satisfactorily when an intelligent [Indian] looks up in your face and asks, 'Had you no good land of your own that you come and deprive us of ours?'"[1] Brown went on to recommend a system of reserves be put in place. He said the Natives should be paid for the rest of the land with a potlatch. Otherwise, warned Brown, "in a few years it will be difficult, they will have got too knowing and trouble will be the consequence."

Brown's recommendation to establish reserves wasn't acted upon for over a decade, but entrepreneurs, swindlers and whisky peddlers spread throughout the region in the meantime. As expert seamen, the Laich-Kwil-Tach were hired to assist with survey work off the mouth of Bute Inlet in the summer of 1872, to locate a route for a railway. Had their advice been sought they could have saved these surveyors, and the nation, a lot of expense. Allowing the Laich-Kwil-Tach a glance at the British charts would have exposed an error, which showed Sonora, Maurelle and Quadra Islands as one island named Valdes. (Read Island had been shown as part of Valdes Island in Vancouver's chart but was found to be separate in a survey in the 1860s.)

Ten routes were proposed for this second transcontinental railway, with Bute Inlet and the Fraser River/Burrard Inlet as the favoured options. Trains were to travel along Bute Inlet, cross over bridges to Valdes Island and Vancouver Island, and continue on to Victoria. The men who surveyed the Homathko River and Bute Inlet were appalled by the extreme difficulty of the terrain, but the Fraser wasn't much better. It was only when more accurate surveys revealed that Valdes was in fact three islands that the Fraser River route won out—and the city of Vancouver was born.

Marine charts were adjusted after surveyor Joseph Hunter released the news of his "fatal" discovery, but the new names—Quadra, Maurelle and Sonora—weren't assigned until 1903. In the intervening years the three islands were simply called Big, Middle and Small Valdes.[2] The narrow passage that separates them became the "unsurveyed channel," leaving its Native name Okisollo ("passage") Channel to fall into common usage, as did the names Chonat Bay ("place that has coho"), Waiatt Bay ("place that has herring") and Kanish Bay (describing its pinched-in-waist shape). A few other local names retained include Quathiaski Cove (for its shape, with an island in the centre),[3] Shellalligan Pass (an Island Comox name for the double-headed sea serpent),[4] and Tsa-Kwa-Luten ("playing place" or "cool spring"). The name Nugedzi Lake[5] was assigned in recent years in honour of Billy Assu, who inherited the name from Wamish.

Wamish may have stepped into his position as one of the head chiefs of the We Wai Kai in the 1870s. He's remembered as the one who brokered peace when he invited many of the Salish tribes from the south to a great potlatch. The Salish were reluctant to attend, fearing a trick, but they came and peace followed. He maintained these ties with frequent trips into Salish territory, accompanied by his daughter Mary. As a consequence, Wamish's gravestone epitaph proclaims him as a "peacemaker among all the neighboring tribes."[6]

Wamish would surely have been among the guests at a potlatch on the Courtenay River in 1876 that was described in detail by Dr. W. Wymond Walkem of Nanaimo. Walkem interpreted the ceremony as the initiation of a We Wai Kai shaman named Chiceete (Chickite in current spelling).[7] The man, known to non-Natives as "Grey-Haired Johnny," was born in about 1846. To prepare for the ceremony, Chiceete fasted in the forest alone for some time, returning in a wild and famished state.

Walkem entered the big house on a seesaw-like plank that doubled as the lower beak of the giant eagle that formed the entrance. Native men in the centre of the house drummed and sang until 8:00 p.m., when all fell silent. "Then a noise with much howling was suddenly heard proceeding from the roof," wrote Walkem. "In a few moments a human body was pushed through the square hole in the roof." Chiceete was suspended by four hooks sewn through the muscles of his upper arms and thighs. His naked body, covered only by a cedar bark loincloth, was lowered three times to the ground. Each time he descended and rose Chiceete shouted out words that were answered by men who stood on the floor of the big house. "No sign on Johnny's face told of the horrible torture he must have been enduring," wrote Walkem.[8]

The final time Chiceete was lowered to the floor he remained there, restrained by the ropes tied to the roof until four large men took hold of him and cut his bonds. When ten other men trooped in, naked to the waist, Johnny gnashed his teeth and forced his way over to them. He lunged at each in turn and bit chunks from their arms. It was a privilege to receive this bite, said Walkem, and each was paid a ten-dollar gold coin. After this Johnny was taken away to have his wounds dressed and salmonberry wine was served, followed by masked dances.

The next day, wrote Walkem, Chiceete hosted a grand potlatch and gave away bales of blankets, tobacco, boxes of crackers, barrels of molasses, boxes of apples, flour and handkerchiefs, to a total value of one thousand dollars. He also burned a large war canoe worth $175 in a show of wealth.[9]

A year after this potlatch, on October 7, 1879, Indian Agent George Blenkinsop compiled a census of the "Kwawkewlth" Indian Agency for the newly formed Indian Reserve Commission. Blenkinsop listed "Tlah-leet-ul," a married man with three female children, as the head chief of the We Wai Kai. (This may have been Chief Clalick, who was taken prisoner by the British navy at Comox in 1865.) Next on the list was "See-wis," who had a wife and two children, followed by "Mack-a-moose," a single adult male. "Tsah-kayt," an adult male with a wife and no children, was at the end of the list, for a total population of 132.

The Indian Reserve Commission made an initial recommendation in 1879 of land to set aside for each band, but creating the reserves was a slow process that didn't wrap up until 1888, when boundaries were set. The government's allocations often ignored requests by Native leaders. Although Tekya held enormous cultural significance, for instance, the We Wai Kai were refused their request for eight hectares (twenty acres) on either side of a stream in Reid Bay and the mountain that backed it. Four tracts were allocated to them on Quadra Island, along with their hunting ground on the Quinsam River, a tributary of the Campbell River.

Also lost to the We Wai Kai were important fishing, hunting and ceremonial sites they had requested, including Hyacinthe Bay,

The Anderson family of Quathiaski Cove and friends pose around welcome figures at Cape Mudge that belonged to the Dick family. The Andersons may have been guests at a potlatch as two of the figures are draped in button blankets. Guests were welcomed through the pursed lips of these poles. The left figure has a "copper" on its chest, a symbol of wealth. Joy Inglis, in the book *Assu of Cape Mudge*, says the copper shields turned on their sides at the top of the poles announce the number of blankets given away at the potlatch. PHOTO COURTESY MARGARET YORKE, MCR 19540

Quathiaski Cove and Gowlland Harbour. From this point on the Native people had to restructure their lifestyle, from one determined by the movement of fish and game travelling long distances across the region, to reserves that represented a fraction of their traditional territory. Setting fixed reserves also caused confusion between the We Wai Kai and the We Wai Kum, both of whom fished on the Campbell River and felt they had a right to land there. An ambiguity in reserve commission paperwork exacerbated their conflicting claims, which had to be settled in court over a century later.[10]

George Blenkinsop returned to Cape Mudge in 1881 to again take the census, this time as part of a national survey. About sixteen big houses[12] lined the beach where a park and swimming pool are today. As was the custom, extended families of up to twenty people lived together in these massive post-and-beam houses.

Sewis and his wife Klah-le-kai-ook had four youngsters in their household. Though the census didn't specify familial relationships, Nun-se, an unmarried man of twenty-five, may have been their eldest son.[11] His name is followed by fifteen-year-old Yah-ko-glass and then two girls—fifteen-year-old Mack-moo-it-sim and Kwin-Kwin-ta-lick.

At the time of the 1881 census, Wamish and his wife Ka-noose-nack had eighteen people in their big house. Two youths, Ya-kowek and O-kwe-la, may have been two of their three children, later known as Nagahu (Frank), Mary and Tom.[13] As befits an important chief, Wamish had a food-gathering station in gʷiǧʷakulis (Gowlland Harbour). He also owned an important ritual attached to gʷiǧʷakulis ("whale between the two") that sounds similar to one described by Island Comox elder George Mitchell.[14] Once each year Wamish's family sent young men into the harbour in a buoyant wooden whale. They rolled stones from end to end inside the whale, to give it the appearance of diving. As the assembled potlatch guests watched, the whale bobbed up and down and sprayed feathers through a blowhole. One year, as the late Harry Assu recounted, four young men were killed as they enacted this ritual. Sabotage was suspected because the line that held the whale to shore was cut and the whale sank.

Wamish's nephew Billy Assu recalled the arrival of the first four

Euro-Canadians on Quadra Island in the early 1880s. His people took the men in and fed them, but their hospitality in no way implied a willingness to hand over their resources. When other white people followed to log, the We Wai Kai realized the full intent of their plans and falsified the loggers' timber marks. "There is a jealous feeling among the Euclataws," reported a timber cruiser in the *Colonist* in 1883, "against the possession by men of land on the Island. They are pulling up the surveyor's stakes, falsifying the blazes and destroying the witness trees."

The loggers proved impossible to stop. The We Wai Kai are a resilient people, as history proves, but by the early 1880s Indian Agent Reginald Pidcock said their

Mary (Wamish) Roberts (1868–1952), left, Mrs. Johnson and an unidentified woman. Mary recalled in her senior years that she travelled with her father, Chief Wamish, when he brokered peace with the Salish bands to the south. She married into a chiefly family on the Campbell River Reserve. PHOTO COURTESY DICK FAMILY, MCR 4425

numbers were so greatly reduced "their former warlike spirit has almost entirely disappeared." While there had once been up to seven distinct groups among the Laich-Kwil-Tach, only the We Wai Kai, We Wai Kum, Kweeha and Walitsma remained. Their combined population was 374 people. The Komenox, Tlaaluis and Hahamatsees had vanished. This sharp population decline was to continue over the coming decades, when the Walitsma combined with other groups.

The We Wai Kai people had the highest remaining population among the Laich-Kwil-Tach at the time of the 1881 census, with 133 people. Only a few of the married couples of child-bearing age had more than two children and the large age gaps between children suggest a high childhood mortality rate. There was just one family with children in a healthy age range from three to eight. Nor were there many elderly people, the oldest being a sixty-one-year-old widower. "Tsuk-hait" (Chickite) and his wife Lass-toal-sel-lass were first on the 1881 census of the We Wai Kai. It may have been this same man, with his name spelled "Chiquite" in a *Colonist* article in 1882, who was arrested after the wreck of the *Grappler* near Seymour Narrows. The shipwreck was the worst known of the Quadra Island area, with the loss of about sixty-seven lives. An officer who investigated the wreck arrested Chiquite at Comox because he had sold whisky he salvaged from the *Grappler* to other Native people. Chiquite served six months in a Victoria prison for his crime. Near the site of this same shipwreck a Laich-Kwil-Tach man found one thousand dollars in the pocket of a drowned Chinese foreman and became an important chief with the potlatch he held.[15]

Potlatches remained the pivotal factor in the social and economic structure of the Native people's lives, yet the ceremony was banned by the federal government in 1884. The decision was influenced by religious groups who felt Native people would not accept Christianity as long as the potlatch remained in force. They also reviled rituals they interpreted as cannibalistic and the apparent squandering of wealth in

The We Wai Kai village at Cape Mudge in 1885 with the schooner *Carolina* in the foreground. PHOTO BY SURVEYOR AND GEOLOGIST G.M. DAWSON, MCR 16982

lavish gifts. The new law proved impossible to enforce for the first few decades, however, because the courts didn't know how to define the ceremony.

In 1886 Chickite presented a dance at Cape Mudge inspired by a play he saw in San Francisco when he was shanghaied to work on a sailing ship. Mike Manson was a guest at the potlatch and wrote about it in his memoirs. "The plot of the play," said Manson, "was that they were all ducks and they had found a good feeding ground." Many young men, with long bills and wings attached to their shoulders, circled the big house as they gathered a large flock to spread the news about a place with plentiful feed. At the end of their dance the ducks' tin bills were knocked off and they were dusted with white flour from small cheesecloth bags, to transform them into white men. "The Indians almost lifted the roof from the house in their glee," wrote Manson, about this parody of white people's hunger for land and resources. Ralph Dick, the current elected chief of the We Wai Kai who claims descent from We-Kai, says his elders taught him to find humour in adversity—which explains the laughter in the big house over the loss of their lands.

Chickite's parody of the fast pace of non-Native settlement was astute. By 1884 about fourteen Quadra Island properties, encompassing 1,305 hectares (3,263 acres), were registered with the Lands Branch as homesteads and timber leases.

The first logging camps on the island were in Gowlland and Drew Harbours. Thomas Earle, a Victoria entrepreneur, bought 65 hectares (160 acres) on the west side of Drew Harbour in 1882. James Miller bought the adjoining 36 hectares (90 acres) to the north in 1883 and W.P. Sayward's crew shipped 37,000 metres (400,000 feet) of logs from Drew Harbour to his Victoria sawmill in June of the next year.[16] Three years later Sayward, for whom the community to the north of Campbell River was named, bought 22 hectares (54 acres) of what's now Rebecca Spit Park.[17] (The We Wai Kai people contend this land was promised to them as part of the Drew Harbour Reserve, allocated in 1879, but taken back to use for Royal Navy gunnery practice and manoeuvres.)[18]

A legendary timber cruiser named Moses Cross Ireland worked for W.P. Sayward and others in the 1880s, assessing the value of standing timber. Ireland's most successful partnership was with young R.D. Merrill of Michigan, who invested in huge tracts on Ireland's advice. (Merrill's descendants still own some of this land in Waiatt Bay and Small Inlet, where they logged for a third time in 1999.) "I have seen timber increase from $1 an acre to $100 an acre," Ireland told a *Colonist* reporter in 1905. "I have seen vast fortunes made by men who bought my timber for a song. They are reputed millionaires, and I am still cruising timber."

Ireland was well into middle age when he moved to the Discovery Islands. He'd logged as a young man on river drives in the state of Maine, then joined the California Gold Rush, and later the Cariboo Gold Rush in BC in 1861. With his earnings Ireland started one of the first sawmills in BC with his countryman Sewell Moody. Their initial shipments from "Moodyville," in Burrard Inlet, were a bust so Ireland dropped out of the partnership and ran freight on the Skeena River until 1880, when he came to the Discovery Islands to log.

Judging by the accounts of Ireland's adventures reported in BC newspapers throughout his life, he was a brave man and an exceptional raconteur. His bold rescues of lost and starving groups in the Cariboo and on the Skeena River prove him to have been a man with dogged stamina and an innate bush sense.

Another man among the first to purchase land on Quadra Island was Reginald Heber Pidcock. Like Ireland, he came to BC for the Cariboo Gold Rush, but there the similarity ends. Pidcock was raised as a middle-class English gentleman, a devout clergyman's son. He and some friends travelled a lesser-used route to the gold fields, via Bentinck Arm. After an eleven-day paddle up a glacier-fed river, they continued by land for many days, with forty-kilogram (eighty-pound) packs. They were so discouraged by the time they reached Alexandria, on the main route into the gold fields, they gave up and returned to Victoria. With the summer before them, they bought a canoe and rifles and set off to explore the east coast of Vancouver Island in search of homestead land. Pidcock's memoir of that summer paints a picture of a young Englishman's hunting and fishing paradise.[19]

At the Courtenay River, Pidcock and his friend got land grants, but Pidcock soon gave up on farming to open a sawmill. Its success allowed him to marry the sister of a fellow settler in 1873. Alice Guillod, who had joined her brother in the Comox Valley, was the daughter of a professional London artist. She captured Reginald's heart with her operatic singing in the settlement's little church. As Pidcock's business expanded he looked for new sources of timber, which is likely what led him to purchase several large properties in Quathiaski Cove in 1882, totalling 128 hectares (317 acres). The land was heavily timbered and had steep slopes that would allow logs to be sent by a chute into the sheltered cove.

Pidcock's plans for Quathiaski Cove, however, took a back seat to other developments in the mid-1880s, when he and a friend began to lay out the townsite of Courtenay on Pidcock's land. But Pidcock had to drop out of the partnership when he overextended his finances with a shipping venture. He lost everything except one of his properties in Quathiaski Cove. (Fortunately Alice retained some of their land in Courtenay in her name, which helped re-establish the family a few decades later.)

With seven children and a wife to support, Reginald Pidcock took a job as the Indian agent for the Kwakwa̱ka'wakw people in 1886.[20] From their home in the old Hudson's Bay Company buildings at Fort Rupert and later from a house the agency erected in Alert Bay, Reginald toured Kwakwa̱ka'wakw villages by dugout canoe,[21] a distance of over 1,600 kilometres (1,000 miles). He travelled from Smith Inlet to Cape Mudge and around the northern tip of Vancouver Island, with his older sons and Native men serving as navigators and paddlers.

While in the southern part of

Alice Guillod sent this picture of herself and Reginald Pidcock home with the inscription: "I write this so you may know who it is, otherwise I am sure you would not, it being as much like my angel as the man in the moon..." PHOTO COURTESY RUTH (PIDCOCK) BARNETT, MCR 19383

the agency, Pidcock and his boys camped on their property on Quadra. "Arrived at Quathiaski, my usual camping place at about 10:30," he wrote in his journal for August 1888. "Here I found Mr. Kay spending his summer in hunting and fishing. He gave us a salmon and was glad to see us." Though his headquarters were at Alert Bay by then, Pidcock may have contemplated a move to Quathiaski Cove because he noted in his journal that he walked his property lines and was disappointed to find none of it was suited for agriculture.

Reginald Pidcock's eldest son Willie was a young adult by the late 1880s and the four other boys were not far behind. As he said in a letter to the Department of Indian Affairs, Pidcock had to make plans for his children's future. His idea, as later events show, may have been to build a sawmill and cannery in Quathiaski Cove.[22]

Added to these prospects, Quadra Island was on the brink of development and settlement. There were a number of logging camps at work and Charles W. Dallas, the island's first non-Native settler, arrived in about 1885.[23] He raised cattle and hogs on a ranch somewhere in the vicinity of Heriot Bay, which was called Dallasville in his honour.[24] Though the exact location of Dallas's ranch isn't known, as he lived as a squatter for about a decade, it likely encompassed the current Heriot Bay Inn site, which he registered as a land grant in 1894.

Glowing accounts by provincial government land agent D.H. McNeil reported in the *Colonist* in 1885 may be what attracted Charlie Dallas to the island. McNeil said the place had many fine swamps, marshes and alder patches ready to drain for the plow. "There is sufficient land known to locate about fifteen families," wrote McNeil. "There is a cranberry marsh on the island and also several places where this popular fruit can be successfully cultivated. There is a stretch of prairie of about 100 acres without a stick of timber on it, covered with a luxuriant growth of grass. There are also other patches of similar land of smaller extent."

McNeil's survey of the Discovery Islands was part of a push by the government to open up farmland all over the province. They offered preemptions of up to 65 hectares (160 acres) at one dollar per 0.4 hectare (1 acre), plus two dollars per 0.4 hectare (1 acre) in improvements such as ditching, fencing and structures. In Canada, the European dream of large farms, the privilege of the gentry, was available to any male British citizen (or anyone eligible to become one). These grants, however, were not available to Native people or to women, unless they were widowed.

Men and women from Britain, Scandinavia, eastern Canada and the US responded to this government propaganda about cheap land and limitless opportunities on the BC coast. This and the arrival of the first transcontinental railway train in May 1887 at Port Moody, near Vancouver brought a flood of newcomers. "The sober and industrious settler need have no fear of want," promised the BC directory for that year. "While elsewhere sad plaints of death and starvation are heard—here the bountiful products of nature waste through want of occupation."

In 1887 a group of disaffected coal miners left Nanaimo after a horrific explosion that killed 148 men. Tom Bell, "Black Jack" Bryant, John Dauton Dixon and Jack Smith[25] were haunted by the memory of hauling corpses from the burnt and twisted wreckage of the mine. Their decision to leave was well-founded—and well-timed. Within months, in January 1888, yet another explosion took seventy-seven lives.

The miners pre-empted land along the perimeter of a vast swamp that runs down the centre of southern Quadra Island. Few had much experience with farms. Black Jack Bryant, for one, came from a long line of coal miners. To leave his profession for an uncertain future in an unsettled place took nerve and determination. But that could be said of all the settlers who followed. Their new life wasn't easy, but it offered limitless personal freedom, adventure and opportunity—or so it seemed at the time.

CHAPTER FOUR

The Rancher Takes a Wife

Loneliness plagued most of the bachelors who settled on the Discovery Islands in the 1890s. They were determined to transform forest land into thriving ranches, though life in the wilderness offered minimal prospects for marriage and families. It wasn't so bad in spring and summer, when they worked in logging camps to earn a grubstake to see them through months of land clearing, but winters were interminable. "Snowed a bit in night," Campbell River settler Fred Nunns wrote in his diary of December 1890. "Got out a few [fence] rails, drizzling rain in afternoon. Feeling very lonely, tired of reading."

Tom Bell of Gowlland Harbour may have been the anonymous writer of a Quadra Island column in the *Weekly News-Advertiser* of Vancouver. In April 1896 he decried the shiftless state of the island's ranchers, forced to work away from home:

> When spring arrives he puts his shack in shape, with a flour-sack inside against the window, to hide the interior from the gaze of the inquisitives; and hies him away, with his blankets on his back, in search of work . . . He must work to support his ranch; he knows not yet how to make his ranch support him . . . In other cases it is lonesomeness; he is tired of batching alone all the Winter and it is ever the same, year after year. He goes out in the Spring and returns in the Fall again, with the geese, with

perhaps enough to support him through the Winter. Perhaps if they had helpmates they could be induced to stay on their claims and cultivate them. It would perhaps be a good thing if the Government could see some method of arranging a way whereby we could have an influx of those Nova Scotia women there is so much writing about . . . Anyway, the country will never be much agriculturally until there are some women on the farms.

Though Bell advocated family life he did not marry for another thirty years. Some of his contemporaries formed fleeting relationships with Native women, and a few, like Jack Bryant, scraped together enough money to return to the "old coun-try" to marry.

Jack Bryant had lived in the US and Canada for twenty years when he returned to Somerset, England, in 1889, where he married his gregarious young cousin Mary Shepperd. At the age of twenty-seven, she was seventeen years his junior, but Jack's proposal presented a good opportunity for marriage in a country where many young men had emigrated to the colonies. Mary is said to have worked in a factory before getting married, one of a few employment options for English women at that time.

Jack no doubt described the beauties, opportunities and hardships Mary would face in a log cabin in the wilderness. But from the relative comfort of her English

Mary Bryant, seen here with her husband Jack, was the first non-Native woman to make Quadra Island her home. She was pregnant with her first child when she arrived in July 1889 and due to deliver in what old-timers called the Big Winter, with a record snowfall that lasted from December 1889 to April 1890. PHOTO COURTESY HELEN (JOYCE) ANDREWS, MCR 7514

existence it would have been impossible for her to imagine the true nature of her new life.

The newlyweds arrived on Quadra Island in July 1889. From Quathiaski Cove, where Mike King and Lewis Casey had a logging camp, they hiked up a steep forest trail the loggers had cut to Jack's homestead. His cabin sat upon a slight rise that overlooked a marsh filled with birdsong and hardhack topped with fuzzy pink blooms and surrounded by massive trees. Jack's plan was to drain the marsh and clear it for use as pasture. Deer came to feed at the marsh and so did a large pack of wolves.

With only a few months left in the logging season, Jack worked away from home as a bull puncher (ox driver) in a logging camp, to save for winter. Later in life, Mary laughed over her many fears, from the wolves to tales of the Laich-Kwil-Tach people's warrior past. When they came to trade baskets for her linens or peered in at Mary's cabin window, she was terrified and barricaded the cabin door with a log. (Another early settler, Emma Yeatman, was haunted by nightmares of the Native people at her windows for the rest of her life.)

Mary longed for news from home, so soon after arrival she walked to Quathiaski Cove in search of mail. Passing steamers dropped the mail

Mary Bryant on her farm at what's now a popular hiking trail east of the community centre. In her senior years she was crippled by arthritis and confined to her home but Mary retained her sunny disposition. PHOTO COURTESY ELSIE (JOYCE) WARGO, MCR 6825

at King and Casey's camp, on a rocky knoll in the southern corner of the Cove. As Mary neared the camp commissary, a bear stepped into her path. She froze as it sniffed at her dress and then stood to place its paws on her shoulders. At this critical moment a man ran out of the commissary and knocked the bear over the head with a stick. He led Mary inside, where she explained her purpose. A letter had come, the man said, but he didn't recognize her name so he had scribbled "there ain't no such person on this island" across it and forwarded it on.[1]

Mary was pregnant when she and Jack arrived on Quadra Island that summer, and Jack's plan was to take her to friends in Nanaimo for her "confinement." To do so required a canoe trip to Comox, the nearest steamship landing with regular boat service to points south. It was a difficult trip, especially in winter—and that winter proved to be one of the worst on record. "The Big Winter," wrote Comox Valley settler Eustace Smith, "came along in 1889–90. The entire district was blocked with snow up to eight feet deep, with no possibility of getting in supplies for two months." Many became famished as the deer died off. Part of what got Jack and Mary through were the many gifts of fish the We Wai Kai people brought.

Eric Duncan of Comox also wrote about that winter.[2] He said the roofs of buildings had to be shovelled day and night "till the piles of pitched snow rose high above the eaves, and it was easy to walk from the ground to the ridges." Most people ran out of firewood and had to dig tunnels to get at their fence posts to keep their fires burning. "At last, after New Year," wrote Duncan, "the wind went north, the sky cleared, and the heavy, damp snow froze to a depth of six inches." The frozen crust allowed people to move about by horse team again, atop the packed snow. The freeze-up came just in time for Mary. She and Jack made their way to Quathiaski Cove and on to Comox by canoe. From there they boarded a steamship to Departure Bay, where Mary gave birth to her son William on January 26, 1890.

Five weeks later, in a thick snowstorm, the couple returned to Quadra Island on a northbound steamer that stopped in midstream off the We Wai Kai village at Cape Mudge. They stayed overnight in an abandoned shack on the beach and then hiked up the hill to Robert

Robert Hall pre-empted land in 1886 that ran east from Quathiaski Cove and across what's now Cape Mudge Road, where he built this squared-log house. The house still stands and is one of the oldest in the northern Vancouver Island region. PHOTO COURTESY KAY NOBLE, MCR 19793

Hall's homestead, near the current Walker Road, where they stayed for two weeks to wait for the weather to break. The last of the "big snow" did not clear off the ground until April.

Robert Hall would have welcomed the lively presence of the Bryants and their baby in his bachelor home. Hall, like Jack Bryant, was a former Nanaimo miner, who had pre-empted land on Quadra in 1886.[3] His original house still stands, with its squared logs and a door made from hand-adzed boards. It's the oldest house in the northern Vancouver Island region.

Tom Backus and his pal "Skookum" Tom Leask[4] joined the non-Native settlers in 1888. They crossed the country together as CPR hands and then worked at various logging camps, which is likely what led them to Quadra. Backus pre-empted land at what's now Quadra Loop on southeastern Quadra, where he built a fine log house from squared timbers. It was a big house for its day, with two bedrooms upstairs, a large living room with a fireplace, and a lean-to kitchen. Backus, who was raised in Ontario, was an experienced hand with a broad axe so he was often called upon to help others build their log homes.

While Backus's homestead showed great promise, the sedentary life of a rancher didn't suit him so he sold the place a decade later and returned to a more nomadic existence as a logger and prospector in the Thurlow Islands area. His friend Skookum Tom, however, made Quadra his lifelong home. His exceptional homestead at Hyacinthe Bay continues as one of a few small farms still being worked on the island.

Tom Leask was a man of legends. He left the Orkney Island of Hoy in his teens and crossed the Atlantic to Montreal. His neighbour of later years, the writer Francis Dickie, remembered Leask as an exceptionally fine person, with a quiet manner and a soft, pleasing voice. Others recalled his machismo humour. But what stood out in many people's minds was Leask's brute strength, matched by a temper that got him into frequent scraps. Herbert Joyce, in a taped interview, said Leask was "one of the toughest, hardest men that this north country ever seen, for tug-of-war or liftin', or pullin', anything like that. He was a real husky, strong man and he worked hard and drank hard." Leask was also known for his barroom tricks. For a bet, he'd chew through heavy beer glasses

Orkney Islander "Skookum" Tom Leask got his Chinook Jargon name for his wiry strength and stamina. PHOTO COURTESY LEWIS AND MARY (LEASK) JOYCE, MCR 6047

called schooners with his double set of teeth and line up the shards to the marvel of his companions.

A legend about Tom Leask says he earned his Chinook Jargon name "Skookum" ("strong") at Haida Gwaii, where he pushed aside a massive boulder that obstructed a canoe launch. Francis Dickie popularized the tale, saying a grateful chief gave Tom his daughter as a bride. The story may only contain elements of truth: Tom likely moved such a boulder, but his children's teacher Katie (Walker) Clarke recalled that Tom met his wife Maggie when her mother, an island settler, moved in as his housekeeper. As Katie recalled, however, Maggie Leask was related to a Haida family named Cross.

Like most of his fellow settlers, Skookum Tom worked away from home during the logging season. He was a valued hand in Mike King and Lewis Casey's camp at Quathiaski Cove in 1890. He also served as a packer on King's lengthy timber cruises.

King and Casey started to log in the Discovery Passage region in the 1870s, from their base at Comox, where they overwintered their oxen teams and grew their feed. They would barge their oxen and hay to their camps, and shove them overboard to swim when they neared shore. Gregarious Mike King was the best known of the partners. He was a tall, handsome man who'd left Minnesota as a young man with his brother Jim. His partner Lewis Casey ran the day-to-day operations, while Mike looked after timber sales and scouted new claims for timber and minerals.

King and Casey's first logging show on Quadra was on the southern tip of the island in about 1886, after which they logged Robert Hall's property in Quathiaski Cove. Their commissary, with its office and store, was a focal point for Discovery Passage residents, who picked up their mail and bought incidentals like flea powder, HP sauce and tobacco from camp provisions.

A greenhorn Englishman joined King and Casey's camp in 1891. Percival (Percy) Smith's upper-middle-class family was new to the area, and he was the butt of jokes in the brawn and swagger of the camp. He was greeted upon arrival by Skookum Tom Leask, who eyed the young man up and down. Historian Rene Harding wrote about their meeting: "'What's yer name, son?' asked Tom. 'Percival, sir,' came the timid reply. Tom's eyes opened wide. 'What did you say?' 'Percival Smith, sir,' he repeated uncomfortably. 'Percival!' the man snorted. 'What a hell of a name!' He shifted a wad of chewing tobacco from one side of his face to the other. 'Percival! We'll just call you the kid.'"[5]

Leask told the boy to put the stock of his rifle up against tree trunks to listen for grouse. "'Oh, and another thing,' Tom added. 'Have you ever heard a harp?' 'Why yes,' said Percy. 'My mother used to play it sometimes.' 'Well, if you don't want to hear a harp again just be sure you remove the shells before you put your ear to the muzzle, eh?'" Though Percy thought Tom's advice was just intended as a joke, he tried the trick and found that he could indeed hear grouse through the stock of his rifle.

Percy attended a huge potlatch at Cape Mudge with Skookum Tom and some of the other loggers in 1891. The We Wai Kai people had purchased impressive quantities of pilot bread and soda crackers, barrels of brown sugar and stacks of Hudson's Bay blankets for their assembled guests. The loggers were shocked to discover that a nine-metre (thirty-foot) Nuu-Chah-Nulth war canoe, ornately carved from a single piece of cedar, was about to be destroyed in a show of wealth. The loggers pooled their funds and tried to buy it for $150 but the chief refused all offers. The canoe was chopped into pieces to toss into the fire and later the charred prow was displayed with pride over the entrance to the big house.

There were many grand potlatches among the Laich-Kwil-Tach through the early 1890s, some of which involved Wamish's nephew Billy Assu, who was in his mid-twenties. Assu stands out as one of the most fascinating individuals of his time and place. "He was, by any standards, a truly great man," wrote Roderick Haig-Brown, who knew Assu in his senior years. "Had the chances of birth and education been different, it is easy to imagine him a leader in world affairs, a delegate to the United Nations or perhaps its secretary-general."

Assu wasn't certain of his exact birth date but he guessed it to be sometime between 1867 and 1869.[6] The facts about his parentage are also obscure, blurred by the passage of time and conflicting accounts. His mother, Annie Kla-pi-ne-ka,[7] is said to have been born of a We Wai Kai mother and a Mamalilikala (Village Island) father.[8] She married Charley Assu, a younger brother of Chief Wamish, but according to some her eldest son Billy (Ya-Kna-Kwas) was born before this marriage, the child of an Italian immigrant.[9] The 1901 census confirms this notion, listing Billy Assu as "EB," to denote European birth.

Whatever Billy Assu's parentage and hereditary rights were, his combination of impressive physical and intellectual strength gave him tremendous stature and power. In his prime, he stood at over 183 centimetres (6 feet) tall and weighed 96 kilograms (212 pounds). "Every morning upon rising," wrote Mildred Valley Thornton in a 1952 article, "he bathed by plunging into the sea. Then he would start out before sunrise to hunt. One day, after a long tramp, he shot a 220-lb deer at 9:30 in the morning and tramped until 3:30 in the afternoon carrying it home to camp on his back."[10]

In the 1890s Billy, like many other Native men and women, worked in the canneries on the Fraser River each summer and fall, followed by a stint in the hop fields of Washington State. Assu was also a recruiter, who hired and managed work crews. With his earnings he held potlatches that advanced his position within his traditional culture. In 1892, as Assu told writer Frances Dickie, he held a potlatch that cost him $25,000. It was attended by 23 tribes, who witnessed Billy's ascent as a chief. The potlatch was described in the *Colonist* on September 6, 1892:

> The Indians of Cape Mudge and Valdes Island are preparing for another big potlatch, which promises to eclipse the one recently given by Salmon River Bill in point of liberality of the gifts and the numerical strength of the gathering. Orders have already been given for 30 canoes, $1,000 worth of bracelets, 700 boxes of biscuits, 2,000 blankets, 600 barrels of flour, 700 trunks, and a great variety of miscellaneous articles. The big event will commence early next week, and will last for several days. Mine host will be Billy Assew, and it is expected that 250 Bella Coola

Billy Assu is in the centre of this family portrait in his big house in about 1918. On the left are his sons Thomas and Frank. On the right are his daughters Susan Quocksister, holding her son Herman, Lucy Chickite with her son Edward and son Harry Assu, seated. PHOTO COURTESY THE ASSU FAMILY, MCR 6775

Indians will swell the gathering. 20 canoes are in port loading up freight for the potlatch, which promises to be one of the biggest held for many years.

Assu's potlatch was one of many among the Laich-Kwil-Tach to be written up in the *Colonist* that year. The first potlatch was in February, followed by one to the north at Salmon River in late August, where 5,300 blankets, 350 boxes of biscuits, 280 silver bracelets and 150 trunks were given away at an estimated cost of eight thousand dollars. Next up was Billy Assu's potlatch in September, followed by Captain John Quocksister's gathering of an estimated three thousand people later that fall.[11]

Indian Agent Reginald Pidcock interrupted a potlatch hosted by Billy's father, Charley Assu, in mid-November 1892. Pidcock attempted to arrest Charley for possession of alcohol but he resisted[12] and Pidcock was surrounded by a hostile crowd. He retreated to Comox and recruited a police officer and eighteen deputies but they were so far outnumbered they left their rifles in Quathiaski Cove, to enter the Cape Mudge village unarmed. They apprehended Charley, his son Billy and Skookum Charley, who the *Weekly News* of the Comox Valley described as "a powerful Indian with a reputation that has made his name a terror for 100 miles around." In all, five men were charged with resisting arrest. Three men paid their ten-dollar fine immediately but Charley and Billy Assu were sentenced to six months of hard labour in Nanaimo.[13]

A potlatch would also have been held to mark Billy Assu's marriage to We Wai Kai noblewoman Mary Naknakim, which took place sometime between 1894 and 1897,[14] when their first child was born. With this marriage Assu acquired important hereditary rights and privileges.

Assu's innate leadership skills were noted by his uncle Wamish. Billy recalled in later years that when Wamish's eldest son Frank Nagaghu died prematurely, sometime between 1893 and 1897,[15] Wamish singled Billy out to take his position. Assu described the hereditary process in a letter he sent to the *Campbell River Courier* in 1956:

> It is true enough that my father before me was not a chief. But the chieftainship has been in my family for years and years. Wamaish was my father's brother and he was chief of all the Kwakwala, as was his father's father before him. My uncle had two sons, with the elder, who was the rightful heir, dying at a young age. My uncle chose me to take his place because he said that his younger son did not have the material that makes a leader among his people. [This son suffered from TB, of which he eventually died.] He called together the tribes of the south, namely, the Point Grey, Squamish, Victoria, Nanaimo, Saanich, Cowichan, Cooper Island, Comox, Church House and Squirrel Cove and adjoining area. At this big potlatch, my uncle named his older son Nagaghu (Big Mountain) and told the gathering that his son would succeed him after his death. Not long after this gathering, Nagaghu died, and soon after his death my uncle, Wamaish, called another large meeting, this time giving the potlatch in my honor and also giving me

the name he had given his elder son, Nagaghu, and he told all those present that after due consideration he had chosen me as his legal heir to the chieftainship at his death. I am not the only member of the family that [Wamish] honored by the large potlatches he gave. Eight years after the one which he gave for me with the West coast Indians as guests, he gave one for my cousin, Mrs. Mary Roberts, calling together the Five Nations of the Kwakwaleth peoples, honoring her who was highly esteemed and beloved by all for her goodness and high standard in our tribal customs.[16]

James Smith of the We Wai Kum Band of Campbell River gave a different account in a letter he wrote to the same newspaper. He said Assu was simply chosen to hold and manage positions on behalf of Wamish's grandson Bill (Quocksister) Roberts of Campbell River.[17] But such arguments were held in check for the duration of Wamish's long life, as he and the other prominent chiefs maintained traditional structures, with advice from young leaders like Billy Assu.

Billy Assu became a Methodist in his youth and attended a church convention, probably in Nanaimo, where his people sometimes worked.[18] He and Wamish, who was also a Christian,[19] made their first request for a missionary and school as early as 1884.[20] Assu's objective, as he later recalled, was for both children and adults to learn to speak, read and write English. He felt strongly throughout his life that his people had to adopt aspects of Euro-Canadian social and economic structures to survive.

The Methodist Church built a cabin in the village in 1888,[21] but the first two missionaries didn't stay long. The Walkers arrived on September 2, 1893, to become the first long-term teachers in the village. Robert and Agnes Walker were dropped off on the beach at Cape Mudge with their few possessions and their two young daughters, Katie and Winnie. The couple had many skills to offer. Both Robert and Agnes had taught children in the Methodist mission at Metlakatla prior to their marriage, and though Robert was just a lay missionary he had a teaching degree and a year of medical training.

Robert (R.J.) Walker and Agnes. Agnes Walker taught in the Methodist mission in Bella Bella and then at Metlakatla in the 1880s, where she met fellow missionary Robert Walker. When the pair decided to marry they had to surrender their jobs, but were later hired as teachers at the We Wai Kai village. PHOTO COURTESY URSULA (WALKER) LEWIS, MCR 20279-21

Many band members were away for work when the Walkers arrived, but those on hand helped them settle in. In the evening some young men came home to the village, recalled R.J. Walker years later. Among them was Billy Assu, then a good-looking youth of about twenty. He loaded the Walkers' bureau on his back and carried it up to the little shack that was to be their first home.

The next day the Walkers invited everyone to attend divine service in one of the big houses, but few came because the elders flatly refused to allow Christian worship in their big houses. It was not until the couple opened their own home the following Sunday that a congregation assembled.

The Department of Indian Affairs sent materials for a school shortly after the Walkers arrived. "[Agnes Walker] was my first teacher," wrote James Martin Smith (Maqualahgulees) some years later, "and I will never forget the patience she exercised in helping an awkward little Indian boy to scratch out letters properly on a slate."[22] Agnes also raised funds for the church. On a trip to her father's home in eastern Canada, for the birth of her third child, Agnes gave numerous talks to benefit the Cape Mudge school and mission.

Billy Assu helped build both the school and a manse for the Walkers, and in 1894 he built his own family a Euro-Canadian-style house. It was the first of its kind among his people, and this break with tradition proved costly. Assu was chastised by the older men and had to distribute five hundred dollars' worth of food in the village as compensation. Billy and Mary Assu's first child, Lucy, was born in Steveston, where Billy worked for the Phoenix Cannery, sometime after the move to this new house.[23]

Billy Assu and the other young men of the village often risked their lives to assist shipwreck victims off Cape Mudge. The sudden drop-off beyond the shelving beach at the cape, combined with low tide and high winds, can pull ships under within seconds.

The wreck of the *Standard*, a cannery tender, was reported in detail in the *Colonist* in June 1892, with a graphic account from William Murray, the sole survivor of its five-man crew:

> The steamer struck the tiderip and sheered, and the waves crashed onto the engine-room, breaking it in and flooding the ship. It wasn't ten seconds before she went down.
>
> I had my life belt right at the engine room door where I could snatch it in an instant, and the other four managed to grab theirs and got in the boat [the steamer's dinghy]. I shoved it clear, and at that very second the steamer sank beneath me.

Billy and Mary (Naknakim) Assu's frame house can be seen through the centre of the tripod erected for a potlatch the Wallaces gave to all the tribes in 1913. PHOTO BY TRIO CROCKER AND COURTESY PAT TALBOT, MCR 9151

I helped the boys in, but before I could get in myself it had capsized. The steamer went down under me, and I saw the three men hanging [on] to the capsized boat. The heavy sea prevented me reaching the boat, and soon all the men were washing from it. The next I saw of them they were all swimming well, and then some heavy breakers came and the deck-hand sang out, "Good-bye, boys, I'm going; I'll take the oar with me."

The seas were running like mountains, and the next time I could look around the fireman and the cook were nowhere to be seen. I saw the captain then. He was swimming well, with a cork tender in his right hand. Then some heavy seas came along and I saw him no more. I swam for the cover of the forward hatch and got it, but had hard work to stick to it. I then tried to make the Cape Mudge side up till midnight, and found I couldn't [so] made for the other side. When halfway over, daylight broke and the sea became calm.

I was still swimming, though not very strong, when, about a hundred yards from the island I saw a man in a canoe paddling towards me. The next thing I knew I was in a comfortable bed, well wrapped up.

Murray was adrift in the water for about fifteen hours before he was rescued, even as Mike King of Quathiaski Cove and Native men from Cape Mudge braved what King described as the second-worst storm he'd ever seen. "I was in the tent that evening, when a klootchman [Native woman] called out that a steamer had gone down. I was out on the water twenty minutes later, and eight Indians stayed there for three hours. We could see nothing of the steamer floating, and heard none of the crew shout. It was just like climbing the sides of a mountain and coasting down."

Ironically, the tug sent in search of the *Standard* was also wrecked off Cape Mudge a few years later. All eight hands were lost on the *Estelle* in 1894, with no witnesses. The authorities surmised the boiler exploded when the boat capsized, because shattered fragments of the tug were found throughout Discovery Passage. The only body recovered was that of Norman McDougall, part owner of the *Estelle*, who was found on the beach with his legs blown off.

An obituary for engineer Herbert Whiteside, who was lost in this wreck, was printed in the newspaper of his native Penrith, England. "He took to the seafaring life, which suited well his hardy adventurous spirit," reported the *Colonist*, in a reprint from the English newspaper, "and in 1890 he went away to Vancouver Island to make his fortune . . . We know that as he fought pluckily for life and battled with icy seas, he cast one glance towards his home and old comrades and native hills; he whispered a loving farewell to his widowed bride, and then, as he sank exhausted beneath the cruel waves, he committed himself to the keeping of the Almighty."

While most of the men and women who braved this coast had a similarly romantic view of themselves pitted against the wilds, some were ready for the services of a settled community. Reginald Pidcock took the lead as Quadra Islanders fought with a parsimonious provincial government for policing, public wharves, mail delivery and a lighthouse. Once achieved these services would attract yet more non-Native settlers to the island, where several communities sprang up and vied with each other for dominance.

CHAPTER FIVE

Quathiaski Cove–The Hub for Quadra Island and Discovery Passage

Things changed fast on the Discovery Islands after the Union Steamship Company of Vancouver began to serve logging camps and settlements up the coast in 1892. With regular transport came a rush to buy and pre-empt land. Union Steamship boats travelled up the mainland side of the islands and made weekly stops at Heriot Bay, leaving Discovery Passage folks to rely upon intermittent service from passing steamships.

The government continued to churn out propaganda to encourage settlement through the early 1890s, with overblown promises regarding the agricultural potential of places like Quadra Island. The push was partly due to the fact that primary industries like logging and mines required local food production. The 1892 provincial directory described Quadra Island as a poor man's paradise:

> The land that is still vacant is covered with timber and has several swamps here and there and is very easily cleared, the soil is beautiful brown loam, well adapted for the raising of good crops. The climate is very mild, with very little snow or frost. The waters abound in fish and the woods in game. Deer and grouse are plentiful, but there are no bears or panthers [cougars] and wolves are very scarce. The cattle and hogs roam at large on

the fine pasture lands and become fat and good for market. The resources of the Island are stock raising and vegetables. Taking everything into consideration this is the best spot on the globe for the poor man to build his home.

The directory also outlined the rules for pre-emptions. The land could not be in use by First Nations people and the applicant had to register for the land and have it surveyed. Buyers also had to live on-site full-time for several years, to block land speculation, but they could apply for a leave of absence if they had to be away for a protracted period. In addition, pre-emptors were required to make improvements up to a value of two dollars per 0.4 hectare (1 acre), at which time they could pay the final one dollar per 0.4 hectare (1 acre) fee to gain title.

A Comox Valley surveyor named Drabble assessed improvements for the region. He noted the value of Robert Hall's work on his 60-hectare (150-acre) pre-emption on what's now Cape Mudge Road in his field book for 1890:

1½ acres cleared and seeded	$120
4½ acres slashed	72
House 22 x 17 hewed logs	150
Ditching	10
Cut down timber near house	50

Though Quathiaski Cove residents weren't on the Union Steamship route, there were enough people in the Discovery Passage region to warrant a government wharf by 1892.[1] It was built on a rock bluff in the southern end of the Cove, in an awkward spot that steamers could only use at high tide. The site was likely selected because it was convenient to King and Casey's logging camp and commissary. "We had to scramble over rocks on hands and knees to get to it," wrote early settler Mary (Hughes) Joyce in her memoirs.

When King and Casey finished logging in the Cove that same year, Robert Hall took over the camp's store.[2] He only sold basic goods like flea powder, lamp wicks and bottled sauces, along with his own farm produce, because most settlers and Native people ordered supplies in bulk from Vancouver or Victoria. A typical biannual order for the Walkers of the Cape Mudge mission included sugar, pilot bread, prunes and apricots in wooden boxes, beans, sacks of wheat and graham flour, tea, coffee, canned milk, lard, syrup, molasses and perhaps a barrel of apples.[3]

Settlers had to go to Comox by canoe or small boat to pick up their food orders, a trip that took two or more days, depending upon the weather and the tides. Herbert Joyce recalled his parents' arrangements to pick up freight, in a taped interview: "They had a big sailboat and they would go down and get provisions that would last them for six months. That was just necessary. And, you know, lots of times they made it fine and other times it wasn't so good." On one occasion his father got stuck on Mitlenatch Island for several days in a storm, with a broken tiller.

The settlers relied upon fish, venison and other wild game for protein. There was a perpetual pot of venison stew on the go in most households. Katie (Walker) Clarke, daughter of the Cape Mudge missionaries, recalled her first taste of roast beef for the rest of her days. Her father brought the neatly packaged roast back from one of his rare trips to Vancouver.

In 1890, an anonymous writer to the *Nanaimo Free Press* described the merits of life on Quadra:

> Some people when they are looking for the makings of a home expect to find one already made to hand with barn, outhouses, fences, aye—and a big fat pig in the stall. Well to all such I would say you will not find that here, except indeed you bring [it] forth. But indeed he will find our woods abound in deer and grouse and waters in fish, and our beaches in clams. Ye Gods, talk about clams, why I have seen the shells used for washbasins among the settlers on Valdes Island.

Tom Bell continued on as the unofficial postmaster for Quathiaski Cove in the early 1890s.[4] He picked up the mail in the Cove and distributed it from his home in Gowlland Harbour. Bell gave up this position in July

The William and Eliza Hughes family built their log home in about 1891 on Cape Mudge Road, just north of the Pinetree Road intersection. PHOTO COURTESY ELSIE (JOYCE) WARGO, MCR 9267

1893, when an official post office was opened in Robert Hall's store, to which Campbell River and Oyster Bay residents rowed to get their supplies.

For the first few months the steamer *Joan* extended its trip from Comox to Quathiaski Cove to deliver the mail, but without a government mail subsidy the service couldn't be sustained. "I see by your last issue the 'Joan' has quit running to this place as it is claimed it does not pay," wrote Tom Bell to the *Weekly News* of the Comox Valley in 1893. "Here we are with a population larger than Read, Cortes and Hernando Islands put together, and mark! each has a post office and a weekly mail service."

When Quadra Island was listed in the provincial directory for the first time in 1893[5] there were an estimated fifty non-Native residents. The vast majority worked as loggers, but among them were a handful of ranchers and a few fishermen.

There were only five women among the Quadra Island settlers in the early 1890s—Mary Bryant, Agnes Walker, Eliza Hughes, Anna Joyce and Alice Pidcock. Mary Bryant must have been thrilled to welcome Eliza Hughes, the second of these women to arrive, especially as her homestead was within an easy walk of Mary's own.

Eliza Hughes and her husband William[6] both had British fathers and Salish mothers, with strong family ties in Nanaimo. Part of their impetus to leave the city may have been a desire to try a new environment for two of their children, John and Sarah, who suffered from TB. William and young John moved to the island first, and built a large squared-log house with a massive chimney and fireplace on what's now Heriot Bay Road, just north of the Pinetree Road junction. Eliza and the three girls—Sarah, Mary and Aleen—followed about a year later, travelling up the coast in the venerable old steamship *Boscowitz* in the spring of 1891.

"We were picked up with a very leaky rowboat and taken to shore," wrote Mary (Hughes) Joyce in her memoirs, "and then a walk to the home of Mrs. Bryant, who kindly offered us rest till father arrived with his two great oxen drawing a sled."[7]

Not much is known of Eliza's parents. Her father, George Hilton, was British and worked in the mines in Nanaimo. Her mother, Qua-Ka-Pas, or Mary, was born in Comox. (She may have met George

The Hughes family women are to the left and William Hughes is on the right with a stick. The man third from the right at the rear is Heriot Bay logger Jack Hanaher. The family to the left of the man with the white beard are the Hoods. PHOTO MAY BE BY JOHN HOOD. PHOTO COURTESY LEWIS AND MARY JOYCE, MCR 6048

Hilton in Nanaimo, where Native groups went to work in the mines and to trade.) Eliza's parents never officially married and it appears her mother, who gave Eliza the Native name Yuetis, raised her within her Native traditions. As a consequence, Eliza never became fluent in English, nor did she learn to read and write.

More is known of Eliza's husband William's family, as her father-in-law kept a diary. William Hughes Sr. came to BC in about 1857 and settled on a homestead in Departure Bay in about 1861. He married Mary Salacelowtz in Cowichan Bay in 1866 and the couple raised their family within the eclectic mix of their cultural traditions. They moved with the seasons to fish by canoe, sometimes travelling as far as the Fraser River, but they also established a homestead in Departure Bay.

The healthful air of the sparsely settled region did not check the effects of TB within the family. John and Sarah died on Quadra in the 1890s,[8] as did Eliza's mother Mary Hilton, in 1896.[9] All are thought to be buried on the family's former homestead on Heriot Bay Road.

Anna Walsh was the next woman to join the southern Quadra Island settlers when she married Alfred Joyce. The couple met in Victoria, where Alfred worked as a plasterer, carpenter and mason to earn a grubstake for his Quadra Island homestead. He pre-empted land on the island in 1888 at the end of what's now Joyce Road, not far from his brother Walter's homestead at the current Francisco Point.

Anna hadn't been in Victoria long when she met Alfred. She was born and raised in Switzerland but went to New York to finish her education. After her schooling she accompanied some friends to California and then on to Victoria, where a childhood friend had married into a Swiss family. Anna was working as a waitress in a hotel when she and Alfred met. After a courtship of several years, they were married in Victoria on October 15, 1892. They spent their honeymoon on the up-coast freight and passenger boat, arriving on Quadra Island two days later.

By all accounts Anna Joyce was warm-hearted and energetic—qualities she surely needed to create a home in a log cabin on Alfred's partially cleared homestead at the start of winter. Anna was equal to the task. She had some practical medical training[10] and an innate love of gardening,

"I know that thou wilt not flight from me nor suffer me to fall," wrote Alfred Joyce in Anna Walsh's autograph book in Victoria in 1890. "I know that thou art ever near to hear me when I call." Alfred and Anna were married in Victoria in 1892 and within days arrived on his homestead on Quadra Island. Though she came from a cosmopolitan background, Anna loved farming and adapted well to homestead life. PHOTO COURTESY HELEN (JOYCE) ANDREWS, MCR 8522

both of which made her a valued member of her new community.

"It is well known that my wife does most of the farming," said Alfred in a speech at a community event in 1906, "at least, she thinks so, for she generally bosses the job, and I must admit that she is perfectly capable of doing it." Their division of duties was typical of life on the island at the time. Anna worked the farm, managed their household and raised and educated their children, while Alfred worked away from home for extended periods to pay for the things they couldn't make or grow. Unfortunately, the Joyces' homestead was too far away to allow for more than sporadic visits with Mary Bryant and Eliza Hughes.

Reginald Pidcock's eldest son Willie was the first in his large family to become a permanent resident of the island in the early 1890s. He moved into the family's cabin at Quathiaski Cove in about 1890,[11] where other family members joined him on occasion. In 1893 Reginald Pidcock began to relocate his Department of Indian Affairs headquarters to the island for months at a stretch. Each time he returned to Quadra Island it required DIA permission. "Sir," wrote Pidcock to the DIA in July 1893, "Should you have any objection to my residing for the next three months at Cape Mudge, Valdes Island? It is within the Agency, and there is now a post office there with fortnightly mails so that I should be within reach of the office in Victoria as often as I am now. My object in requesting your permission is that my wife and family are at present residing there."

The Pidcocks built a fine new house on a bluff that overlooked Grouse Island in 1893–94. It was described in the *Weekly News* as a grand home "that cost way up in the figures" and was likely financed through the sale of some of Alice's lots in the new town of Courtenay and a small inheritance she received. As Pidcock remarked in his letters to the DIA there was hardly enough to spare from his thousand-dollar annual salary to cover more than a few years of boarding school for his eldest boys—though his wage was twice that of the average logger of the time.

The Pidcocks' new house with its stone foundation was indeed grand, compared to other island-ers' log shanties. On the main

Anna and Alfred Joyce replaced their log cabin with a frame home in about 1905 and as the family grew the house expanded, as seen in this sketch by Campbell River artist Sybil Andrews. "There is an old-world charm about the vine-clad house," wrote a Vancouver journalist in 1925, "with its rose gar-den nearby and the hops spreading all over the verandah." The tall structure remains and is now the James Pottery Studio and showroom at the end of Joyce Road. PHOTO COURTESY GLENBOW MUSEUM, MCR 993.12.34

floor of "The Big House," as it was called, were a large kitchen, a din-ing room and a parlour with a heat-efficient Rumford fireplace. Later a conservatory was added for Alice's fuchsias, geraniums and canaries. The central staircase led to numerous bedrooms and a washroom, where water was piped in from a barrel on the hillside.

By 1894 Alice and all the children were in permanent residence on Quadra,[12] joined by Reginald in summer and fall. Alice brought a touch of culture to the community, with her refined education and sensibilities. She was a gifted pianist and singer, with a passion for opera. Alice was also an experienced midwife and stayed with expectant mothers for up

The Pidcock family's new home built in 1894 in Quathiaski Cove on what's now Pidcock Road was a grand place islanders called "The Big House." PHOTO COURTESY DAVID PIDCOCK, MCR 12722

to two weeks. At least eleven of the babies she delivered were named for her or other members of her family. Alice remembered each with a gift at Christmas for the rest of her days.

The island's many non-Native bachelors were overjoyed by the arrival of women and children. "The boys in the logging camp just loved to see two little girls," reminisced Katie (Walker) Clarke of the Cape Mudge mission. "They made the greatest fuss over us. Those big lonesome boys, that's what they were."

Loggers were a tough breed, proud of the strength, nerve and skill required by their dangerous industry. Fights were a regular feature of camp life, but when a lady and children appeared in their midst they were bound by a strict code of conduct. The rest of the time they were hard-as-nails loggers, without the balancing influence of wives and family. It was a lifestyle that led many to alcoholism, a habit some encouraged among the Native people who worked in the camps as well. Native women were urged into prostitution and alcohol abuse, though it was illegal to sell alcohol to Native people. Agnes and Robert Walker led a campaign to keep whisky peddlers away from Cape Mudge Village after the tragic deaths of several young people. The death of Sally, a twenty-four-year-old Cape

Mudge woman, hit the news in Victoria, where her naked body was found in a clump of bushes. The marks on her body and a string around her neck suggested she was murdered but her killer was never found.

Foremost in Agnes's mind, however, was the death in 1895 of a Native woman named Susan, who was killed in an alcohol-related accident. Susan had not touched a drink for several years, wrote Agnes in her memoirs, until she and several friends stopped at Edgar Wylie's trading post on Read Island. Wylie stood them all drinks, which led to a spree. With far too much whisky in them, the four women paddled to another island to sleep it off. In their stupor they neglected to secure their canoe properly and it drifted away with Susan asleep on board. When one of Susan's companions discovered the canoe adrift she ran for help, but she was too late to save Susan, who fell overboard and drowned. The drifting canoe, with eleven unopened bottles of whisky in it, was recovered quickly but Susan's body was not found until two days later.[13]

Edgar Wylie, a former police chief from North Dakota, was fined three hundred dollars for illegal liquor sales. A few years later, Wylie was again charged when two young men from Cape Mudge, one of them a chief's son, drowned after drinking too much at Wylie's hotel. Their bodies were never recovered.

From then on, Billy Assu and Robert Walker took turns patrolling the beach when whisky sloops were in the area to ensure they didn't stop at Cape Mudge.

There was otherwise little contact between the We Wai Kai people and the many non-native settlers who arrived in increasing numbers. Men like Robert Willson of Surrey, England, and Frederick Yeatman, who had a large family, received a ready welcome when they came to the island to assess its homestead potential. Alfred and Anna Joyce advised Yeatman on his best options and Fred pre-empted land off what's now Smith Road, near Cedar Road, in 1896. He filed his pre-emption papers and then wrote to Alfred Joyce to enlist his assistance:

Dear Sir, I am writing a few lines to say I am coming to live on Valdez Island in about a month or 5 weeks. I have taken up that piece of land near Mr. T. Backus. Have you any fowls to sell as I want to get about 1 doz & if you have them I wouldn't bring any up with me. If you have not got any to spare perhaps you may know of someone that has. If you would kindly let me know I would esteem it a favour. I wrote to your brother I think over a month ago—about a piece of land near him for a neighbour of mine. I thought perhaps he had not had the letter as I have not had an answer yet. He talks of coming up the same time as me to look at it. Hoping this will find you quite well, I remain yours respectfully, F.C. Yeatman. P.S. if you have any fowls please say what they are worth.

Journeyman carpenter Robert Willson pre-empted a homestead near Tom Backus, on the west side of what's now Fox Road at Quadra Loop, in 1895. A few years later he fell in love with young Arlette Michaelson, when she came to stay with her friends the Hughes after the death of her father. Arlette was a third-generation coastal girl, the granddaughter of French sea captain Louis Page, a veteran of the Crimean War, who came to Victoria in 1859 and later settled near Nanaimo. She was a good

Robert and Arlette (Michaelson) Willson with their children Clovis, Jane and Pearl outside their log home on what's now Fox Road. This was Robert Willson's second of three homes on the island. PHOTO COURTESY GRACE (WILLSON) MCPHERSON, MCR 4076

The Yeatman family's home shortly after it was built in 1896 on what's now Smith Road, east of Cedar Road. Seen here is Fred Yeatman with his son Rob on the horse. On the porch are his sons Tom, Sam, Fred Jr. and James. Standing at the porch, from the left, are Robert Willson, Emma Yeatman and Arlette Willson. PHOTO BY JOHN HOOD AND COURTESY PEGGY YEATMAN, MCR 4251

choice as a wife, though she was only sixteen and had to marry against the wishes of her mother, who hoped her daughter would marry later to forestall child-bearing. The two were married in 1900 and the babies soon followed in their 5 x 7–metre (16 x 22–foot) log cabin overlooking Sutil Channel. A neighbour helped with the delivery of their first child, and when Robert was asked years later how people fared without medical care back then his simple reply was, "We didn't need any." "How do you mean you didn't need any?" asked interviewer Ed Meade. "We didn't need any. We never got sick."

Those who did have ailments had to walk or row to Comox for medical care, or go to Robert Walker who served as an emergency medic. His family remembered the tortured groans of Native people and settlers alike as Walker used his heavy pliers to extract their aching teeth.

Robert Willson put his carpentry skills to work on the island's first school, a log structure built south of current Pinetree Road in 1895. "I helped clear the ground," recalled Willson, "helped get the logs out, helped put it up and I done what bit of finishing work there was there. 'Course there wasn't much, just put the floor in and window and door. And I made the desks and the stools for the kids to work at and a blackboard for the teacher and made her a little bit of a desk. But that was a nothing job." The island's bachelors were eager to help Willson, wrote Mary (Hughes) Joyce. They "all began to shave and dress more carefully and make their Sunday calls" after schoolteacher Kate Smith of Steveston, a family friend of Willson's, arrived in the fall of 1895.

The government required a minimum of ten pupils, with eight in regular attendance, to provide a teacher for a rural "assisted" school. Humble as the little school was, with its drafts and oil drum heater, it also served as a place of worship and as a courthouse.

The school was too distant for young Katie (Walker) Clarke of the Cape Mudge mission to attend but she and her family paddled around to the Cove on the snowy Christmas Day of 1895 to ride from there in the Pidcocks' jingling ox sleigh to the "school closing." It was a grand event. Most of the island's non-Native settlers packed into the schoolhouse to

Very few families could afford to send their children to school by horse. Most children walked great distances and in one case a father carried his young son on his shoulders, bringing the child to school each day to maintain the minimum enrolment requirement. Seen here in 1908 are Brud (Gordon) and Ethel Letson at the Walker's Homewood Farm in 1908. PHOTO COURTESY JOY (WALKER) HUNTLEY, MCR 5559

The island's first teacher, Kate Smith, outside the log school that opened in 1895 on Heriot Bay Road, to the north of Pinetree Road. PHOTO COURTESY JOHN PHILLIPS, MCR 5359

watch with pride as fourteen students[14] took prizes for proficiency in academics, deportment and attendance. Some gave recitations, including the Yeatman and Pidcock boys, followed by cake and candy.

From then on young Katie (who many years later taught school on Quadra) begged to attend the school. It was five years or more before her father acquiesced and cleared a trail up the steep bank behind the village to connect with the trail that's now Cape Mudge Road. It was a long walk for Katie and her siblings. They had to leave the house at first light, with a storm lantern swinging between them, for their ninety-minute hike through stands of gigantic fir trees. "I remember walking to school four miles," wrote Katie in her memoirs, "through the loveliest timber. Nothing could beat Valdes's beautiful straight trees. My brother used to worry about them coming down on us as we walked but the fir, cedar and hemlock didn't break like that. It was like a park through there."[15]

Though she was a bright child, Katie felt she wouldn't make the honour roll for academics so she was determined to distinguish herself through perfect attendance. When a heavy snowfall came that first year Katie's parents tried to persuade her to stay home but she was not to be stopped. She sank deep into the wet snow with every step until she finally reached the silent schoolhouse. No one else had come to school. so Katie lit the fire, dried her clothes, ate her lunch and trudged home. The next day, with snow still falling, she decided to stay home—only to find that her teacher and some classmates went to school that day. As a result, Katie lost her perfect attendance record.

With no church on the island, Katie's father held services for the settlers in the school, at the Pidcocks' home or in front of the massive hearth in the Hughes family's log house near the school. "What pleasant gatherings the settlers had when [Mr. Walker] came to my father's house twice a month to hold services!" wrote Mary (Hughes) Joyce in her memoirs. "The people came from Heriot Bay, Quathiaski Cove and the Cape. What a pleasant memory to look back and imagine one can hear again those dear old hymns sung, such as 'Rock of Ages' sung without music, led by Mr. Walker."

As more settlers arrived there was a push for regular freight service at Quathiaski Cove to rival the upstart new community at Heriot Bay, where the Union Steamship Company stopped weekly. Those who collected their mail in the Cove never knew when it would come. "If you happened to be listening, if you just heard a steamer whistle," wrote

Walter (holding a baby) and Mary Joyce (fourth from the left), the Hughes sisters (seated and standing behind the girl in the white blouse), Cordelia Bull (with baby), Hosea Bull (with platter) and perhaps the Hood family at a picnic on Mitlenatch Island. The photo was taken by John Hood, a professional photographer who moved his family from Vancouver to Quadra for the duration of the tough recession of the early 1890s. PHOTO COURTESY ELSIE (JOYCE) WARGO, MCR 9275

Mary (Hughes) Joyce, "you would go to the Cove and see if papers, perhaps a month old or more, had arrived." Another resident complained that sometimes they'd go to the Cove to find a steamer had passed by without stopping. Under these conditions, Quathiaski Cove storekeeper Robert Hall closed his post office on June 1, 1896, in deference to a new post office that opened that same day in Heriot Bay.

Several months later Robert Hall, George Warren and Edward Levine made one of their regular trips to Comox for supplies. Hall proudly paid off the last of a debt to a creditor in Comox and loaded his provisions in George Warren's new boat. They were within sight of home when the boat, likely overloaded with supplies, capsized. Hall and Levine's bodies were never found but by some miracle trapper and logger George Warren washed ashore, where he was found unconscious but alive.

Robert's nephew Dick Hall, who had just emigrated from England, inherited his uncle's estate, including the Quathiaski Cove store and 144 hectares (355 acres). Together with his own pre-emption in the Cove he now owned 209 hectares (515 acres).

Not long after Robert Hall was lost at sea, the wharf at the Cove was demolished by a storm.[16] "Our first wharf floated away through the Narrows," wrote Anna Joyce in her memoirs. "And were the settlers sorry? I should say not." Reginald Pidcock soon lobbied the federal government for a new wharf. It was built in 1897, farther to the north in the Cove near where Pidcock Road now drops down to the beach.

Dick Hall sold his uncle's store to the Pidcocks in 1899[17] and they relocated it to the head of the new wharf, with Willie in charge. Willie presided over a long counter with weigh scales, paper and string. He filled orders from customers all over Discovery Passage, for canned goods, garden supplies, tools, books, ready-made clothing and bolts of fabric from the shelves that lined the walls. Barrels and boxes littered the floor and above the counter hung lanterns and water buckets in all shapes and sizes.

Another of Reginald Pidcock's causes involved lobbying for a lighthouse at Cape Mudge. It went into operation in 1898 to warn mariners against the dangers of the long shoals. The first light was mounted on

Cape Mudge lighthouse, seen here in about 1900, opened in 1898 to warn mariners away from a long shoal, with a steep drop-off, on the southwestern tip of Quadra Island. BCA F-03690

a square block of a building that cost $1,225 to build. John and Annie Davidson, Scottish immigrants, were the first keepers. They shared the twenty-four-hour watch, operated a hand-held foghorn when required and lit the coal-oil lantern on the roof beacon every night.

The Cape Mudge lighthouse went into operation just in time for a rush of traffic through Discovery Passage as boats of every description headed north for the Yukon Gold Rush. Barking dogs aboard these boats were answered by a chorus of dogs at Cape Mudge Village, and the occasional fog-bound ship anchored offshore, where passengers swapped news of the outside world with islanders.

W.E. Anderson, a man who would play a vital role in the twentieth-century economy of Quadra Island, passed by the new Cape Mudge lighthouse on his way to the Yukon Gold Rush in 1898. The Andersons had bought passage on a ship with an inexperienced captain, as they later discovered. "We arrived at [Seymour] Narrows too soon, for the tide was coming in at a terrific rate," wrote W.E. Anderson's brother in his memoirs. "There were four men on the steering wheel to keep the boat straight. As we came close to the Narrows, the captain ordered [them] to turn into the bay and as the boat made the turn the swift tide turned the boat over on its side and dumped all the freight off the bow of the boat." The boat quickly righted itself, but not before four heavy sled dogs crashed through the 5.5-metre (18-foot) ship's railing and plunged overboard. The crew had two hours to retrieve the dogs and gear from the freezing water, while they waited for the tide to turn. Anderson and his family continued on to the Yukon, where they made a fortune—much of which was invested on Quadra Island about a decade later.

The little community of Quathiaski Cove had begun to take shape by the late 1890s and showed great promise—though the new village in Heriot Bay, with its post office and weekly steamship connections to Vancouver, posed a serious threat to its long-term success.

CHAPTER SIX

A Tale of Two Villages

The history of the venerable Heriot Bay Inn, still with us over a century later, is illusive—thanks to a long line of maverick owners and a checkered past full of twists and turns. The HBI (or the "Hibee") has had an adventuresome life.

Its first incarnation may have been as the Hotel Dallas, operated by the island's earliest non-Native settler and rancher, Charlie Dallas. The word hotel conjures a grand vision for what was probably just a spare one-room shanty occupied by the occasional sportsman or between-work logger.[1] Charlie's hotel in Dallasville was mentioned through the mid-1890s in the Quadra column in Vancouver's *Weekly News-Advertiser*, but since Dallas lived as a squatter its exact location in Heriot Bay isn't clear. In May 1894 he registered for land in Heriot Bay, on the current site of the hotel, but dropped his claim within months for reasons not explained. His immediate successor was Hosea Arminius Bull, who hailed from Dallas's home state of Missouri.

Bull may have taken over Dallas's buildings or erected his own hotel on the site in 1894. Herbert Joyce, who grew up on the island, first recalled the hotel as a jumbled combination of logs and timber frame located near the current Cortes ferry dock. "It was like one big house built onto another, the first one," said Joyce. "It was a long, low, rambling affair and it was hard to say just which way it faced."

It may not have been fancy, but Bull's hotel was large enough to host the non-Native residents' first dance in 1895, with Hosea sawing on his fiddle. The *Weekly News-Advertiser* columnist thanked Mr. Vroom of Cortes Island, who brought the Cortes and Read Island school-teachers to the dance. "A very enjoyable time was had till Sunday morning, when all left for their homes."

Fun as Bull's hotel was, it didn't have a liquor licence so it wasn't profitable. Instead, Bull earned a living by various means. He sold bread to the British navy ships that came to Drew Harbour to practise manoeuvres and opened

Hosea Arminius Bull. MCR 8523

The first Heriot Bay Hotel was a "ramshackle joint that faced every which way," somewhat to the east of the current site. Hosea and Cordelia Bull adopted a child in Vancouver, which perhaps led to this orphanage picnic at the hotel. Seen here are Hosea Bull's second wife Helen and community leader Frank Xavier Gagne in the front right. PHOTO COURTESY HERBERT JOYCE, MCR 5986

Hosea and Cordelia Bull holding Cecil in the doorway of their store and post office in Heriot Bay in about 1900, with an unidentified First Nations group. PHOTO COUR-TESY SHEILA BULL, MCR 20392-12

a store in the bay in 1894.[2] His clientele included settlers and the many loggers who worked in camps at Hyacinthe Bay and Village Bay.

Hosea Bull had many talents. Prior to his move to Quadra, he'd held a string of jobs in Steveston, where he arrived in about 1887.[3] At different times he worked as a bookkeeper, a cannery night watchman, a farmhand and the manager of a lumber company. He's also rumoured to have been a preacher, though his granddaughter Sheila Bull laughed over this possibility. He was brought up in a strict Christian household by Hezkiah and Abigail Bull on a twenty-hectare (fifty-acre) pig farm, but he was not a religious man. That, however, would not have stopped Bull from passing himself off as a preacher, said Sheila. "Old Hosea Bull would turn his hand to anything, if he thought it would make him some money. He was the rebel, the wild one with a keen interest in women, cards, gambling and drink."[4]

Sheila Bull emphasized the fact that her grandfather was a

philanderer, a claim borne out by his circumstances. When Bull and his wife Cordelia arrived on Quadra they had a youngster named Samuel West with them, who attended the island's first school. Cordelia didn't claim the lad as her own, but he lived in their household and used the surnames Bull and West interchangeably.[5] And a few years after their move to Quadra the couple adopted an infant from a Catholic orphanage in Vancouver whose birth certificate says he was the natural son of Hosea Bull and a young woman named Mabel Davis.[6]

Hosea Bull had become the dominant force in Heriot Bay when Charlie Dallas dropped dead in a logging camp in January 1896 at the age of sixty-nine. "The deceased was eating his dinner when without the slightest warning he fell from his seat to the floor," said the *Weekly News-Advertiser*. "His friends instantly went to his assistance but the vital spark had flown and Charlie Dallas had suddenly crossed the dividing line between life and eternity." Within a few years of his death the name Dallasville was dropped in favour of Heriot Bay.

The many logging camps near Heriot Bay ensured its rise as a commercial hub. On June 1, 1896, Hosea Bull added a post office and store to his services and within a year there were thirty names listed for the

Cordelia, Cecil and Hosea Bull in about 1900. PHOTO COURTESY SHEILA BULL, MCR 20392-13

community in the provincial directory. By 1899 there were eighty-three names on the list, compared to four for Quathiaski Cove. (Directories only captured a small percentage of the actual population and rarely included women and children, but for Heriot Bay's directory Bull included every known resident, including women and children.)

Bull applied for a liquor licence for his hotel at the annual sitting of the provincial licensing board in 1898 and 1899. He was required to get signatures of support, which was easily done among the loggers, but Reginald Pidcock and Robert Walker urged against it for fear of the negative effects upon Native people.

Pidcock did have a sincere desire to represent the interests of local Native bands but he had other objections as well. Bull's licentious social and moral values ran contrary to Pidcock's beliefs, plus the man was a decided threat to the success of Pidcock's sons' business interests in Quathiaski Cove.

The Hughes sisters—Sarah (seen here), Mary and Aleen Selecelwit[7]—were exceedingly beautiful women of mixed Salish and British ancestry. Their parents' farm was on Heriot Bay Road, north of the Pinetree Road intersection. MCR 8486

Hosea Bull cut a wide trail from the beach at Gowlland Harbour (at what's now Camp Homewood) to Heriot Bay so loggers and residents on the west side of the island could patronize his businesses. The first official road followed in 1897, built by Walter Hughes, who got a one-hundred-dollar contract to clear a cart track along what's now Heriot Bay Road. Eventually the road ran up from Quathiaski Cove to what's now called Telephone Hill and turned north to reach Heriot Bay. (West Road did not come into being for another two decades.) Mary (Hughes) Joyce and her siblings helped with the work. "I have seen my father and other settlers digging with pick and shovel," wrote Mary in her memoirs, "and with a long pole to pry out roots, onto which we children would hang with all our weight to help heave them out."

Walter Joyce, an English settler with a fine homestead that overlooked what's now called Francisco Point, fell in love with Walter Hughes's beautiful daughter Mary. She was an ideal choice for a wife. Unlike some of Walter's peers, who married city girls or brought their sweethearts from the old country to share the privations of homestead life, Walter's wife was a well-adapted partner. The couple had to endure hardships of another type, however, when they married in 1898. Mary's Native ancestry was not acceptable to Walter's brother Alfred, who avoided them for the remainder of his life.

Mary travelled on horseback to visit her parents, taking the trail that's now Cape Mudge Road for her weekly visits. When this path was upgraded to a road, she drove a horse cart to their home and carried on to Heriot Bay to sell eggs, vegetables and sometimes mutton and beef. "I have had my two-wheeled cart upset going over a root on our narrow roads," wrote Mary. "Oh, what a great disaster at the time! Unhitch the horse, and right the cart after great heaves, then load on boxes and children and go on happily again."

The new road allowed settlers to drive to Heriot Bay to attend social functions organized by Hosea Bull. His picnic of July 1896 ended with a dance at the hotel and was described in the *Weekly News-Advertiser* as a grand success. The next year Bull invited everyone to the island's first May

Walter Joyce got a land grant at what came to be called the Jones' Farm on Sutil Road, at Francisco Point. He married Mary Hughes of Quadra Island in 1898 but suffered from depression following a bout with influenza in 1919 and took his own life. Mary was left with a large family to raise. PHOTO COURTESY HERBERT JOYCE, MCR 7839

Day picnic, held in late May to celebrate Queen Victoria's birthday, which became a much-loved tradition on the island and continues to this day. Fifty people gathered for his picnic and foot races in 1897 at what's now Rebecca Spit Park:

> The ladies of the island spread tablecloths on the green and covered them over with most of the good things that little boys and hungry men know what to do with. After all had satisfied the cravings of the inner man, the games commenced, the programme containing foot races, three-legged races, etc, etc. All seemed to enjoy themselves and before leaving for home all joined in singing, "God Save the Queen."

May Day picnics to celebrate Queen Victoria's birthday have been a tradition on Quadra Island since Hosea Bull of the Heriot Bay Hotel organized the first one at Rebecca Spit in 1897. The men seen here in the back, from the left, are Alfred Joyce, unknown, Walter Joyce with a flag, William Hughes, Robert Grant Sr. and Charlie de Veine. The four women standing are Cordelia Bull, Aleen Hughes, Mary Hughes and Sarah Hughes. Seated in front are Johnny Hughes, Harold Hood, Roy Hood, Hosea Bull with Cecil, Sam West, Eliza Hughes and Weaner Jones. PHOTO BY JOHN HOOD AND COURTESY HERBERT JOYCE, MCR 4074

A few months after Bull's inaugural May Day picnic, Alice Pidcock invited everyone to attend a second gathering to celebrate the Diamond Jubilee of Queen Victoria's reign on July 28, 1897. All of the non-Native residents (save the Bulls) came out to share a meal on the grounds of the new lighthouse at Cape Mudge. Though Katie (Walker) Clarke was only a child of seven, she recalled every detail of the day:

> All the neighbors and friends gathered there to honor the Queen. The Pidcocks took all the Cove people and those living near on their tug the "Quathiaski." A large table cloth or a number of them, were spread under the trees, the children raced around like wild things getting acquainted, especially the three Walkers. We did not see our neighbor children very often and had been looking forward to this picnic for weeks. Such a spread of good food. Mrs. Bryant had fattened and cooked a delicious suckling pig, apple in its mouth too, in spite of it being June. Mrs. Yeatman had a chicken pie made in a milk pan. The Pidcocks brought oranges, candies and cookies from their store. Our Mother was very proud of her green gooseberry pies, the first of the season. Mrs. Joyce had brought several delicious roast chickens. All these were enough to excite us to the highest pitch besides salads, jellies, cakes and many other kinds of pies.
>
> Lunch was always the first thing on the programme. After a rest we usually had sports, racing and a ball game, everyone taking part. But this year we were doomed to disappointment. It had been a very wet June. Deluging rain seemed to descend on us at a moments notice and the weatherman did not wish us to celebrate the Queen's Jubilee. We just had the table nicely set and the fire going well for the tea when down came the rain. Not just a gentle shower but a deluge. Everyone grabbed something and we all tumbled into the new boathouse and everyone congratulated everyone else on how lucky we were that a nice new building was there on such a day. We had our wonderful meal and Mrs. Pidcock called us all to sing "God Save the Queen."[8]

The island's non-Native settlers celebrated the Diamond Jubilee of Queen Victoria's reign in July 1897. The gathering was a rare treat that Katie (Walker) Clarke, the child to the left of the girls with the white bonnets, remembered in detail for the rest of her life. PHOTO BY JOHN HOOD AND COURTESY HERBERT JOYCE, MCR 7493(A)

The feud between Hosea Bull and Reginald Pidcock came to a head in 1899. It started when Pidcock reported Bull to the provincial chief of police, with a charge that he was "keeping a very disorderly house" at Heriot Bay. He asked that several key witnesses be subpoenaed to give evidence against Bull, whom he said sold "large quantities" of liquor without a licence. And he reminded the police chief of the serious stabbing at Bull's hotel at New Year's, the result of excessive drinking.

To retaliate, Bull wrote to the Department of Indian Affairs to say Pidcock had opened a store, contrary to the rules of his posting. "I do not own a store, either directly or indirectly," responded Pidcock to the DIA. "My sons bought out the store of Mr. R.H. Hall and they manage their own business and I do not in any way have anything to do with it, having in mind the section of the Indian Act to which you refer in your letter."

Pidcock was vindicated when charges were laid against Bull for illegal liquor sales under the guise of a private club. "The trick resorted to by Bull," reported the *Colonist* on February 5, 1899, "[was to have] all his customers register in a book." An investigation revealed that Bull paid everyone's club fees for them. "He had a set of club by-laws and rules and regulations all drawn up according to the law, and had been doing a rushing business for some time." Bull was fined two hundred dollars for this infraction, plus expenses.

Bull applied again at the next two annual sittings of the liquor licensing board but Pidcock continued to block him. When he applied in 1901 Pidcock pushed to have Bull's whole operation shut down. He claimed that even large logging camp operators like Sayward and Haslam didn't want Bull to be licensed because drunkenness had an adverse effect on their men's work.

Though Reginald and Alice Pidcock's children were now young adults and all the lively fun was happening at Heriot Bay, they were urged not to go. "Mrs. Pidcock didn't like us going to dances at Heriot

Reginald Heber Pidcock of Quathiaski Cove, centre, in a family portrait taken just before his death in 1902. Seen with him are his wife Alice to his right and her niece Carrie Green standing on his left. In the back row are the Pidcocks' sons—from the left, William, George (Hugh), Herbert and Reg. In the front row are Mary, Harry and Daisy Pidcock. PHOTO COURTESY RUTH (PIDCOCK) BARNETT, MCR 6923

Bay," recalled Dolly Smith, who came to live with the Pidcocks as a companion to Alice. "Oh she was indignant at us for going to a place like that!"

When Reginald Pidcock passed away quite suddenly in March 1902, the rivalry between Heriot Bay and Quathiaski Cove lost some of its vigour. Pidcock died in Victoria at the age of sixty-one from cancer of the liver, the day after his eldest daughter's marriage to the son of one of his long-time friends. He had continued to paddle his canoe throughout his large Indian agency almost to his very last days (the new agent got a gas engine shortly after he took over the job).

Though Reginald was sorely missed by his family, not much changed after he passed away. Alice Pidcock had long been the de facto head of the family, by virtue of Reginald's long absences. And the boys were busy with the various family enterprises in Quathiaski Cove, with their mother acting as their financial backer and partner.[9]

In the years that followed Reginald Pidcock's death, several more of his children married. Herbert wed his mother's young companion, Dolly Smith of Black Creek, in 1903. An auburn-haired beauty with a zest for life, she came from the same upper-class English background as the Pidcocks and shared their keen enthusiasm for fishing and hunting. Dolly was also an accomplished horsewoman. Herbert and Dolly built a stylish house near "mater," on their own land in the Cove.

Mary Pidcock also married into the Smith family. Cecil "Cougar" Smith, her husband, was renowned as a cougar bounty hunter and guide. Mary was a great sportswoman too, and was touted in the Columbia Coast Mission newsletter as "a typical woman of the West, able to turn her hand to anything; can handle a boat and tackle the most lively of Campbell River salmon."

The Pidcock boys divided their business and household responsibilities. William managed the store and post office and Harry looked after the farm. George, Herbert and Reginald ran a sawmill they opened in about 1900, and they were licensed to run the family's tug and steam donkey for their logging operation. As a sideline enterprise they sold deer meat and hides and they sometimes hired out their steam launch or their horse and wagon to deliver passengers and freight from the Cove. As George noted in his journal, it took two and a half hours one way to haul lumber by horse and wagon to Heriot Bay.

George Pidcock was the businessman, the one who brokered their log sales and kept the accounts. His notation-style journals provide a glimpse into not only the boys' business interests but the family's lifestyle.

By the time of Reginald Sr.'s death, the Pidcocks lived in comfort and style, compared to other islanders. Most of the extras came from Alice's investments and inheritance. Between the various family members, the Pidcocks owned most of Quathiaski Cove and Grouse Island, where they browsed livestock. Their large home, graced by Alice's prized piano, was surrounded by an orchard, a hayfield, gardens and a tennis court.

Though Alice's sons were hard-working coastal labourers, she liked to observe the social conventions she was brought up with. Everyone had to "dress" for dinners served by Alice's Chinese cook, and convene at the sound of her little bell.

The Pidcocks became fast friends with police officer Henry Fred Morgan Jones when his headquarters was transferred from Shoal Bay on East Thurlow Island to Quadra Island in 1902. Jones bought Tom Backus's farm and log house on the east side of the island (now Quadra Loop). He built a new frame house there for his young family, complete with a fully modern bathroom and a gravity-fed water system. From Quadra Island, Jones patrolled a huge district that extended from Powell River to the Thurlow Islands.

One of the more notorious cases Constable Jones handled was the apprehension of a thirteen-year-old girl from a cagey First Nations prostitute named Kitty Coleman. Kitty was a seasoned offender by 1905. Her name had first cropped up in the Attorney General's records in 1893, when she serviced a client who went on to commit a murder in an isolated logging camp on Read Island. She was back in the news in 1896 when she tried to sell a girl in her employ to a logger.[10] Her exploits in the 1905 case made the headlines in newspapers as far away as London, England. The shock factor was that Kitty's girl was of mixed race and looked white:

Mr. C.J. South [superintendent of the Children's Protection Act] left for the North on the steamer "Cassiar" on a knight errant mission of rescue. His purpose is to bring away the young girl, Edith Grant, now being held by an Indian woman named Kitty Coleman, at Quathiaski Cove. Mr. South says he has ample evidence to prove that the Coleman woman is a procuress who is bringing up the girl for immoral purposes. The woman is a full-blooded Indian but . . . the child is almost purely white. Mr. South will leave the "Cassiar" at Heriot Bay, where he will be joined by Provincial Constable Jones, and together they will proceed by canoe to Quathiaski Cove. Accompanied by the stalwart constable, Mr. Smith does not anticipate any great difficulty in securing the girl, and expects to be back in the city by Thursday morning.

(C.J. South also had a tarnished reputation in 1905, the result of a charge a few years prior of the sexual abuse of a nine-year-old orphan. Several children came forward with charges, but when the case went to trial the prime witness was too nervous to testify so South was acquitted and exonerated.)

Though Edith's mother belonged to the Cape Mudge Band, South took the girl. The authorities contended that because she appeared to be white she did not fall under the Indian Act and therefore could be removed. As reports in the provincial Attorney General's records state, the unnamed girl's mother and the chief of the We Wai Kai demanded her return. When Edith was eventually validated as a Native youth she was, presumably, returned to her mother.

Constable Jones's workload increased when the Heriot Bay Hotel got a licensed bar around 1906.[11] Old-timers said the Bulls "threw away the key" when they got their licence. The hotel was open for business day and night. "It got actually out of hand once in a while," recalled Herbert Joyce. "The fishermen and the loggers and the miners, they could never get along extra good and if they got too much to drink it would cause lots of dissension and a few fights and what have you. The miners was the worst."

Most of these men prided themselves on their prowess as hunters—but accidents were common and sometimes fatal. Fred Yeatman and his eldest son Tom bagged a deer at Brown's Bay, north of Campbell River, in November 1903 and then took different routes to circle back to their departure point to flush out more game. Tom reached their agreed meeting place but his father never showed up. Tom tried to follow what he thought were his father's tracks in the snow but a two-day search brought no results, so he went back to Quadra Island. Every able-bodied man in the district joined in successive search parties to comb the forest but they found no trace of Fred Yeatman.

Emma Yeatman was left with seven children to raise in a log house, on a ranch that was only partially established. Alfred Joyce

When Emma Yeatman's husband went missing in a hunting accident in 1903 her neighbour Dick Hall proposed but Emma felt he simply wanted to increase his land holdings and refused him. They were both Welsh but she was over ten years his senior. Emma is seen here in 1917. PHOTO BY ROB YEATMAN AND COURTESY PEGGY YEATMAN, MCR 6123

canvassed for money to assist the widow and her children. Her eldest son Tom ran the farm and some of the younger ones got jobs in logging camps. It wasn't an easy life, even before Fred went missing, but they got by. In her heart Emma wondered if Fred had deserted her, overwhelmed by the intense drudgery of their homestead life. She carried that secret fear for eight years, until Fred's skeleton was found by some hunters at Brown's Bay, trapped beneath a fallen log.

To add to the family's difficulties, two years after Fred disappeared their log home burned to the ground. The community again rallied to their assistance and built the Yeatmans a fine new house from milled

Tom Yeatman was just seventeen when his father died in a hunting accident but he got a job in a logging camp to support the family. The younger boys soon followed him and later the brothers ran their own outfits, as seen here at Hyacinthe Bay in about 1912. PHOTO BY ROB YEATMAN AND COURTESY PEGGY YEATMAN, MCR 6224

Two years after Fred Yeatman died, the family's log home on Smith Road, west of the Cedar Road intersection, burned down. The community volunteered time and funds to build Emma and her children a fine new home that still stands. Seen here are Rob with his bicycle, Emma and Dot Yeatman on the porch. PHOTO COURTESY ROB AND PEGGY YEATMAN, MCR 6344

lumber, complete with a stone foundation and a brick chimney. The house still stands on a lovely farm midway down Smith Road.

The early settlers paid a high price for their dreams of freedom and affluence, urged on by a government that wanted every corner of the province developed. The carrot they dangled was cheap land, and plenty of it—and a prosperous future. But despite all of the hard work it wasn't farms that brought wealth to the islanders. It was timber and salmon.

CHAPTER SEVEN

New Settlements on Northern Quadra Island

L ogging practices were in transition in the 1890s, when northern Quadra Island became a major logging and mining centre on this part of the coast. Many camps still used the heavy oxen teams of former years, but some began to switch to horses to pull their logs to tidewater. Horses ("hay burners") were light and fast, but neither method allowed loggers to haul from more than a few kilometres inland. Under these circumstances, contractors looked for dense, straight stands of fir and steep seaward slopes, where they could more easily skid the logs to the sea.

Hugh Grant's camp at Granite Point, at the entrance to Kanish Bay, was typical of the day. He had about twenty-five men on his payroll and he operated as a free agent to negotiate the best log prices from a choice of mills. But the industry was in flux and small operators like Grant were about to be nudged aside by "big-time operators." Of the ten camps at work in the northern Quadra/Okisollo area in 1891, several were managed by foremen who worked directly for the large sawmills. Their presence signalled the start of a shift toward corporate logging.

Despite a few short articles in the *Colonist* calling him "the well-known Valdes Island logger," not much is known about Hugh Grant. According to the 1891 census he was a thirty-eight-year-old widower from Nova Scotia.[1] Grant started logging on Quadra Island in 1887 and while he wasn't particular about the ages of his men, he preferred eastern Canadians. The other camps on northern Quadra, however, had a wide ethnic mix of men from Sweden, Ireland, Finland, Scotland, Austria and all parts of Canada and the US. While most camps had Chinese cooks (who were paid half of what Caucasians earned), Grant had a German-American cook named Henry Bowman. The real anomaly in Grant's camp, however, was that Henry Bowman had his wife Teresa and their three daughters with him. Teresa was the only non-Native woman for many kilometres around, at a time when women and children were not welcome in camp.

Hugh Grant broke new ground in other ways as well. He was the first in the region to experiment with the use of float camps, to allow his crew to work on the steep grades of Granite Point. Grant towed two massive scows from Victoria in 1890 at considerable cost. He butted the scows up to shore and used one for his oxen team and equipment and the other as accommodation for his crew.

When Grant finished his timber claim at Granite Point, he and

Loggers were required to bring their own bedrolls to camp and used hay from the horse team's feed or fir boughs as mattresses. The itch from bedbugs was a constant problem. PHOTO COURTESY ARNOLD CAMERON, MCR 13312

his brother John and a friend pre-empted adjoining properties south of Maude Island, at what came to be known as Grant's Bay. They logged back as far as Grant Lake (now Morte Lake), but in the late 1890s Hugh moved on, to prospect and explore in northern BC.

The largest logging company at work on the Discovery Islands in the 1890s was Royal City Planing Mills, owned by John Hendry, an eastern Canadian by birth. Hendry and his partners also owned lumberyards and mills in Nanaimo and New Westminster, and in 1886 he bought timber land at Village Bay Lakes. In 1889–90 Hendry amalgamated his various interests (including the pioneering Hastings Sawmill of Burrard Inlet) under the new name BC Mills Timber and Trading Company. The cumbersome name didn't catch on. Most preferred to simply stick with the old name, Hastings Company.

From the 1890s until World War I Hastings logged extensively on the islands, with each camp assigned a letter of the alphabet. Their regional headquarters was located at Bickley Bay on East Thurlow Island and later at Rock Bay, on northern Vancouver Island.

Logging companies weren't concerned about destruction of habitat or the needs of First Nations residents. Nature was limitless in her ability to recover—or so they assumed as they skidded logs down streams they left choked with debris.

With few rules to restrict them, the Hastings Company reshaped the Village Bay Lake chain in the early 1890s. They dammed and flooded it all the way back to Stramberg Lake and Shadow Brook at the northeast end of the lakes to form one large mass that allowed them to log the perimeter and boom their logs before they were shot down a flume on Village Bay Creek.

These alterations would have gone unnoticed, except for the fact that Village Bay Creek was a key fishing site for the We Wai Kai Band, who had a reserve at its mouth. They asked their Indian agent to intercede but Pidcock's requests came to naught.

In July 1894 Hastings was granted permission by the Department of Indian Affairs to cut a road through the Village Bay Reserve at no fee. And as the owners of Hastings could foresee a decade of work at the lakes, they wanted to buy the 4.5-hectare (11-acre) reserve. The Native people flatly refused, but the company built a temporary camp on their land anyway. "When I stated that I thought a sum of $30 [per annum] would be reasonable compensation," wrote Indian Agent Pidcock a few years later, "I meant for the trespass that the company had already committed."[2] Whether or not this paltry sum was ever paid isn't recorded.

When the We Wai Kai people found their salmon run completely blocked, Billy Assu once again called upon Pidcock. "I found on examination that the flume has been built directly down the centre of the stream," wrote Pidcock, "with heavy cross logs totally obstructing the stream and preventing the Indians, except in some few places, from catching the salmon."

The negotiations and complaints continued. In the end the company's concession was to erect a small fish ladder in their flume. As Pidcock reported to the Department of Indian Affairs, it was too small to be of any use. This same scenario played out again years later. In September 1909 Fisheries officer A.F. Lloyd (stationed in Quathiaski Cove) went to Village Bay Creek with George Pidcock to cut out yet another logging company's dam. When it was cleared they estimated twenty thousand fish passed through the stream in one afternoon.[3] When loggers dammed the creek yet again in the teens the Native people took the matter into their own hands and blew it up in the middle of the night.[4] A few coho and chum still spawn on this creek, and in 2006 a Salmon Enhancement group counted five sockeye in a fish trap at the outlet of the stream.

Hastings opened Camp C in Granite Bay in the 1890s.[5] The site had huge stands of Douglas fir in a valley that was ideal for railway logging. Hastings first experimented with the use of trains in the Fraser Valley on the lower mainland in the 1890s, and then sent a former CPR train called "Old Curly" to Granite Bay in 1901, along with several other engines for nearby camps.[6] From this beginning, the use of trains revolutionized the industry as they allowed loggers to haul from many kilometres inland.

By 1908 Hastings had eight kilometres (five miles) of track at Granite Bay along what's now Granite Bay Road. It was the first railway on the island. They also had five steam donkeys in use, another relatively

John Hendry of the Hastings Company bought a CPR engine used in transcontinental railway construction in the 1890s to experiment with hauling logs in the Fraser Valley. It was a success so he sent the engine to his camp in Granite Bay in 1901, where an engineer nicknamed it "Old Curly" in reference to Satan, when the engine made a sudden movement and nearly killed him. The train is now on display at Burnaby Heritage Village, near Vancouver. PHOTO BY HENRY TWIDLE AND COURTESY MARION ADAMS, MCR 6012

new piece of technology at the time. Over forty men worked in this camp,[7] with a daily output of 5,100 square metres (55,000 board feet) of timber,[8] enough to warrant adding two more locomotives in 1908.[9]

Most of the Hastings Company's crews were recruited through Vancouver hiring halls but they also employed local men. Southern Quadra Island rancher Frederick Yeatman worked on the booms in Granite Bay in 1903. He sent a letter to his wife via a steamship that called at Granite Bay and later went to Quathiaski Cove. It was the last letter Emma received before Fred died in the hunting accident, and she kept it for the rest of her days:

My Dear Emma, I suppose you have had a letter from me before this—I wrote last Sunday, but it would be a long time in reaching you as the boat is on her way up when she calls here & don't call again for a week. I hope this will find you all well; as I am thankful to say I am quite well. Have been working on the boom the last week & riding up & down on the train, the camp is two miles in from the beach. I don't know as I will be able to send my washing home. I have plenty of clean clothes to last quite a while, but if I see anyone coming that way I may send some; if not I might wash a little. I don't suppose I shall be able to come home until I come for good, unless I walk home. I may possibly do that but it is a pretty good walk. If you are sending some papers you can send a map of the island. I think there is a broken piece with the island on it. And send the compass too. If there is any roadwork going on you can let me know & the amount of money to be spent & I would come home—but I suppose they won't do it till spring. I don't know as I have

The Hastings Company had a reputation for keeping their older hands at work, as seen here in the Granite Bay camp in 1916. Company foreman Percy DesBrisay may be the man in the dark shirt and suspenders at the top of the stairs. On the bottom to the left is Charlie ("Dutchie") Neuberg. PHOTO BY HENRY TWIDLE AND COURTESY REINO LUOMA, MCR 3885

any more to say now. Hoping you are all well, I remain your affectionate, Fred.[10]

Though Henry Bowman broke with tradition in the 1890s and brought his wife Teresa to camp, there were still very few women among the loggers a decade later. In this male-dominated atmosphere, prostitution was a lucrative business. Some non-Native women travelled the coast by boat with their pimps to "service" the logging camps. Native women also came to the camps under the protection of male family members who claimed a share of their earnings. Such was the case when Reverend John Antle of the Columbia Coast Mission, a new seagoing medical and religious service, visited Granite Bay in about 1905:

> While conversing with the foreman, I glanced across the bay and the gleam of colour caught my eyes. The sun was shining brightly on the trees and on red blankets strung out on lines by the Indian women. I called the foreman's attention to this beautiful picture. "Yes," he said dryly, "very pretty indeed, but not so pretty at four in the morning. You ought to hear those women screech!" Then came the story. The women used to visit logging camps at night, returning to their own encampment in the morning.

The women's nighttime yells, continued Antle, were the consequence of arguments with their protectors. "I was intensely shocked," wrote Antle in his memoirs, "and resolved something should be done." He marched over to the encampment and told the Native men to leave but they pretended not to understand English. "So I proceeded to the camp where the women were sitting and addressed the most intelligent looking of them. Her name I found out later was Tessie, a notorious character on the coast." Antle was pleased to see the little group paddle out of the bay early the next morning.

Shortly thereafter Reverend Antle went to see Indian Agent George DeBeck (Pidcock's successor) at Alert Bay to demand something be done about prostitution. The agent initially agreed to support Antle's cause but later recanted. "He stated," recalled Antle, "that he did not feel called upon in his position as Indian Agent to spend his time chasing Indian whores around the coast."

As far as Antle was concerned, Indian agency officials were in collusion with the large timber companies. And he may have been right because logging had become big business and prostitutes, like good grub, were required benefits.

The Sunday following Antle's visit to Granite Bay the loggers held an "indignation meeting" to protest his interference. Other camps likewise damned Antle, whose Anglican bishop asked him to back down for fear of toppling the mission. But Antle was a determined man with strong convictions. He persuaded his bishop to accompany him to a meeting with A.W. Vowell, the head of the Department of Indian Affairs in BC. During a heated exchange, Vowell suffered a minor heart attack. When he recovered he capitulated to the feisty missionary and agreed to support Antle's push to eradicate the prostitution of Native women.[11] (His efforts did not succeed, however, until Native leaders like Billy Assu of Cape Mudge formed a patrol of Native men to enforce anti-liquor and anti-prostitution rules set by the band a few years later.)

By the early years of the twentieth century the Hastings camp was large enough to give the appearance of a tidy little settlement. It ran along both sides of the mainline track about 4.8 kilometres (3 miles) back from tidewater. There were the usual camp buildings, from the cook shack to the bunkhouses, and quite a number of loggers had their own shanties.[12] There were also some farms along the track, most of them owned by Finnish settlers.

It was stories of the Yukon Gold Rush and Sointula, the Finnish utopian community to the north on Malcolm Island,[13] that stirred Konstantin Wilhelm "Wilho" Stenfors's desire to immigrate to Canada. Stenfors sold his home and possessions in Finland to pay for his family's move, but when he arrived in 1901 it proved hard to find a place to live at Sointula. Maria and Wilho joined the many Finns who lived at Nanaimo, but with Wilho's minimal English all he could get were odd jobs. After nearly two years in a cramped one-room cottage they pre-empted land at Granite Bay in 1903, along with their Finnish friends

Wilho and Maria Stenfors' son Art in about 1923 on their Granite Bay farm, which was bordered by the current Granite Bay and Newton Lake trail roads. The Stenfors were one of many Finnish families who settled at Granite Bay after logging camps and mines opened there. PHOTO BY HENRY TWIDLE AND COURTESY GEORGE PUTTONEN, MCR 6689

Jacob and Frederica Larsen.[14] Both families built houses from massive log slabs, with Finnish elements like exterior stairways to the second storeys and saunas out back.

There were no other bona fide settlers at the bay when the two families arrived, other than a few loggers who had become semi-permanent residents. William Stramberg was the foremost among them. He lived in a shack on company land at what came to be called Stramberg Lake.

Granite Bay was probably not an easy place to live, with the mess of logged-over terrain and the isolation, but it had great promise. Government land was cheap and plentiful and the Hastings camp offered both an outlet for farm produce and seasonal employment for surrounding residents.

A Finn named Alfred Luoma was the next to join the Stenfors and Larsen families. Luoma came to the bay from Sointula when the utopian community failed. He pre-empted a large property at Granite Bay in

1906[15] and the next year, in the chapel of the Columbia Coast Mission's boat, he married Susanna Kayala, a Finn he had met at Sointula. That same year Alfred's brother Emil emigrated from Finland to establish a home at Granite Bay for his wife Amanda and their three sons, who followed in about 1909.[16]

When the Lucky Jim gold mine opened in the early 1900s, Granite Bay became a mini-boomtown. Hugh Grant appears to have been the first to find gold at Granite Bay, as he told the *Colonist* in 1892 that he'd found promising ore. "He has also some beautiful samples of white marble, granite and other valuable finds," said the article. "Mr. Grant is convinced he has a good thing at his island home besides timber." Grant does not appear to have raised the capital to open a mine, though his assay samples came in at $109 per 900 tonnes (992 tons) of gold-bearing ore and 1.4 kilograms (50 ounces) of silver.

The Hastings Company, however, was well positioned to finance a mine, so they registered Lucky Jim and several other claims in 1900. Their assay samples showed valuable streaks of gold, silver and copper in a seam near their mainline track, about 3.2 kilometres (two miles) inland from the bay. Though they only shipped 18 tonnes (20 tons) of ore from

Alfred and Susanna Luoma's house on Granite Bay Road is being restored by the current owners. PHOTO COURTESY GEORGE PUTTONEN, MCR 6686

Granite Bay in 1906–1907, Lucky Jim showed enough promise to inter-est investors like George Mumford of New York and Vancouver banker Eric Hamber. With these new partners, Hastings formed a subsidiary mining company, the Great Granite Development Syndicate Ltd.

Lucky Jim investor Eric Hamber was an astute young business-man on a meteoric rise. He'd started out as a bank clerk in Vancouver and later married the daughter of Hastings Company's president John Hendry. When Hendry died in 1916, Eric Hamber took over as presi-dent of Hastings, leaving Hendry's nephews in charge of daily opera-tions. By 1936 he was lieutenant-governor of the province.

Lucky Jim brought Hendry, Hamber and their associates tidy prof-its for the first few years. In 1908 they hired William Law (who later

Alfred Luoma, left, with child on his knee, got a land grant in Granite Bay in 1906, after he left the failed Finnish utopian community of Sointula on Malcolm Island. About a year later he married Susanna Kayala, who he had met at Sointula. The family went home during the Russian Revolution to support the cause but are thought to have been killed upon arrival, as traitors, although one daughter may have survived. Seen here from the left are Sylvia on Alfred's knee, Willie, Aino (behind Willie), Harold, Susanna and Elma. PHOTO BY HENRY TWIDLE IN ABOUT 1916 AND COURTESY GEORGE PUTTONEN, MCR 6688

The Lucky Jim gold, silver and copper mine was staked by the Hastings logging company in about 1900. It was a valuable but short-lived mine, with only a bit of surface work continuing after about 1911. PHOTO LIKELY BY HENRY TWIDLE, MCR 6006

This giant flywheel, which remains at the Lucky Jim mine site in Granite Bay, ran a compressor to pump water from the mine shafts and to run drills. PHOTO BY JULIE (LUOMA) DOUGLAS

bought a homestead in Hyacinthe Bay) as their superintendent. They shipped 78 tonnes (86 tons) to a smelter in Ladysmith in 1908 and the next year production increased to 305 tonnes (336 tons). In about 1910 they installed a huge iron flywheel, fired by a steam boiler, to pump water from the mines and run air drills in the 34-metre (110-foot) main shaft. They also hired Alfred Luoma to build five log bunkhouses and cook shacks along the railway tracks. (Both the flywheel and the remains of the original cabins can still be seen at this prized heritage site.)

Numerous other mines were staked in the wide belt of crystalline limestone that runs from Granite Bay to Bold Point, by a small army of tenacious prospectors and city investors. Among them were Rising Star, Stampede and the Anaconda, where an adit was driven in from the shores of a small lake in 1914. A mine called the Gold Exchange was staked by former south Quadra settler Tom Backus, in the same belt as the Condor, Geiler, Cormorant, Pelican, Hook and White Swan. None of them gave significant returns.

The Columbia Coast Mission became a vital service for men who worked in dangerous industries like logging and mining in isolated areas. But Reverend Antle had to use his considerable skills of persuasion to sell his cause to the loggers at Granite Bay:

> It was evening and the day's work was over. After much maneuvering we were all, or nearly all, gathered in one of the bunk houses and I was standing in the middle of a circle of strange faces endeavoring to explain the objects of the mission and my reason for the visit. After a while it seemed to be impressed upon my audience that, as someone remarked, this was "no graft" [swindle]. The doctor then took the floor, and in a few well-chosen words outlined the hospital and medical work.

Many of the men became subscribers, which entitled them to free service at the mission's hospital and aboard their ships. "I am sure we tramped back over the ties with much lighter hearts, feeling that we had made a goodly number of friends and supporters in one of the most important camps on the coast," wrote Antle.

Wilho and Maria Stenfors's seventeen-year-old son Arthur was thankful for the mission's services. He was working for Hastings as a brakeman on the railway in 1907 when he was "terribly crushed" between the skids of the landing and a railway car. He was taken immediately to the hospital at Rock Bay, where they despaired of his life. But a month later he was "practically as well as ever."

The Columbia Coast Mission covered Arthur's medical costs and his workmates paid his family's living expenses because by 1907 Wilho and Maria were dependent upon their son's income. "The boys at Granite Bay Camp put up handsomely for him," wrote John Antle in his newsletter, *The Log*, "so that he had no worry about the support for his mother and sisters while he was in hospital."

Arthur walked with a heavy limp for the rest of his days and was limited in his capacity to work, but as long as Hastings was in business he was assured of a job. When his father Wilho died of a heart attack in about 1911, Arthur took full responsibility for his mother and his siblings.[17]

Arthur's eldest sister Irene married Hastings blacksmith William Stramberg a few years before their father died, at the age of sixteen. Although Stramberg was twenty-two years her senior, he was considered a good catch.

William Stramberg had a better education than most of his fellow loggers. He had left his home in Pictou, Nova Scotia, for the allure of the West and somewhere

Herman Stenfors, left, was born in July 1903 and is thought to have been the first non-Native child born in Granite Bay. His twelve-year-old sister Irene and his father acted as the midwives at his delivery. Also in this photo is Dutchie Neuberg, famous all over the coast as an exceptional musician and entertainer. He worked as an assistant blacksmith to William Stramberg in the Hastings camps and lived with the Stenfors in the off-seasons. PHOTO BY HENRY TWIDLE AND COURTESY ROS LUOMA, MCR 4394

Irene Stenfors, a Granite Bay Finn, married logger and blacksmith William Stramberg. They're seen here in about 1917 with their children Vida (Carlson) and William Jr. The Strambergs were living in one of the old Lucky Jim mine cabins at the time of this photo but later started a farm below the mine, where they built a house that still stands. Irene was much younger than her husband and used to walk to southern Quadra Island to attend dances. She kept a pet monkey for company and had an exceptional flower garden. PHOTO IS LIKELY BY HENRY TWIDLE AND IS COURTESY ROS LUOMA, MCR 4391

along the line became a certified blacksmith. He was hired by Hastings at Thurlow Island in 1901, then transferred to Granite Bay later that year.[18] The quality of his work was so exceptional, his daughter Vida (Stramberg) Carlson recalled, that men came to him from all over the coast to have their equipment repaired. "If Bill can't fix it," they said, "no one can." Men who had a set of tools forged by Stramberg considered themselves very lucky.

Stramberg also had a winning personality. He was sought after for his lively conversation, his musical talent and far-reaching interests that included paleontology and anthropology. "The window ledges were always covered with his rocks," said Vida.

William and Irene lived in his cabin at Stramberg Lake for a time, and then moved to various Hastings camp buildings. It was over a decade before they got their own place just below Lucky Jim mine.

By 1910 a small village had formed on the waterfront at Granite Bay, atop a deep midden from an ancient First Nations village. The community was listed in the provincial directory for the first time that year, with twenty-nine names. Among them was Joseph Dick, the stepson of Hosea Bull of the Heriot Bay Hotel. With a gold mine in operation and a large logging camp, Hosea bought a quarter section at Granite Bay and built a combined hotel and store at the head of the freight and passenger dock.[19] Joseph and Jean Dick had living quarters upstairs and in 1911 they added a post office to their operation.

Within a year of all these improvements and additions to the community Lucky Jim's thin seams petered out. Hosea Bull sold the hotel and store in 1911 and the next year the Great Granite Development Syndicate sold their interests in the mine to a company that tried without success to revive it.

Yet Granite Bay remained a busy community, in spite of the failed mine. The Hastings Company had seventy-five men at work in its logging operation in 1911, according to the census. The only woman in camp was Lela Henderson, the wife of railway engineer Charlie Henderson. Lela stayed with her husband as he moved from camp to camp, until her premature death in 1919 at Rock Bay.

Henry and Agnes Twidle saw potential at Granite Bay and bought the store and hotel from Hosea Bull in 1911. The Twidles were an intriguing couple. Neither fit the working-class profile of the majority of their fellow residents—particularly Henry, with his photography and butterfly collections. Henry had the benefit of a first-class education

Twidle's Granite Bay store, built originally to also include a hotel, is on the right. The house in the foreground belonged to Henry Twidle's nemesis Henry Bull and family. PHOTO IS LIKELY BY HENRY TWIDLE, COURTESY MILT ADAMS, MCR 7843

in England, where he'd served as a private secretary to a wealthy man who had also promised him an inheritance. He immigrated to Canada in 1903 and became a bookkeeper in Vancouver, where he met Agnes through one of her relatives. Shortly thereafter Henry took a job as a timekeeper and store manager at the Hastings Company's Rock Bay headquarters, where he brought Agnes when they were married in 1907.[20] When he wrote home to tell his benefactor of his marriage he never heard from him again. Agnes's family wasn't keen on the match either. Henry had nothing to offer but his charm and good education.

Edward DesBrisay, whose father was the Hastings Company's superintendent, recalled his boyhood visits to the Twidles' little store, where general supplies could be purchased over the counter. Shelves of dry and canned goods lined both walls and you could see to the back of the store, into the Twidles' quarters, where Henry's butterfly collection was on display. Henry was an interesting man to talk to and young DesBrisay admired the slick runabout boat he used for fishing and transport in the days before a road existed between Granite Bay and southern Quadra Island.

Henry Twidle is best remembered now for his exceptional

Agnes Twidle in the parlour at the back of her and Henry's store at Granite Bay, with Henry's butterfly collection on display. PHOTO BY HENRY TWIDLE AND COURTESY JESSIE LUCAS, MCR 9108

Henry Twidle shot this photo of himself and his wife Agnes in front of their home in Granite Bay. Henry's sister-in-law Jessie Lucas described him as a lithe man. "I have a picture in my mind of Henry," wrote Jessie, "nearing a dock and jumping very gracefully from the boat to the wharf to tie it up." PHOTO COURTESY J.H. DALTON, MCR 6951

photographs of loggers, camps and settlements around Quadra Island. While many of his photographs and glass plates were destroyed when the childless couple left Granite Bay later in life, some were retained in private collections. His adept skill and sharp eye for detail provided an evocative record of coastal life at the time.

A school opened in Granite Bay the same year the Twidles arrived, in 1911. The government provided a one-hundred-dollar grant and the Hastings Company donated materials for a one-room school and a three-room teacherage on the Stenfors family's land, not far from the beach. Twelve children were enrolled that year but the numbers fluctuated with the vagaries of the logging industry. Sometimes the trustees had to search for a teacher with children to plump up the roster, or bring in children from elsewhere to board with Granite Bay families. The school inspector reported the students didn't make rapid gains because most spoke Finnish at home, so their English grammar and spelling lagged.

Across Quadra Island from Granite Bay, on the east coast, was another little settlement at Bold Point. Moses Ireland, the pioneer

Granite Bay School in about 1911. The Luoma and Stenfors families built the Granite Bay School on the Stenfors' land close to the current bridge, at the intersection of the Granite Bay and Newton Lake trail roads. PHOTO BY HENRY TWIDLE AND COURTESY J.H. DALTON, MCR 9120

logger of the region, established a cattle ranch there with his wife Julia in about 1901.[21] Like a few other autonomous loggers of his day, Ireland needed a place to overwinter his horse teams and accommodate his crews.

Moses was in his fifties when he married Julia Ward, a widow with two children and a granddaughter. For the first few years Julia remained in Victoria, where she worked as a seamstress, but in the early 1890s she moved to Moses's home on Subtle Island, off Cortes. The family relocated their hotel and store to Bold Point. By the time of their move Julia's son Bernard Ward was old enough to help with the large ranch Ireland established at Bold Point, along with the store and hotel.

A small community formed around the Irelands' hotel. There were sufficient residents and logging camps in the general area, including southwestern Read Island, to warrant a government wharf, which was built in 1910. About this time a telegraph line was installed from southern Quadra, and in 1911 the Irelands opened a post office, with Julia's granddaughter Sadie as postmistress.

Bernard Ward was in charge at the Irelands' hotel bar in 1902 when he ran afoul of the law by selling liquor to Native people. To dodge the expense of a conviction he fled to the US, where he stayed for a year in hopes his transgression would be forgotten—but as soon as he returned he was brought before local judges Dick Hall and Robert Walker and fined three hundred dollars. A year later the hotel was destroyed in a forest fire, and when Ireland replaced it he had to apply for a new liquor licence. He got a petition signed by loggers in several nearby camps but was opposed by another petition signed by Quadra and Read Island settlers and several foremen of local logging camps. "Mr. Ireland had for several years past," reported the *Colonist*, "had a liquor license for the Bold Point Hotel. It appeared that it was in his absence during the past couple of years that the infringements of the law for which the convictions took place, and Mr. Ireland manfully assumed all responsibility for the same, but for all this his application was refused."[22]

Bernard brought a common-law wife with him when he returned

Moses Cross Ireland (left) of Bold Point in his senior years, with Jack Perkins and perhaps his granddaughter Sadie in the doorway. Ireland was a colourful figure, known for his bravery, vigour and bush sense. He came to BC in 1862 for the Cariboo gold rush and stayed on to run freight on the Skeena River before moving to the Discovery Islands as a logger and timber cruiser. He ended his days at his Bold Point ranch in 1913 but was buried in Vancouver. PHOTO COURTESY RAMONA VANSTONE, MCR 19923

from the US. Lilly Joy Wilson was a devout Theosophist, embracing the new religious movement that spurned marriage and incorporated elements of the occult, including a belief in communication with the dead. Lilly Joy, who was eight years Bernard's senior, no doubt kept some of the irregularities of her life and beliefs to herself because she was accepted as a regular columnist for the Columbia Coast Mission's newsletter. In one of her articles she described her first year on the island: "We had a Christmas tree for the two little ones that were at the Point that year, and Old Santa appeared in all his glory, though the tree was laden with only homemade gifts, and devoid of its usual burden of city sweets, the love and goodwill made up for all deficiencies. It was a white Christmas, and I shall never forget how sweet the voices of the boys [loggers] sounded as they sang when they rowed into the bay over the icy waters, and came trooping into the room with their merry Christmas greeting; or the evening that followed, with stories and songs, accompanied by the twang of Jack's guitar."

Bernard and Lilly Joy moved to Read Island in about 1905, where Bernard ran his own logging camps, and while there the couple sanctified their union.[23]

Moses Ireland regained the liquor licence for his Bold Point Hotel after Bernard and Lilly Joy left Quadra. Ireland had already joined the ranks of BC folk heroes when a *Colonist* reporter interviewed him in 1905. He gave a dramatic account of a life full of adventure and said, at the age of seventy-five, that he was still timber cruising. "Although I am not as active as I used to be, I can stand just about as much hard work and exposure as when I broke the [log] jam at Beal's Bar," said Ireland. "I suppose I must go like all the rest of them, but I am not going to quit cruising until they carry me out of the woods."

True to his wishes, Ireland died in 1913 in the midst of his busy life. He was still in the employ of Merrill and Ring and Company, with whom he'd worked from his earliest days in the Discovery Islands. The *Daily Province* of Vancouver published a lengthy obituary for Ireland:

There have always been legends about Moses Ireland. A few facts about him are common property. For instance he was beyond all doubt the father of timber cruisers in BC. His uncanny instinct for picking out the best timber in a given tract of wild land and for estimating its worth correctly, added many millions to the fortunes of the timber merchants of the Pacific Coast. In recognition of this fact a certain Seattle lumberman paid Moses Ireland a pension to the day of his death. It is also common knowledge that Ireland had perhaps the coolest set of nerves of any man on the coast, the hardest set of muscles and the steadiest brain. His last days he spent in peace not far from the big timber.

Julia Ireland and her family closed the hotel and saloon[24] sometime after Moses passed away but they maintained the ranch, store and post office. When Julia died in 1917, she was buried in the new cemetery on southern Quadra Island. She left a considerable estate, valued at $6,817, an amount that would have supported an average family for eight years. Her son Bernard's wife Lilly Joy died sometime before Julia's death in 1917. She was buried in a grave surrounded by a wrought-iron fence draped in roses on the edge of the farm field at Bold Point, though any trace of her grave has long since disappeared.

Bernard Ward, his niece Sadie and her husband maintained the small store and post office at Bold Point for several decades, though the community became a backwater after the Irelands' deaths.

It was fitting that Bold Point should fade into quiet oblivion after Moses Ireland died. It marked the passing of an era of dreams of freedom and limitless potential. A new age was set to dawn, when the world was changed forever by rapid industrialization and the devastation of World War I. But there was still room for individualism in the little communities of southern Quadra, at Heriot Bay and Quathiaski Cove, where old rivalries continued.

CHAPTER EIGHT

The Slippery Quadra Island Postmaster

Heriot Bay had become the main centre for the region when Cordelia Bull passed away prematurely in June 1905 at the age of forty-four. A few months later, as the *Colonist* newspaper announced, Mrs. Helen Dixon, an expert with a gun, returned to Vancouver from a successful hunting trip in Heriot Bay. She bagged a brace of grouse and a large buck. Shortly thereafter Hosea remarried, taking as his wife a widow named Helen Dick. These women may have been one and the same, for Helen had a need to conceal her identity.

New Zealander Helen Bull was different things to different people. Her women friends, who came from diverse social spheres, admired her energy and organizational skills. Theodora Walker (missionary R.J. Walker's second wife) thought well of her, as did the eccentric feminist Lilly Joy Ward of Bold Point. But Tommy Hall, who stayed at the Heriot Bay Hotel while he attended school, remembered Helen as a stern disciplinarian he called "The Old Grey Mare."

She was the Old Grey Mare to Hosea's son Cecil too. Cecil was only seven years old when his father remarried. It was a difficult transition. Helen, who was in her prime at the age of forty-four, was loaded with ambition and a yen for the better things in life. She'd already raised a family in New Zealand and had no time for pampering an ill-mannered boy. "I am grateful for your trouble," wrote Helen to a friend who took

Helen Dick (later Bull) in her native New Zealand with her daughter Edith Tompkin. Helen moved to the opposite end of the globe after her former business partner shot at her point-blank. The bullet deflected off the busk of Helen's whalebone corset and her erstwhile killer got a seven-year sentence. Helen's New Zealand descendant Ingrid Sage has written a play about the affray. PHOTO COURTESY BEVERLY UPTON

care of Cecil during one of the Bulls' absences, "for I know what a trouble Cecil can make if he likes." Her methods of discipline could be harsh, including the time when she shoved the boy's head into a water barrel on the steamship dock for so long a logger intervened. (If Cecil was a "wild country boy" it was surely the result of being left to his own devices. He slept in the attic of the hotel with the loggers and sawmill workers and spent the rest of his time, when he wasn't in school, in the kitchen with the Chinese cook.)

Helen was a self-determined woman at a time when most of her sex were dependents. Back in New Zealand, she left her failed marriage after her three children were grown and joined her friend Annie McWilliam selling crystal work, wax and paper flowers, and panels for ball dresses. Helen went on to run several small hotels until about 1892,[1] when she persuaded Annie (also estranged from her husband) to purchase the City Hotel, a small establishment on one of Reefton, New Zealand's main streets. Helen served as the manager of the hotel, but the pair

The *Cheakamus* at the Heriot Bay dock, built in about 1902 in front of the Bull family's hotel and store. PHOTO BY ROB YEATMAN AND COURTESY PEGGY YEATMAN, MCR 6339

weren't in business long before they were forced to sell at a loss that Annie McWilliam later claimed bankrupted her. Helen went on to run a boarding house for a time until she was hired as the manager of a tea room in one of Wellington's landmark historic businesses, the Kirkcaldie & Stains Department Store.

Helen could have kept the messy details of the dissolution of her and Annie's partnership hidden in the past, had Annie McWilliam not decided to take the law into her own hands in 1898. As she later claimed in an account published in the New Zealand press, Helen owed her £2,250 and her paltry attempts at repayment added insult to injury.[2]

Annie's solution to the problem was to pay a visit to Helen's tea room, along with one of her daughters. Helen watched the pair closely and probably heaved a sigh of relief when Annie finished her tea and approached the till to pay. But instead of pulling out her wallet she drew a gun and fired at Helen point-blank. Annie's aim was true but the bullet deflected off the "busk"(top edge) of Helen's heavy whalebone corset, leaving only a bruise above her heart. Helen ducked and ran for a back storage room, followed by more bullets.

In the court case that followed, Annie McWilliam gave a garbled and vitriolic account of their history together. Midway through the trial she changed her plea to guilty. She had fully intended to kill Helen, she told the court, and she had no remorse.

Helen decided to move to the other end of the globe to be well away from Annie McWilliam when she finished her seven-year sentence. Washington State and BC, the jumping-off places for the Yukon Gold Rush, were good choices for a woman with her business instincts.[3] Some said Helen ran a brothel in either Seattle or Vancouver prior to her arrival on Quadra Island, but no records have been found for this phase of her life, when it's possible she lived under an assumed name.

Where and when Helen Dick and Hosea Bull met is also a mystery but Hosea must have seemed a good prospect. His diverse income base—from logging and timber cruising to hotel, store and postmaster contract—were distinct advantages, and Heriot Bay was loaded with potential. His property had a splendid view and there was a new government dock (built around 1902[4]) in front of the hotel and store. All that was needed was Helen's refining touch.

Helen took over the store, a 6.4 x 18.2–metre (21 x 60–foot) structure Hosea built in the spring of 1904,[5] with overflow hotel rooms upstairs. Though the store was her official domain, Helen also took a keen interest in the hotel—where she was seen by most as the primary active force. "When the hotel came under the management of the second Mrs. Bull," recalled Katie (Walker) Clarke, "it took on a whole different atmosphere." Helen liked things to be classy; no expense was spared on new trappings. Her vision was to cater to both the tourists and the "boys," as she and others called the bachelor loggers and miners. The two clienteles made for a tricky mix that required a degree of finesse and entirely separate accommodations.

About a year after they were married, the Bulls built a boat to use for cruises and for transporting their guests. As Lilly Joy Ward wrote in the Columbia Coast Mission's newsletter, the new boat could seat twenty "visitors of that noted hunting and summer resort." Over three hundred people showed up for the launch of the *New Zealand,* which was described in detail by Lilly Joy in July 1906:

Long banquet tables, draped in snowy linen, sparkling with silver and crystal, and garlanded with silken flags, and cut flowers, were spread beneath the luxuriant maple trees upon the lawn before the hotel, presenting a most captivating scene. At the stroke of twelve, the guests assembled upon the pier and beach to witness the ceremonies of the christening.

Master Cecil Bull, dressed in a spotless suit of white duck, acting in the capacity of "Commander" of the Heriot Bay fleet, took his stand upon the upper deck of the launch, and gracefully invited all guests who could find standing room to come aboard.

Seventy-five people crowded on board to watch two young women clad in gossamer gowns christen the boat. They recited poems and draped a wreath of cedar sprays and maple leaves "dripping with the salt waters of the bay (typical of Neptune's kiss to the bride)" over the bow. "Cheer after cheer rang out from every throat," continued Lilly Joy, "until the crowd was hoarse with shouting."

The Bulls' guests were seated at tables "spread with all the delicacies of the season," and a few were invited to speak about the successes of the pioneer community. Mary Bryant reminisced about her first years on the island in the 1890s and thanked Hosea Bull for the many comforts he

Helen and Hosea Bull launched the *New Zealand* in 1906, shortly after they were married. They held a gala party beneath the giant maples on the lawn of the Heriot Bay Hotel to christen the boat. PHOTO COURTESY SHEILA BULL, MCR 20392-39

provided them at Heriot Bay. "In the old days we had to go [on] long wearisome journeys by little row boats, which took us many days, and sometimes weeks, to the nearest settlement for provisions. Now we have our post office and store within an hour's walk. We have all the enjoyment of country life, with the advantages of the city within our reach."

Walter Joyce was the next to speak. "My heart swells with pride to realize the changes that have taken place in our island, and yet those old days were happy ones too. So here I invite you to drink to the good old days," said Joyce, "and the people who blazed the trail over which the feet of future generations will tread, when the pioneers of Quadra Island will be only a memory."

Hosea Bull, who was next to speak, described the success of his enterprises:

> I hope to make Heriot Bay a resort that you will all be proud of. You have been my neighbors and patrons for many years, and although it has sometimes been a hard uphill struggle for me to meet the many demands upon my finances to make Heriot Bay what it is today, still I intend to keep on trying to bring it up to your ideal of what the principal resort of Quadra Island should be. As for our launch, there are many kinds of launches, but the very best launch that a man can make is when he launches into matrimony. And that kind of launch will give him more real happiness than any gasoline launch that was ever launched.

Helen Bull wrapped up the speeches with her address:

> I feel truly grateful to the "boys" for having chosen me to respond to their toast. I hoped when Mr. Bull was asked to say something for our little launch he would speak about her since she is just at this moment my "pet hobby." I always knew that he had a deep-seated reverence for that kind of "launch" and his pet theme, "women."
>
> Now, just a word for "our boys," I have travelled the world over and can truly say that never have I met with more courtesy

The launch for the Bull family's boat, the *New Zealand*, included a dinner on tables covered in white linen beneath the maples at the Heriot Bay Hotel. The festivities included a tug-of-war between the loggers and miners. MCR 11375

> than among "our boys." They are true "diamonds in the rough," and no more generous and kindly hearts beat in the breasts of any men. They know that I speak the truth since I have chosen from among them the man in whose keeping I place my heart. To me the prince of them all, my dear old "chum."

The rest of the day was spent in races and a tug-of-war between the loggers and the farmers, "which was won easily by the loggers." And that night a string band entertained the crowd until dawn with a lively dance.

Later that summer, Bull must have persuaded the authorities he was now a respectable citizen, with his old liquor offence deep in his past, because he was appointed as a Justice of the Peace in August 1906. He and several other local JPs tried minor offences at the island's school.

The cost of a new store, the boat and elaborate parties outstripped the Bulls' income by 1907. To dodge their debts they took a lengthy trip

Other side of the tug-of-war between loggers and miners, Heriot Bay. MCR 9376

to Australia and New Zealand, financed by swindling Hosea's timber cruising partner Mr. Myers.

Hosea's son Cecil was boarded out with Alfred and Anna Joyce that September when the Bulls set off on the first leg of their trip, with a stop in Victoria and another in Seattle. From Seattle, as they told everyone, they would go to San Francisco, and from there to Australia by boat.

Hosea had arranged to meet Myers in Victoria to pay him his share of a recent timber sale of twelve thousand dollars but the Bulls skipped town just prior to the appointed time. (Hosea later said the real problem was that his finances were in such a muddle he didn't know exactly how much was due to his partner.) When the Bulls didn't show up Myers notified the police and charged Hosea with grand larceny. The police traced the Bulls in Seattle and had Hosea incarcerated to await the arrival of Canadian officials. Myers, however, also went to Seattle, where Hosea's glib tongue won the day. Hosea persuaded Myers (who later confessed he had been hoodwinked by Bull numerous times) to accept one thousand dollars in cash and the remaining three thousand in a cheque.

When Myers got back to Canada he found Bull's cheque was worthless and once again called upon the police, but by this time the Bulls were long gone. When Myers learned Hosea had received a twelve-thousand-dollar bank draft on a London bank for the log sale he realized the Bulls had to be headed across the US by train to New York and then on to London. As it was now impossible to reach Hosea Bull, Myers's lawyer advised him to drop the case. "Myers considers himself extremely lucky, as compared with the majority of the people who have had business relations with the astute Bull," said the *Colonist* newspaper. "[Bull] has debts everywhere it seems, and paid nobody he could avoid. The Kelly Douglas Company of Vancouver [store wholesalers] is stated to be one of the firms who are heavy losers on account of their dealings with the slippery Quadra Island postmaster."

Things did not go well at Heriot Bay during the Bulls' lengthy absence. They had barely left when manager William Glennon hosted a giant masquerade ball with no holds barred. The liquor flowed freely throughout the weekend and one of the logging crews bought more whisky to continue the spree at the Okisollo Channel camp off northern Quadra. Two of the men served Billy Assu's mother Annie Kla-pi-ne-ka whisky in camp, and she was later brutally murdered. In the end the accused was exonerated of all but illegal liquor sales to a Native person.[6]

Some have suggested that it was the murder of Billy's mother in 1907 that led him to crusade against alcohol use, but by that time he had championed abstention for more than a decade. Back in September 1904 Assu had asked the resident missionary at Cape Mudge, Reverend J.E. Rendle, to write to Indian Agent George DeBeck to describe the problems brought by the Heriot Bay Hotel and a new hotel in Campbell River:

> Some of the people get drunk at Bull's and other places and come to me to have their wounds dressed. A white man by the name of Lord Bacon supplies whiskey from these bars to any

Indian wanting it, it was only a week ago that a man from the village got liquor from him at Bull's, and then was tried and fined $10.00 by a mock court. All the people wish to see the law enforced and at this time seem in earnest. This is the second letter I have had to write to you this week on this subject.

The Bulls had to face up to the infamy of Glennon's mismanagement of the hotel and their many debts when they returned to the island in the spring of 1908. In family stories of this time, Hosea blamed his troubles on Glennon, who he said embezzled them. This alibi must have served its purpose because a few years after their return the Bulls were able to build a fine new hotel on the current site.

A grand celebration was held on December 27, 1911, to open the new hotel, but within a few months, on May 11, 1912, it was destroyed by fire. Young Tommy Hall, who boarded at the hotel on school nights, was shocked when he returned on Monday to find it a blackened mess of burnt timbers, chimneys and bedsprings. The Bulls must have had the hotel well insured because they quickly replaced it. The new hotel included a dance hall on the top floor and nineteen bedrooms on the

Hosea and Helen Bull replaced the first Heriot Bay Hotel in 1911 with the build-ing seen here but it was destroyed by fire within months of opening. It was quickly rebuilt and opened in 1912. The lounge and kitchen of the current Heriot Bay Inn are all that remains of the 1912 structure. PHOTO COURTESY HERBERT JOYCE, MCR 7676

upper storey. It had a large office where travellers gathered around the fire to await the late-night arrival of the Union Steamship boat from Vancouver and a hallway that separated two halves of the hotel to isolate the loggers from the sportsmen and tourists. The loggers' saloon had a high bar fronted by a brass rail, with spittoons at the corners, and the loggers and tourists each had their own dining rooms. The store was moved into the hotel at this time as well, attached to one end so it had its own entrance.

The exterior of the new hotel was beautifully appointed. There were baskets of geraniums and nasturtiums hung along the nine-metre (thirty-foot) verandah that doubled as a summer dance floor, and at its far end was Helen's aviary of rare canaries. The grounds included a tennis court and lawns that stretched down to a beach fence draped in roses.

The staff at the hotel and store included girls in white dresses who waited on the dining tables (only the best of the waitresses could serve the tourists), a Chinese cook, a Chinese gardener, a bartender, an odd-jobs man and a bookkeeper.

Behind the hotel were a barn (a place long-time resident Bill Law hinted sometimes doubled as a brothel) and a large kitchen garden. To the west of the hotel was a stylish cottage the Bulls rented to city folks for long-term stays. And yet farther to the west, around the bay, was Hosea Bull's sawmill, near land donated to the community by the Bulls so visitors and residents could enjoy the sandy beach. (The government wharf built at that end of the bay years later blocked the drift of sand and changed the quality of the beach.) The Bulls also donated a strip of waterfront for a public walkway that ran from Esplanade Park to the hotel.

The Bulls had high aspirations for their hotel, though they were cognizant of the fact that the boys, with their pranks and brawls, were their mainstay. A notable habitué of the bar was Lord Huey Horatious Nelson Baron Bacon, "the only Lord in America." Some believed there were shreds of truth to his claim to nobility because he was a well-educated man and could recite at length from the classics when he was in his cups.

One day, Bacon sent word to his enemy John Hanaher[7] to meet him at the Heriot Bay Hotel for a duel. Old-timer Bill Hall told the tale as he heard it from his Uncle Charlie. "The bar was full, waiting to see

Hosea and Helen Bull, on the left, with summer guests Bishop Scholfield of Victoria (with the cleric's collar) and his wife on his right. To the Bishop's left is: Helen Bull's daughter-in-law Jean Dick. Mrs. Letson, a regular Vancouver visitor, is seated at the tea table. Waitresses Jennie and Mae Millar stand by the centre post, next to Mae and Velma Anderson of Quathiaski Cove, in darker dresses. Next is Lizzie Law of Hyacinthe Bay and Reverend Fred Comley of Quadra, seated. Next to him are Mrs. Whipple, wife of the Quathiaski Cannery storekeeper, Margaret Haslam the Heriot Bay schoolteacher, Theodora Spencer (later Walker) the Valdes Island schoolteacher and unknown. MCR 4249

the shootout," said Hall. "Bacon came in wearing a .45 six-shooter and asked if anyone had seen Hanaher," and Charlie Hall plied him with double shots of whisky until he passed out.

Later Hanaher arrived wearing a .44 with a long barrel and said, "I see Bacon's not here. I didn't think he had guts enough to show up." Charlie Hall listened to the man's rant and plied him with the same potent drinks he gave Bacon. When Hanaher passed out, Hall and the boys tied him in bed face to face with Bacon. "When they awoke some time later they started yelling and cussing each other. They said when they got loose they'd get their guns and shoot everybody in Heriot Bay and burn the hotel down. They was so set on revenge they forgot their feud and never did get around to having a shootout," recounted Bill Hall.

Hosea's sawmill did good business through these years. It was located at the foot of what's now Antler Road and employed six people, all of whom lodged at the hotel. Among them were Helen's nephew and her son Joseph and his wife Jean, who had immigrated with Hosea and Helen upon their return to Canada. It was also at this busy time the Bulls built the combined store and hotel at Granite Bay, which they sold when the Lucky Jim mine failed.

The Bulls were proud of the fact that Heriot Bay surpassed all the little communities in the region, including the new tourist village of Campbell River. They had biweekly steamship connections to Vancouver by 1910 and ninety-six men were listed under Heriot Bay in the provincial directory. Nearly half were loggers, sixteen were farmers and/or ranchers and thirteen were miners, along with a boat builder, two cooks, a fisherman, a clerk, a bookkeeper and a sawmill operator.

A compromise was struck between Quathiaski Cove and Heriot Bay folks when it came to the big event of the year, the May Day picnic. Sometimes it was held at Cape Mudge lighthouse and at other times it was at the Maxwells' chicken ranch on Rebecca Spit. On at least one occasion, in 1901, the picnic was held in Campbell River, where Billy Assu of Cape Mudge Village and Johnny Moon of Kelsey Bay played host. "We had invited all the white people in the vicinity to attend," Billy Assu told the *Colonist*, "nearly all of whom responded to our invitation, and we had quite a large gathering numbering 300 persons." (This anomalous blend of Native and Euro-Canadian celebrants for May Day doesn't appear to have been repeated for many decades.)

The Rebecca Spit picnic grounds were on Winfield and Louise Maxwell's big farm field. Not much is known about this childless couple. She was a Mexican by birth and came to Canada in 1900; he was an American logger who had been in Canada since 1888. The Maxwells and their friend Robert Kelly were listed in the Heriot Bay directory as "chicken fanciers." The Maxwells' log home was somewhere in the vicinity of the knoll at the first narrows of the Spit.

It was always hard to get out the door on time on the morning of the May Day picnic. The women packed an elaborate meal, the farm animals had to be tended and everyone had to be turned out in their finest attire. The Anna and Alfred Joyce family set out late one year but they made good time with their horse and buggy, thanks to their frisky "Indian ponies," until they came up short behind Jack Bryant. He and his boys sat atop an old sleigh that was being dragged down the trail by their oxen team. Mary Bryant and the girls had wisely gone ahead on foot, while their menfolk transported the big picnic basket, which was covered by a white cloth. "And when our horses seen him they were frightened," recalled Herbert Joyce in a taped interview, "because he had that white cloth around this basket. His oxen and him wouldn't move off the road and our horses wouldn't go by so there was lots of swearing. [Dad] had to get out and drive Bryant's team up in the woods to allow ours to get by—and away we went again."

Seen at this May Day picnic at Rebecca Spit in 1902 are, from the left: Herbert Pidcock, Mary Holmes, Aleen Hughes, Harry Pidcock, Mary Pidcock, Jack Bryant, Lillian Hood, Annie Davidson, Mrs. Davidson, John Davidson (the lighthouse keeper), Willie Pidcock, Dick Hall, Roy Hood, Dick Bryant, Tom Yeatman, Rob Yeatman and George Yeatman. From the right rear is Katie (Walker) Clark, Winnie Walker, Daisy Bryant, Alice Bryant, Mary Bryant, Alice Pidcock, Dot Yeatman, Emma Yeatman, Ray Yeatman, Fred Yeatman Sr., Fred Yeatman Jr., Reg Pidcock, George Pidcock and Gordon Hood. PHOTO MAY BE BY JOHN HOOD AND IS COURTESY ROB AND PEGGY YEATMAN, MCR 4363

"Everyone brought a picnic lunch and just set it down on long table-cloths on the grass," recalled Grace (Willson) McPherson, who grew up on the island. "Then you just sat down where you wanted to." After the picnic they sang "God Save the King," followed by the excitement of foot races, with cash prizes of up to fifty cents. There were the usual two-hundred-yard dashes and novelties like a race with a hard-boiled egg on a spoon, three-legged races, a pipe race (you had to dash to a line, light a pipe and return with it alight) and a blindfold race. "[Mr. Bull] was one of the greatest sports in the world for children," recalled Herbert Joyce. "They had a sack race for the little kids and he got in and put one sack on each foot and beat everybody."

As the day came to a close Mr. Maxwell set up his gramophone to amaze his friends. "Children would crowd around it, gazing in wonder at the box that could talk," wrote Bill Law. "After the picnic a dance would be held in the hall above the hotel," he continued. "There would be a pianist and Mr. Bull with his fiddle and the dance would continue until 6:00 a.m., when breakfast would be served." Everyone went to the dances, young and old, but loggers had to leave their caulk boots at the door. As the night drew on the children were bedded down in the hotel rooms to sleep.

Hosea and Helen Bull, with their hotel and store, were at the centre of the non-Native community's social scene. But while these enterprises brought the Bulls success they didn't create much work for islanders. The Pidcocks, however, had already embarked on a business in Quathiaski Cove that was to become the island's major employer.

CHAPTER NINE

The Finest Salmon-fishing Waters in the World

There were non-Native settlers scattered about in various spots on the southern end of Quadra Island by the economic boom years at the start of the twentieth century. With transport being mainly by foot, each area had to have its own school. In 1910 Hosea and Helen Bull donated land for a school in Heriot Bay, at what is now the junction of Hyacinthe Bay Road and West Road. Unlike the log cabin that served as the non-Native settlers' first school, this one was built of milled lumber, with funds and labour donated by islanders.

Katie (Walker) Clarke was the first teacher at the new school. Her parents, Robert and Agnes Walker, formerly of the Cape Mudge mission, lived on their farm in Gowlland Harbour, which they bought in 1904. They named their property Homewood Farm (today it's Camp Homewood). Katie had finished grade school on Quadra Island and passed her entrance exams for high school, but her parents couldn't afford to send her to the city to continue her education until Reverend Antle of the Columbia Coast Mission interceded. "Mr. Antle and Mother had a heart to heart [and] he suggested that I could work for my board as there were women in the city who were glad to give a home to a high school student in return for companionship and help with their children. When he left that evening he said, 'Don't worry Kate, we'll get you to school okay,' and he did."

Heriot Bay School's first teacher was Katie (Walker) Clarke, who was raised on the island. PHOTO COURTESY KATIE (WALKER) CLARKE, MCR 6781

Katie's pupil Tommy Hall had to row across the head of Gowlland Harbour and walk from there on an old skid road that came out near the school. The route took two hours each way so he boarded at the Heriot Bay Hotel, along with a few others in similar circumstances. To pay for his keep Tommy milked a cow, built fences, fixed waterlines, delivered groceries and helped Helen Bull in the store.

Children who attended the old log school got a new building in 1905. By then, the "Old University," north of Pinetree Road, was in a sad state. "I'll invite the readers of your paper to

Heriot Bay School shortly after it opened in 1910 on Hyacinthe Bay Road near the West Road intersection. PHOTO COURTESY KATIE (WALKER) CLARKE, MCR 6913

come and see the little children huddled around the stove trying to keep warm," wrote an islander in the *Colonist*, "and on rainy days [or] snowy days trying to keep their books from getting wet."

After much debate about a new location for the school, they decided to build on Daniel Smith's property near the current Department of Highways works yard to better serve children who lived in the Cove and those at the southern tip of the island. Smith agreed to donate some land but as he no longer lived on the island the property transfer was slow. When islanders were finally ready to build only $850 of

The Hall family outside their home in Gowlland Harbour. Standing on the porch are: Mary and Pierce (William) Hall, with William's brother Charley in the doorway. The children, from the left, are Beatrice, Ann, Tom, Mary, Bill and Bob. The older children had to cross the harbour by boat and then hike a trail to Heriot Bay School. It was a long trip so in winter the eldest child Tommy worked for the Bulls at the Heriot Bay Hotel for his bed and board. When Tommy was at home he worked on the farm. "I swear that I packed brush to the clearing fire," recalled Tommy later in life, "before I was off the bottle." PHOTO COURTESY HARRY HODSON, MCR 16315

the original grant allocation remained. The result was a "shack" one islander likened to a woodshed, but it was a vast improvement on the Old University.

The first teacher in the new Valdes Island School was an inadvertent agent of change for the Pidcock family in Quathiaski Cove. William Pidcock fell in love with Mary Holmes, who boarded with his family at the Cove, but she was not easily won. When Mary returned to her family in Victoria, William's heart went with her, though there was no time in the Pidcock brothers' busy schedules for lovestruck mooning. They added a cannery to their businesses at the Cove in 1904,[1] which achieved their father's long-held vision.

Native men and women did most of the fishing for the cannery, from dugout canoes that were well-suited to the job. They used very simple gear—a length of "cuddy hunk" (heavy cotton line) wound onto a wooden spool, a flasher made from the bowl of an old spoon to attract

Canners like W.E. Anderson of Quathiaski Cove had exclusive rights to fish in a set area around their canneries. Anderson relied mainly upon fish taken by hand from small boats but also had a fleet of about five seine boats. In this 1912 photo, salmon are being brailed into the hold of a packer boat before being taken to the cannery. PHOTO BY HENRY TWIDLE AND COURTESY MARION ADAMS, MCR 5128

the fish and make the line flick from side to side, a herring rake (a long pole with nails spiked along the lower half to spear bait fish) and a choice of hooks. They tied their lines to their legs above the knee with a climp knot that released at the tug of a fish. Once a salmon was reeled in beside the boat it was gaffed aboard in one deft motion and clubbed.

In an August 1905 article about two sport fishermen who spent their summers in Discovery Passage the *Colonist* newspaper said Quathiaski Cannery was the only one in BC ("or perhaps in the world") whose catch was taken entirely by hand, with about fifty men and women in their employ. Their total catch for that season was about sixty thousand fish, for a pack of four thousand cases.

In 1905, sport fisherman L. Layard met one of the Pidcock boys on the fishing grounds in his dugout canoe. He was using two handlines and his catch for the day, from 3:00 a.m. to 9:00 p.m., was 706 salmon.[2] He and the other fishermen had to bring their own daily catch into the cannery because the family's boat (nicknamed "The Little Stinker" for its unreliable gas engine) was not suitable as a packer.

At the wide cannery door, the fish were unloaded by the Chinese crew, who scrubbed and butchered the fish to the approximate size of the cans. These chunks went to women who worked on the line, where they trimmed the fish to fit precisely into the cans. The Chinese crew cleaned the rims of the cans, added salt, soldered the lids and loaded them onto flats they shoved into the "retort" machine, to remove the air. Then the cans were shellacked and made ready for the labels.

As the 1901 census shows, the majority of We Wai Kai people were experienced cannery workers by the time the Quathiaski Cove plant opened. Most listed cannery work as their primary income, though they had to travel huge distances to work in Fraser River and Rivers Inlet plants before Quathiaski Cannery opened.

Census figures also show the Native people's population was still on a sharp decline. By 1901 there were only 105 people left in the band, compared to 133 in 1881. While the premature death rate among the elderly seems to have decreased by 1901, with Wamish at age seventy,[3] the childhood mortality rate was still high, with big gaps in ages between the children in many families.

Cape Mudge Village in about 1915, when a number of the communal big houses had been replaced by single-family homes. PHOTO COURTESY SHEILA BULL, MCR 20392-2

Sixteen band members could speak English by 1901, including some children who attended school for a few months in winter. Their families pulled them out of school when they moved to seasonal food-gathering sites or went to work in distant canneries.

Billy Assu continued to host lavish potlatches that brought his family prestige at the start of the twentieth century. When his uncle Wamish died in January 1903, his names and positions became a matter of contention. Wamish's grandson William (Quocksister) Roberts of Campbell River was understood by some to inherit Wamish's rank and privilege, and his mother Mary (Wamish) Roberts held a potlatch in his name to affirm the fact, but the question remained open in the minds of others.

The Pidcock family of Quathiaski Cove also faced a divisive issue when William Pidcock followed Mary Holmes to Victoria to win her hand. His departure called for major restructuring of the family's businesses. With one less family member involved, in 1906 the Pidcocks sold the cannery and store to Victoria druggist T. Atkins, who enlarged the cannery, added new machinery and bought a steam launch to serve as a fish packer. Atkins ran the store and post office, and hired Fritz Rathgerber to oversee the cannery—but he didn't keep the labour-intensive operation long. He sold it in 1908[4] to Vancouver businessmen W.E. Anderson and Frank J. Comeau.[5]

Not much is known of Frank Comeau, but Anderson was a man blessed with a winning combination of energy, integrity and good luck. He sold his interest in a sawmill in Ontario in 1898 to try his luck in the Yukon Gold Rush with his brothers and a friend. Where thousands failed, Anderson made a fortune from two claims at Hunker Creek that became Klondike legends. He bought his claim for twenty dollars, reaped an impressive profit and then sold it for five hundred thousand dollars to a man who went on to make a million from it.[6]

W.E. Anderson's wife and family were with him when he sold his Klondike claims and moved to Vancouver. He invested in a number of ventures, including the little cannery at Quathiaski Cove.

A year after Anderson and Comeau bought the cannery it was razed in the middle of a busy packing season. Reverend John Antle of the

The Quathiaski Cannery was opened in 1904 by the Pidcock brothers but they sold the labour-intensive business in 1906 to druggist T. Atkins, who in turn sold the cannery within two years to W.E. Anderson and Frank J. Comeau. Under Anderson's direction the cannery developed into a thriving business. MCR 20126-31

Columbia Coast Mission was tied up at the cannery dock on August 31, 1909, when fire ripped through the building:

> About two o'clock in the morning the cannery was discovered to be in a blaze and we woke up to find the flames roaring over us and the paint frying on our boats and deck gasoline tank. Dr. Kemp and I cut and shipped lines as soon as possible but the vacuum under the cannery created by the fire was so great that our united efforts could not move the boat from the wharf. But Engineer Evans was busy with his engine and in the nick of time the welcome puff puff was heard, and I was glad to escape to the wheel house and give the bell that set her forging ahead to safety. I do not think that the boat could have remained at the wharf another minute without catching fire in all probability exploding the gasoline tank.

The cannery's normal pack for the season was 6,500 cases but all that was left after the fire were 500 cases yanked aside before the building was fully engulfed. Comeau dropped out of the business after the fire and the next year Anderson reformed his company, with Vancouver wholesale

Quathiaski Cove, c. 1920. The "China House" is on the far right, above is the court-house and jail built in 1912. The large building in the centre is the cannery. To the left is the sawmill and the Anderson's home and store at the head of the government wharf. MCR 20126-84

grocer W.H. Malkin, who held a one-quarter share. The partners rebuilt the cannery on a much larger scale.[7]

By 1911, when the census was compiled, the cannery had a crew of twenty-seven people, most of whom lived on-site. Albert Nye,[8] the cannery manager, was among Anderson's highest paid employees, at one thousand dollars per year. W.E. Anderson and his nephew Melvin ran the store and thirty-two-year-old Wu Lee earned four hundred dollars per year as the foreman of a sixteen-man Chinese crew. Lee worked under an off-site overseer who paid all the men's living expenses. The crew who gutted the fish and operated the cannery machines earned three hundred dollars per year. Many of them were married men in their twenties and thirties, with wives back home in China. After the canning season most returned to Chinatown in Vancouver, where they lived in cramped dormitories to await the next canning season.

In those pre–World War I years cannery operators got the exclusive right to own seine boats within an allotted territory. Anderson's Area C boundaries encompassed a forty-eight-kilometre (thirty-mile) radius, from the Oyster River to the Adams River. He had one or two seine boats in use in 1911, with a crew of eight fishermen from Scotland, Russia, Prussia, Norway, Nova Scotia and Germany. The head seine fisherman earned one thousand dollars per year, while the rest got four to eight hundred dollars per season.

None of the seine boat crew were First Nations people. Though they knew fishing better than anyone else, it was illegal for Native people to work on mechanized boats—based on a ruling the Canadian government said was designed to limit the fish harvest.

Anderson persuaded the Pidcocks to sell him their sawmill site in about 1911,[9] as part of his expansion of the cannery. "It was a bad time to sell," George Pidcock later recalled. "The war started shortly after and the price of lumber boomed."[10]

The Andersons lived on-site for most of the year and their daughters attended the little school on Heriot Bay Road. Margaret Anderson entertained a constant round of guests through the canning season, selected by W.E. from the many international sport fishermen and locals who came and went from the Cove. Their large house sat on pilings at the

Laich-Kwil-Tach families lived in cabins on the southern shore of Quathiaski Cove for the canning season. Some worked in the cannery from the age of about ten hauling baskets of cans to the women who worked "on the line," trimming the fish to fit the cans. This photo is dated 1912. PHOTO COURTESY TIM WOODLAND.

north end of the cannery complex, across from the store, at the head of the wharf.

The handline fishermen were paid fifty cents for a tyee of 13 to 32 kilograms (30 to 70 pounds) and ten cents for any fish under 13.5 kilograms (30 pounds).[11] Like a few other canners, W.E. Anderson paid with tokens rather than cash. As the tokens could only be spent (or cashed in) at the company store, it made good economic sense for Anderson. He also felt the system kept family men from squandering their wages. However, the token system was scrapped in about 1917 in response to continuing complaints. As cannery workers said, you couldn't use your tokens to go to a dance or to pay your debts.

The various ethnic groups among Anderson's crew kept to themselves. The Chinese men, who lived at the southern end of the complex in a huge "China House" on pilings, were not welcome at the northern end, where the store, the post office and the Andersons' home was. To the south of the China House were the Native people's cabins. During off-hours the Native men played lahal by the light of beach fires, a guessing game involving two opposing teams accompanied by drums and songs. Sometimes the Native men played cards through the night with loggers from one or another of the nearby camps. The games occasionally erupted into fights, and as a result the trail that skirted the shore behind the cannery was called "Blood Alley."

On the hill behind the cannery was a small bunkhouse for the seine boat crew at the intersection of Pidcock and Heriot Bay Roads. (The place still stands, though it's long since been enlarged and used as a private residence.)

While cannery workers had to live on-site, the handliners worked and lived at their favourite fishing grounds. Some camped on shore in tents and others built shacks from driftwood. As the cannery output grew, shantytowns popped up near the best fishing grounds—below the bluffs at Cape Mudge ("Mudge City"), at Francisco Point and at Poverty Point (later called April Point).

W.E. Anderson was remembered by most as an exemplary employer and a generous sponsor of community projects. When Harry Assu reflected back upon his fifty years as a commercial fisherman, he said Anderson was the best man he ever worked for. When one of the daughters of cannery carpenter and night watchman Robert Willson was born with club feet, the Andersons paid for a series of treatments by expensive Vancouver specialists. "The

W.E. Anderson made a fortune in the Klondike Gold Rush and invested it in a number of BC businesses, including the Quathiaski Cannery. The cannery quickly became his main concern and the family lived on site for a number of years before building a winter residence in Shaughnessy in Vancouver. Seen here from left to right are Elva, Mae, W.E., Margaret and Valma Anderson. PHOTO COURTESY ED MCALLISTER, MCR 20126-54

government didn't spend five cents on people in those days," recalled Mae (Anderson) McAllister, "and there wasn't help for anyone except people like my mother and father."

While the Andersons and their cannery had come to dominate the Cove, the Pidcock brothers were still very much at the forefront of local development. The boys earned their living as loggers after they sold the cannery in 1906, when they bought two yarding engines, a 9 x 10 Washington and later a 10 x 12 Washington road engine. They logged their own extensive properties in the Cove and purchased more land as well.[12]

With so many demands upon his time George Pidcock didn't marry until 1913 when, like his brother William, a young schoolteacher captured his heart. Eleanor Starrett was the perfect daughter-in-law for Alice. Eleanor loved music and the arts, not fishing and horses (like Herbert Pidcock's wife Dolly)—but while Eleanor adored Alice, her rural life on Quadra proved a hardship. The house George built for her was in an isolated spot across Uncak Channel (in northern Quathiaski Cove), a rowboat ride away from anywhere.

Understandably, Eleanor spent as much time as possible at her mother-in-law's large house, which was close to all the action at the cannery, store and government dock. A steady stream of boats of all kinds delivered shipments of cans and other goods. Tugs tied up at the dock to wait out bad weather or get water and residents from the whole region congregated there to shop at the cannery store or wait for the freight boat. "The steamships came in twice a week," recalled Eve (Willson) Eade in her memoirs, "and brought fresh goods and also the daily papers from Vancouver. Everyone who could went down to meet the boat as the mail came in too, so that was a great event."

W.E. Anderson subdivided a few lots from his extensive land holdings on the hill behind the cannery, which expanded the village. Amelia Smith of Black Creek, with two children married into the Pidcock family, bought a lot on the south side of the junction of Heriot Bay and Pidcock Roads, where she lived on a semi-permanent basis in Sunset Cottage. On the opposite side of the street was the region's first official police station and courthouse, built in 1912. The building included a large courtroom on one side, two jail cells in the back and living quarters that looked out over the Cove.

The region's first police constable Henry Jones, who had been on Quadra since 1902, died suddenly after a strenuous tour of duty in 1907. He had just tucked his little girl in for the night and was on his way downstairs when he collapsed with a heart attack. Constable Lines replaced Jones, to become the first officer quartered in the new police station with his family.

Seymour Bagot tried the cases at the new courthouse as a local Justice of the Peace and his family bought Constable Jones's property at Quadra Loop. The Bagots had much in common with the Pidcocks as Eleanor Bagot, the matriarch of the family, was an aristocratic Englishwoman. She had raised her family in Australia and then immigrated with her children to BC as a widow. "[We] arrived at Vancouver in July 1907 on the steamer *Manuka*," wrote Seymour Bagot in his memoirs. "Several weeks later we heard of the house on Quadra Island. On inspection that property was found suitable for our family needs so my mother purchased it."

Amelia Smith, at the rear in this photo, had two children who married into the Pidcock family of Quathiaski Cove. She's seen here holding a child's hoop and stick toy, with May Marshall (centre) and her children and Dot Yeatman in front. May Marshall's husband was the constable for the region, with their combined home, jail and courthouse seen behind this group, at the corner of Pidcock and Heriot Bay Roads. PHOTO BY ROB YEATMAN AND COURTESY PEGGY YEATMAN FAMILY, MCR 6355

Eleanor Bagot was English but she raised her family in Australia. They immigrated to Canada after her husband died and bought Forest Lodge from the Jones family, at what's now Quadra Loop. On the left is the log house built by the original owner Tom Backus. Beside it is the large frame home Constable Jones built. The houses faced into the farm fields and beyond to the sea and mainland mountains. PHOTO COURTESY PEGGY (BAGOT) DEMARLER, MCR 6738

Eleanor's children—Peggy, Diana, Jack, Arthur and Seymour Bagot—revelled in their new life on the island. Their farm, Forest Lodge, was an exceptional place. It had two large houses—the four-bedroom house Jones built and Backus's old log house. Both overlooked an expanse of islands and the mainland mountains. The farm also had a bearing orchard, barns and 6.8 hectares (17 acres) of pasture.

Another new family of these years was the Nobles. Like the Bagots, it was a chance encounter that sent them to Quadra Island. Newlyweds Thomas and Vivien Noble stopped in Vancouver on their way to Australia and happened to meet Dick Hall in a hotel lobby. Hall wanted to sell his large acreage on Quadra Island so he could return to Britain. The island sounded ideal to the Nobles, as did the established farm on what's now Cape Mudge Road, near the Walker Road intersection. The talk of mines on northern Quadra was also an attraction for Thomas.

The Nobles fixed up the Halls' old squared-log house from the late 1880s to be their new home and named their place Hillcrest Farm. Both Thomas and Vivien were keen farmers. With a bit of a family income from Thomas's railroading family in Britain, they added conveniences like automatic watering devices in the barns and a heated greenhouse.

There was an interesting mix of young people on the island by 1910, between the grown children of the first settlers and newcomers of various nationalities and circumstances. The Andersons, Bagots and Nobles organized swimming parties, plays, musical

Vivien Noble and two of her three sons, whose names were not identified in this photo. When Vivien died due to what her husband believed was faulty surgery, he kept all her personal belongings as she had left them for the remainder of his life. His descendants still own this collection, which includes things like her purse with the coins and hairpins inside. PHOTO COURTESY BRUCE NOBLE, MCR 20191-33

Harry Pidcock was the first to bring a car to the island when he bought a Hupmobile in 1911 to take his mother up the steep hill to church services at the school, where she played a portable organ. PHOTO COURTESY DAVID PIDCOCK, MCR 12721

Emma Yeatman supervises the antics of her children and their friends. Seen here, from the left, are Rob Yeatman, Dot Yeatman, Archie Simons, Frank Yeatman, Ida Roberts and perhaps Nels Roberts in the Yeatman's dining room on Smith Road. Photo taken by Rob Yeatman with a camera extension and "flash lights." PHOTO COURTESY PEGGY YEATMAN, MCR 6219

fetes and picnics. A telephone line that was cabled across Sutil Channel from the mainland to the Bagots' farm in 1911 established their place as a phone station. From there the line continued on poles to Quathiaski Cove and by cable across Discovery Passage. When the Bagots and Andersons both had phones the young people could arrange a party with only an hour's notice.

It was a new era, with more to life than just grubbing out an existence—but there were warning signs for those who paid attention to the news in Europe. A war was brewing and while many sensed its approach, no one realized it would beggar the Western economy.

CHAPTER TEN

The Land of Milk, Honey, Canned Fish, Giant Firs and Precious Spuds

A lot changed for the We Wai Kai people on the cusp of World War I as they struggled to regain a modicum of autonomy under Billy Assu's determined leadership. The band started their own logging company in 1912, perhaps as the result of a soured deal with a logging company the year prior. The band signed off a right-of-way through their Drew Harbour reserve to Abbott Timber Company, allowing them to run a rail line through the centre of Quadra Island to a log dump in Drew Harbour. But when a harsh recession struck shortly thereafter, in the buildup to World War I, the company ran into trouble and dodged the agreed-upon annual right-of-way fee of fifty dollars. To add insult to injury they also refused to compensate the band for trees they took beyond the right-of-way.

Abbott's camp of wood and canvas shacks was to the south of the current intersection of Smith and Arbutus Roads and their rail line ran parallel to Cape Mudge and Heriot Bay Roads. The owners had expected to work on southern Quadra Island for six years but they were forced to sell the company within the year, as log prices dropped during the deepening recession.

A company called Wilson and Brady took over from Abbott and tried to swing a deal with the We Wai Kai to log their land at Drew Harbour but the band refused. The tough-minded manager of Wilson

Abbott Timber Company, and later Wilson and Brady, ran a railway logging operation through south central Quadra Island during World War I. In 1919 their camp was burnt out by a forest fire that also wiped out several farms. John Garat, a boy living in the camp, recalled the engineer covered the train with wet canvas and ran the engine through the flames to get everyone from the camp to the beach at Drew Harbour. PHOTO COURTESY HELEN (JOYCE) ANDREWS, MCR 8810

and Brady was not to be deterred, however, as Harry Assu recalled in his autobiography. The company offered his father Billy a bribe to push a contract through. When he said no, Wilson and Brady got new Indian Agent William Halliday on side and a deal was signed by twelve band members when most of the headmen were away for seasonal work. Only one of those twelve men was literate. "Too bad that man learned how to write," said Harry Assu. (There was, however, enough remaining timber for the band to log on the Drew Harbour Reserve in 1919 at a $23,000 profit, plus wages.[1])

The band borrowed three thousand dollars from the Department of Indian Affairs to buy a steam donkey. Under the DIA's paternalistic system of the day, the band was required to get permission before they logged on their reserve. They also had to agree to clear and seed the sixteen hectares (forty acres) they logged at Cape Mudge, as the

DIA was determined to turn the Native people into farmers. And they had to send the proceeds from their log sales to the DIA, who paid the men their wages using a slow bureaucratic process. Billy Assu, who had logged off and on since his youth, served as the manager for their logging operations.

Billy Assu was in his prime in 1911, when he urged the elders to accept a new structure for the band.[2] They formed a village council, an innovative system for bands at that time. The council met monthly and operated under a set of legally struck bylaws.[3] Their main purpose was to eradicate alcohol abuse and prostitution, using Native constables appointed by the council for enforcement.

The Council may have also played a role in the resolution of the debate that followed the death of the band's leading hereditary chief Jim Chickite, who claimed descent from Sewis and We-Kai. He drowned in a storm at sea on Christmas night in 1912. Dissent over leadership must have followed his premature death because Indian Agent Halliday came to the village to help settle the choice between John Chickite (the son of the late chief and son-in-law to Billy Assu) and Major Dick, the nephew of the late chief. An election was an unusual move at a time when the Native system of governance through hereditary chiefs was still in effect.[4] Indian Agent Halliday reported on the outcome of the election to his superiors:

Alert Bay, BC, March 1st, 1913: With reference to your letter of January 21st No 4270II-56 regarding the election of a new chief for the Cape Mudge or Wewaiakikai band to succeed the late Chief Chikite who was drowned on Christmas night I have the honor to inform you that on Wednesday last February 26th I was at Cape Mudge and called the people together to a meeting and acquainted them with the contents of your letter. The matter impressed them very favorably and an election was held. There were two candidates proposed, namely John Chikite the son of the late chief and Major Dick a nephew of the late chief, and who inherited the potlatch rank of the late chief. After a close ballot John Chikite won the election by two votes and was declared elected. The only objection that could be made against the new chief is his youth as he is only about 20 years of age. He is married to a daughter of Billy Assu who for years has been the real though not the nominal chief. Assu and some of the older men promised to act as advisers until the young man had learned a little of the responsibility of his office.

The Indian name of John Chikite is Yakoglas.

Your obedient servant, signed William Halliday, Indian Agent.

John Chickite had many weighty matters to consider at a young age. The band's new logging company required attention, and as Wilson and Brady's use of the right-of-way through Drew Harbour Reserve remained contentious it too had to be monitored. There was also a push by younger band members to turn away from the old traditional lifestyle to adopt mainstream values.

Only a few Native men enlisted for war service in 1914, because, as with most other islanders, they performed essential services as fishermen and loggers. But as the war dragged on these rules slackened, though men with problems like flat feet or bad teeth couldn't join up. With so many men enlisted it became difficult for logging companies like Wilson and Brady to keep a crew. "Old Bill Brady had to handle his crew with velvet gloves or he wouldn't have anybody to work with," recalled Herbert Joyce. "One morning the conscript guys and policeman come along and took about half his crew and while they were rounding up some of them, some of the boys took to the woods. They didn't want to be conscripted. So, by gosh, Monday morning come and Brady didn't have enough [men] to do nothing. But the bunch they took, two-thirds of them come back. They were rejects and what have you."

Islanders like Bill Law, Jim Law, Herbert Pidcock and the Bagot brothers were readily accepted as soldiers. They were fit men who were used to hard physical work and as hunters they were expert shots with a rifle. Herbert Pidcock enlisted with the 67th Battalion in 1915 and was sent to the front, where he served as a sniper. Like so many on the front lines, he was gassed and sent to a hospital in England to recuperate for eight months. For the remainder of the war he ran donkey engines, logging Britain's forests for the war effort. Fifty-three-year-old James Ford of Hyacinthe Bay enlisted in 1917, when the army began to accept older men. He spent the duration of the war in France, leaving his wife Georgina to manage their farm and family on his army pay of thirty dollars per month. Years later Georgina bragged to her grandchildren that she was not only able to live within these narrow means but she saved a bit as well.

Those left behind were consumed by thoughts of the war. People like Helen Bull—whose son Joseph enlisted, as did her stepson Cecil at the age of seventeen—worked hard for the war effort. Helen organized fundraising events and work bees to fill emergency kits for the Red Cross in an old shack islanders rented for the purpose in Heriot Bay. She sent $1,260 (including $800 from W.E. Anderson) for the troops one year, the equivalent of about four annual family incomes. We Wai Kai women also gathered together to knit socks and sew flannel shirts for soldiers.[5]

Fourteen-year-old Archie Walker of Vancouver tried to enlist but he was too small to convince anyone he was of age. Instead he got a job as a whistle punk (relaying signals between the loading crew and the steam donkey engineer) at Wilson and Brady's camp. Old Bill Brady, a veteran American woodsman, made the boy work as a dishwasher for the first few months, as Archie recalled in his memoirs:

> The cookhouse was a combination cookhouse with dining room attached. A great stove about 10 feet long fired by wood was the cooking means. The top was one great sheet of smooth metal which was used for frying eggs, hot cakes and steaks. The dining room contained two long tables about 50 feet long and at the door was a steel triangle that was hammered on by the cook or night watchman to wake the men, then again to call the men to their meals. I was told to pick out a bunk in the bunkhouse, which was a building about 16 feet wide and 60 feet long with bunks top and lower all around the building, with straw mattresses. A great home for bed bugs.

During my stay in camp one of the hardest things to put up with was the bed bugs. It was the worst infested place that I was in in my life. For me they were bad as their poison set up a blood condition that brought on a permanent itch. I got in such terrible shape that I had a permanent rash and it was said that I had the seven year itch. I finally went over to Campbell River to see a doctor. He gave me some ointment but when I got to sleep in a clean bed the itch disappeared.

The camp crew consisted of one cook, two waiters or flunkies, one dishwasher, one bull cook who's [sic] job was to cut wood and light fires and be general help around camp. One blacksmith and timekeeper who doubled as storekeeper in which was kept logger's needs such as shoes, socks, tobacco.

I did finally get to go out into the woods. The camp at this time was running two sides, each side consisting of one donkey and one spar tree. Spar trees at the time were a straight fir tree of about five feet diameter at the base and of good sound wood. The foreman would pick the tree then the high rigger would put on his climbing spurs and with me as attendant would start up the tree.

Evenings in the bunkhouses fell into a sort of pattern. There would be horseplay, jokes such as water cans on top of doors to trap the unwary, clothes knots, all types of problems to circumvent to get in or out of bed. One evening in the dining room I put a cherry in the end of a spoon and shot it at a pal across the table but he ducked and it hit another logger right in the eye. I stayed away from the bunkhouse as long as I could but finally had to go in. I was spared, he never said a word about it. I sure was glad for, to me, he looked mighty big. Then in the evening there was the poker and blackjack games which kept me broke.[6]

The freedom to log on the same licence system as non-Native operations—and retain their earnings—was one of the key issues for the We Wai Kai people when they addressed a Royal Commission that toured the province in 1914. The villagers packed into the schoolhouse on Cape Mudge Reserve to listen to Billy Assu's impassioned and articulate plea, which was paraphrased in a commission report. Many people lived in a famished state, said Assu. It was a struggle to survive within non-Native strictures, under legislation that stripped them of their traditional rights.

Assu also provided the basic facts about the We Wai Kai Band for the commission. There were ninety-six people on the reserve, with twenty houses and twenty children, including some from various Laich-Kwil-Tach bands who attended their day school. Their teacher was the resident missionary Reverend J.E. Rendle.

"How are we to live?" asked Assu. His people were confined to their reserves, but the Indian agent and others had told them the land was not actually theirs—it was held in trust. "A white man can come into the country and remain a certain number of years upon a place and the Government says it's his. Why isn't this same right applied to the Indians?"

Speaking on behalf of the elderly, Assu said one old person received the paltry sum of $1.25 per month in government assistance.

The Department of Indian Affairs supplied the lumber and some of the labour needed to build Quadra Island's first school at the We Wai Kai village in 1893–94. The sturdy building remained in use for many years. PHOTO COURTESY JOHN PHILLIPS, MCR 5360

In former days this person and others would have been well cared for through the potlatch system. "None suffered through poverty while it was permitted to continue, as the potlatch was for the benefit of all," said Assu.

Billy Assu no doubt met the impassive gaze of the commissioners and concluded nothing would come of these meetings. If things were to change, he and other Native leaders had to work around the blocks and foils of Euro-Canadian society.

Many non-Native islanders also lived in deep poverty by today's standards. Yet the depth of the recession of the war years—unchecked by the government through price and wage fixing, which was later used during World War II—encouraged people to adopt a co-operative philosophy and take group action.

The roughly three hundred residents of Quadra Island pooled their resources to complete an impressive array of community projects with donated labour and raised funds. Women were the backbone of many of these achievements. For the first time, with so many men overseas, they took overt roles in community development and began to be listed in provincial directories with their professions. In the 1918 directory, Helen Bull was listed as the manager of Heriot Bay Store for the first time. Both Elizabeth Ford and Jean Dick, whose husbands were overseas, were listed as farmers.

Among the community achievements of the war years was the formation of a farmers' co-op that allowed people to shop at better rates. Islanders also formed a Women's Institute, opened a cemetery for non-Native people and built a community hall and a church.

Prior to the opening of the new cemetery, pioneer residents were simply buried on their homesteads or their bodies were shipped to Vancouver. It was the sad death of sixteen-year-old Alice Bryant, the child of the island's first non-Native woman settler, Mary Bryant, that galvanized the need for the cemetery. Mary's son-in-law Frank Gagne, an energetic community leader, directed the work.

Alice died of diphtheria in June 1913 and was buried on her parents' homestead until the cemetery was ready two years later. Her remains were disinterred to become the first burial in the little cemetery on

Heriot Bay Road. (Her gravestone, installed that year, mistakenly gives her year of death as 1915.)

Ironically, the next to be buried in the cemetery was the midwife for whom Alice Bryant was named. Alice Pidcock, the pillar of her family, died as the result of a stroke in May 1915. As her son George remarked in his diary, nearly everyone in the community crowded into the cemetery in the spring rain to pay their last respects.

Agnes Walker passed away within weeks of Alice Pidcock and was also buried in the little cemetery. Her memory was dear to many, due to her firm belief in her Methodist faith and her work at her husband's side at the Cape Mudge mission. The death of these two community leaders signalled the end of the island's first generation of non-Native pioneers.

Alice Pidcock had long wished for a church on the island, and her death sparked the realization of that goal, with a donation of three hundred dollars in her honour from two Englishwomen. The Pidcock estate gave one hundred dollars and the rest was donated by the Anderson family and raised through bazaars, parties and concerts. A total of $1,600 was collected, and St. John's Church was built on land donated by Amelia Smith on the south corner of Heriot Bay and Pidcock Roads. Fred Comely of the Columbia Coast Mission led the volunteer construction team and the Anderson family donated an organ. The chancel was dedicated in the fall of 1917,[7] with an agreement that the church could be used by any Protestant denomination and for social functions, though there were to be no dances or alcohol on the premises.

Fred Comely did not stay long to enjoy his new church.[8] A tea party was held on a fine summer day in August 1918 in the "Old Pidcock House" as a send-off for Comely and his wife and to celebrate the nuptials of the first couple to be married in the new church. After the tea party, widower Robert Walker and island schoolteacher Theodora Spencer walked up the hill from the Pidcocks' house to be married by the Columbia Coast Mission's founder Reverend John Antle in St. John's Church.[9]

Reverend Alan Greene of the Columbia Coast Mission was the next minister assigned to the district. Alan Greene was a lively man with a tremendous sense of play, lots of energy and a commitment to the service of his parishioners, no matter their faith, or lack thereof. In 1919

St. John's Church in Quathiaski Cove was non-denominational. It also served as a venue for community services. "Once a year a dentist from Courtenay would come to fix all the school children's teeth," recalled Eve (Willson) Eade in her memoirs. "A dentist's chair would be set up in the church and there we would have all the dental work done at one time. No needles those days to take away the hurt and while someone was in the chair the others waiting their turns would be peering in the windows so you didn't dare cry or those peeping in would think you were a baby." The church lost its resident minister in the 1940s. It was sold in the 1970s and torn down. PHOTO COURTESY *COURIER-UPPER ISLANDER* NEWSPAPER, MCR 10522

Greene purchased Amelia Smith's cottage[10] next to St. John's Church for his bride Gertrude. The Cove proved a happy home for Gertrude and the five children she raised there over the next seventeen years. Though Gertrude was on her own for much of the time, as her husband patrolled his large parish by boat, she was an active participant in community life. It was not an easy life for Gertrude but she shared Alan's dedication to his calling.

The cramped quarters of an old shed in Heriot Bay used for dances and fundraising events throughout the war made clear the need for a community hall. Frank Gagne and his young wife Daisy Bryant (the first non-Native born on the island) invited friends to her parents' log house to discuss plans. At this and a subsequent meeting, labour and five hundred dollars in cash donations were pledged.

The hall was built near the site of the current Quadra Children's Centre on land donated by veteran settler Tom Bell. The location was central to both Quathiaski Cove and Heriot Bay. Within a month of the little meeting at the Bryants', the hall was far enough along to host a dance, as Anna Joyce recalled some years later:

Reverend Alan Greene of the Columbia Coast Mission bought Amelia Smith's Sunset Cottage in Quathiaski Cove for his bride Gertrude. The couple's children have fond memories of their childhood home. When they left in the 1930s the community presented the Greenes with an inscribed silver tea service that's now in the Museum at Campbell River collection. PHOTO COURTESY ALAN GREENE JR., MCR 8428

> Many of the ladies helped with the shingling and laying the floor and with lunches for the workers. All was ready on March 16th for the first entertainment [except for] a door for the kitchen. Mr. Gagne produced that from somewhere, carrying it for two miles through the bush. The place was decorated with greenery in honor of St. Patrick and the first dance was held in the new place. Of course it did not look much, but we did enjoy that evening to its limit and felt very important.[11]

The Valdes Island Social Club was formed to manage the hall, with Frank Gagne as club president. Under his leadership the hall was expanded before the year was out to include a 7 x 21–metre (24 x 70–foot) dance floor, a large dining room, a poolroom and a canteen. A public wharf was added down the hill at Tom Bell's beach in southern

Gowlland Harbour, to accommodate the crowds who came from far and wide to bimonthly dances on the hall's exceptional "sprung" (floating) hardwood floor.

Frank Gagne had an infectious zest for life and his community projects were carried out with terrific enthusiasm. He was also a gifted orator, who could rally everyone on side. Frank had been on Quadra Island for over a decade by this time. He'd left his native Gaspé, Quebec, in about 1900 to work for an uncle in Seattle on a stern-paddled steamboat. But Frank had a restless soul and in 1902 he took a job in a logging camp at Jervis Inlet as a skid greaser (oiling the skid roads to facilitate the movement of the logs) and two years later he leased the Pidcocks' sawmill in Quathiaski Cove, to use as a machine shop. In 1906 he gave that up to log in Gowlland Harbour[12] but by 1914, when he married Daisy Bryant, he was logging for Hosea Bull in Drew Harbour and lived at the Heriot Bay Hotel.

A prohibition on alcohol sales across the country was declared

The Valdes Island Social Club's hall started out as a small structure but was quickly added to, as seen here in about 1920, to include a kitchen, ladies' dressing room and billiards room. The hall was the finest in the region, with a dance floor made from New Brunswick maple. The words "Valdes Island" were inlayed in wood on one of its walls. People came from many kilometres away to attend bimonthly dances at the hall. PHOTO COURTESY CATHERINE (GREENE) TUCK, MCR 19799

in November 1917, the same year the Valdes Island Social Hall was opened, which meant loggers were forced to dance without the helpful crutch of a few drinks to get things rolling. The strictures of the prohibition were also a blow for Hosea and Helen Bull, until it presented a new opportunity. Several poor island families distilled liquor on the sly, so the Bulls converted their swift little boat into a rum-runner for the remainder of the prohibition.

By the war years, the tables had completely turned for the old rivals, Heriot Bay and Quathiaski Cove. The 1919 directory lists twenty-five names for Heriot Bay (down from 121 in 1905) and thirty-five names for Quathiaski Cove.

The Valdes Island Copper Company's mine in northern Gowlland Harbour provided much-needed work during the war. Pierce Hall, who lived nearby with his family, worked many of the mineral claims there on his own for years but he didn't have the capital to go beyond surface work. L.W. Nestelle of Seattle staked claims in 1903 but he didn't get far either.[13] It was A.F. Rolph, with nineteen claims in the "Copper Mountain group," who got the mine underway in 1910. By the end of the war the mine was a substantial operation, with housing for ten miners on the beach at the Hall family's homestead, where a massive pier jutted far out into the shallow mud flats.

When armistice was declared in 1918, Wilson and Brady blew their whistles non-stop and ran their two trains up and down the track. Some enlisted men, like Cecil Bull and Joseph Dick, returned as decorated heroes. Others, like Bill Law and George Haskins (who had a farm at what's now Haskins's Trail), brought home English brides. Even young Jim Law, who enlisted at the age of fourteen (passing himself off as sixteen) made it through the heartbreak of the trenches, though it was an experience he could never talk about.

The end of the war was a cause for celebration on Quadra, but ultimately the soldiers had to restart their lives. Joseph Dick took over Hosea and Helen Bull's rum-running business at Heriot Bay and George Haskins took a job as a teamster for the copper mine in Gowlland Harbour. He didn't want to leave his wife alone, however, so he left before dawn every day to hike past the Bryants' homestead and down to the dock in southern Gowlland Harbour; from there he rowed to the top of the harbour. Veteran Charles Gow opened a machine shop and the People's Store in Quathiaski Cove, looking to compete with the high prices at the cannery store.

"Soldiers settlements" were established throughout the Discovery Islands, as a way to put returned soldiers to work and open more agricultural land. Grant's Bay (below Maude Island) was divided into sixteen-hectare (forty-acre) blocks for soldiers—but with no road access the men didn't stay long on what turned out to be substandard farmland in an isolated part of the island. Many returned soldiers, especially single men in search of freedom and fresh air as they struggled to recuperate from the mental and physical anguish of the war, became handliners. They lived in the little shantytowns at Poverty Point (now April Point) and

Dollie (Smith) Pidcock and her son Reg went to England to stay with aunts for the duration of World War I, after her husband Herbert was gassed while on the front lines as a sniper. When he was released from hospital he served in the English forestry service, taking down trees for military use. Herbert's release papers said he was in A1 condition but he never recovered from being gassed and died at the age of 53. "Where he had been a man of splendid physique," said his obituary, "who could carry a 72-kilogram (160-pound) deer out of the bush more easily than the average man could walk unburdened, after the war he was never fit again." PHOTO COURTESY PIDCOCK FAMILY, MCR 14825

Cape Mudge, where they built driftwood shacks. In the peak years for handliners, there were up to three hundred men and women working the prime fishing grounds off Cape Mudge. Their average daily catch was fifty fish per boat.[14]

An influenza epidemic followed the returned soldiers home and claimed more lives in the western hemisphere than the war overseas had done. At one point on Cape Mudge Reserve every able-bodied adult was ill so they had to hire a non-Native man to haul wood and water.[15] Their kin at Kelsey Bay (who had already suffered radical depopulation) lost so many people most of the survivors left the reserve. A few families joined the Cape Mudge Band and others moved to the Comox Reserve. (Some decades later the band officially amalgamated with the Comox people.)

Arlette Willson of the non-Native community died of influenza in 1918 at the age of thirty-five, leaving a young family of seven behind. Robert Willson had to continue his work at the cannery so he hired a housekeeper and relied upon his eldest daughter Jane to manage the household, the farm and the younger children. The Andersons of Quathiaski Cannery wanted to adopt Robert's two youngest daughters but he refused to part with any of his children.

Some childhood diseases still prevalent at this time, like diphtheria, were known to be preventable—but health care information was not readily available. Gertrude Greene, the wife of Reverend Greene of the Columbia Coast Mission, initiated a chapter of the Women's Institute on Quadra in 1920,[16] a rural woman's organization that provided health care information. The club also offered a cherished opportunity for isolated women to socialize, share experiences and undertake community work, like the maintenance of the social club's hall and the cemetery.

A Women's Institute was formed in Cape Mudge Village as well and the band used a handsome profit from logging their Drew Harbour reserve to build new houses. Gone were the days when the old men of the village said that if people wanted white men's houses they should go live with the whites.[17]

"My father called all the people together and told them, 'We have made good money so we can modernize the village,'" recalled Harry Assu in his autobiography. The men towed their steam donkey around from

Drew Harbour to Cape Mudge and used it to pull down the last of the big communal houses. (The deep pits from those houses were flattened and became part of what's now a park that runs along the beach between the current band office and a swimming pool.) By 1925 the massive project was complete and Cape Mudge Village was touted in the *Comox Argus* newspaper as a model village. In fact the We Wai Kai people were far ahead of many communities in the district, with their own electrical and water systems. "The village is up-to-date in every respect," reported the *Argus*. "They also boast of a fine water supply in their houses. Many beautiful homes are added every year with fireplaces and other conveniences. Lately a fine Community Hall has been opened."

The man with the practical genius to make most of these conveniences possible was John Dick Jr. (or John Star Dick), a self-taught man who could do anything he set his mind to. He was a man of high rank who held the name We-Kai in a direct line of descent and gained important privileges through his arranged marriage to Maggie Frank of the Comox Band.

Ralph Dick cherishes the memory of his grandfather, John Dick Jr., for his impressive range of skills, from fishing and boat building to electrical systems and construction. John was born in about 1888 and though the day school was available in his childhood he didn't attend it for long,

Billy Assu with Emma Cranmer on the right and his second wife Annie Moon on the left. The other people are not identified. PHOTO COURTESY WEDLIDI SPECK, MCR 11345

Mary Bryant stands on the right in the doorway of St. John's Church in Quathiaski Cove. Directly below her is Gertrude Greene, who was instrumental in forming a chapter of the Women's Institute on Quadra Island. The institute provided health care information and a social outlet for isolated women. Mary Joyce (later Butler) stands at the rear, second from the left. Helen (Joyce) Andrews sits with her son Alfred on the far right, next to Mrs. Clandening and Theodora Walker and her girls Joy and Ursula. PHOTO COURTESY HELEN (JOYCE) ANDREWS, MCR 8843

so he had to teach himself to read and write. As an adult he ran the band's logging operation for years and maintained the books. He was also a churchwarden and the official record keeper for births, deaths and marriages in the village. He built over twenty gillnet boats and a seiner. Billy Assu praised the man at his death many years later and acknowledged it was John Dick Jr. who led the work of the reconstruction of the village.[18]

There were also huge changes within We Wai Kai social structures during these years, when some families began to weave non-Native conventions into their age-old traditions. Whereas Jimmy and Louise Hovell had to keep their Christian wedding in Vancouver in 1913 a secret from the elders, some couples now married within both traditions.

Many marriages were still arranged by parents, as was the case with Mary Wilson and Oscar Lewis, who were married in October 1917, though they barely knew each other. "All the adult males in the village

The We Wai Kai people's village at Cape Mudge was considered a model of success all over the coast. They installed running water and an electrical plant years before such services were available elsewhere in the region. PHOTO COURTESY MRS. DESMARAIS, MCR 8715

had a meeting in the Community House," recalled Mary in later years. "There was much talking and singing." In what amounted to a village potlatch the older men decided Mary and Oscar should be married. Mary's mother told her to gather her clothes and a friend told her she now belonged to a man and must do his cooking and look after him. After this six men took Mary from her parents' house to Oscar's parents' home. Three months later, on January 17, 1918, they were also married in a Christian ceremony in the village.[19]

The next year seven other couples followed suit by taking their marriage vows in a group ceremony, though some had been together for many years and had young families. They were married by Methodist Minister Peter Kelly, an ordained Haida man.[20]

The forty-year ban on potlatching was enforced with devastating effects in 1922 when a major arrest was made after Dan Cranmer's potlatch at Village Island. "People came from all over, from Lekwiltok to Smith's Inlet," recalled Cranmer years later. "Three to four hundred

The Dick family and friends in about 1940. At the rear, second from the left is Frank Assu, Maggie (Frank) Dick sits at centre and John Dick Jr. is standing to her left. Mona Dick is behind the boy in the front row and to her left, wearing matching dresses in the front row, are Violet and Dollie Dick. Bob Clifton is standing at the back on the far right and Ethel Assu is sitting on the step in front of him. PHOTO COURTESY THE HAMATLA TREATY SOCIETY AND JUNE JOHNSON

men, women and children turned up. The second day a XweXwe [Sxwaixwe] dance with the shells was given to me by the chief of Cape Mudge. I gave him a gas boat and $50 cash. Altogether that was worth $500. I paid him back double. He also gave me some names."[21]

Billy Assu must have suspected someone would report the potlatch because he placed a Christmas tree atop his pile of gifts, which were valued at an estimated ten thousand dollars. As reported in the *Colonist*, Assu said this was how he acknowledged numerous kindnesses from friends—but his Christmas tree was "suspiciously late, and his generosity seemed out of all reason," said the newspaper.[22] Twenty-nine people were arrested in this series of back-to-back potlatches. Seventeen were sentenced to terms in Okalla Prison, including Billy Assu. "When Chief Billie Assu planned to make himself solid with the tribe," said the *Colonist*, "by giving away forty sewing machines, forty gramophones, many blankets and loads of jewelry, the shadow of the white man's law was the only skeleton at the feast. For the white man's law forbids the potlatch, under pain of imprisonment with option of a fine."

Indian Agent William Halliday offered Assu and the others a reprieve. If all the chiefs surrendered their masks and dance regalia and swore to give up potlatching their sentences would be suspended. Cape Mudge elders met to consider this request and voted to comply, to secure Billy's release. Billy's nephew Jimmy Hovell was one of many quoted in the minutes of this meeting:

> I pledge myself to do away with the old customs, but would like to enquire from the Crown Authorities their opinion as to what I should do with my belongings. I have been gathering for a final potlatch. What am I to do with my things? I have about $2,000.00 cash owing me, what will become of that? Some of this was lent before the law was put in force. I only learned the facts of the law three years ago.[23]

It was a very sad day when all of the We Wai Kai people's masks, head-gear and dance aprons were loaded onto a barge and taken away. Many pieces were sold and others were stored in a warehouse in Ottawa. After this event potlatching ceased among the Laich-Kwil-Tach, though facets of it continued within accepted Euro-Canadian celebrations.

Closer ties were established between Natives and the rest of the Quadra community in the 1920s. Numerous We Wai Kai people could now speak English and men from many nationalities worked together at the cannery, on the fishing grounds and in logging. Their respective schools, however, remained entirely separate.

In 1923 the non-Native community of southern Quadra Island got a new school, for an enrolment of about twenty-five students, on its site near the Heriot Bay Road and School Road junction.[24] To brighten their schoolyard the students planted broom that spread throughout the area and down Telephone Hill. "The school had a well for drinking water and a large wood stove at one end of the room," wrote Eve (Willson) Eade in her memoirs. "The pupils took turns getting in wood and water and cleaning blackboards. The plumbing was two outdoor privies, one for girls and one for boys. Just outside the school fence was a swamp that froze over in winter."

All the non-Native schools hosted May Day celebrations in 1923,[25] in renewed patriotic fervour encouraged by the federal government. Each crowned a May Queen and had maypole dances and foot races. The festivities were repeated at the annual community-wide May Day picnic.

One of Eve's schoolmates, Mary Vosburgh, was the child of Jessie Assu of Cape Mudge and a non-Native logger. After her mother died Mary boarded with a family and attended the non-Native school. She suffered taunts for her Native ancestry but when Mary told her teacher kids called her a "dirty Siwash" (Chinook Jargon for Native), the woman's response was, "Well, you are, aren't you?"

Other families with Native ancestry, like the Halls of Gowlland Harbour, left that part of their heritage behind. Pierce Hall of Kansas married Mary Silva in 1900. Her mother was a Cowichan woman and her father was Portuguese. The Halls sailed up the coast in their sloop *Black Maria* in search of land and settled at the northern end of Gowlland Harbour in 1902, where they raised a large family. As the girls came of age Mary urged them to

James Hovell (seated next to Oscar Lewis) lost his mother as a child and was raised by relatives, including his uncle Billy Assu. Billy arranged for James's marriage to Louise Maqua, daughter of the chiefly Homiskinis family of Salmon River. Louise's family took her to Cape Mudge in two rafted canoes with boards across them, where Louise sat in her regalia. When they arrived at Cape Mudge Billy Assu, as James's elder, waded into the water and carried Louise ashore to the traditional big house where a gathering was held to mark her marriage to James Hovell.
PHOTO COURTESY DICK FAMILY, MCR 4422

marry fair-haired Swedes—"and your children will be lovely," she told them.[26]

A more enlightened teacher was hired for the Valdes Island School in 1924. This was Donald Capon's first teaching assignment, at $960 per year. Everything was new to the city boy. On one of his first days, as he recalled years later, he arrived at the schoolyard to find the children huddled in silence at the far end of the field. In hushed tones they told him to creep up to the fence. "Then the children jumped up and whooped and a grouse flew up into the fence. They yelled, 'Grab him Mr. Capon,' which I did. 'What will I do with it now?' I asked them. 'Ring its neck Mr. Capon.' So I did and took it home to Mrs. Moorhouse to cook for dinner."

There were four little schools on the island (Granite Bay, Heriot Bay, Valdes School and Cape Mudge) when a new one was built in 1922 in northern Gowlland Harbour. It didn't last more than about a decade, however, as it was destroyed in a fire and not replaced.

The second generation of non-Native kids may not have got the

The old English tradition of crowning a May Queen and children dancing around the maypole was revived in schools across Canada in the 1920s. May Queens were selected at the Valdes Island and Heriot Bay Schools in 1923. Seen here at Heriot Bay School are, from the left, Doris Kilgour, Queen Eliza Johnson and Dorothy McKenzie. PHOTO COURTESY DOROTHY EDMONDS, MCR 8732

education some of their parents had, but they were a self-reliant lot who could make anything work. The Beech family of Gowlland Harbour converted an old Model T Ford into a dual-purpose tractor and car. They lengthened the frame and installed two gear systems, one for low-speed tractor work and a higher gear so they could drive the island's dirt roads. As a tractor, the Model T ran on wheels made from an old bed frame.

Property prices on the island were affordable for the few who had anything extra to spend in the recession years of the early 1920s. A 17-hectare (43-acre) farm with a four-room house, a barn, a chicken house, an orchard of one hundred trees, 0.8 hectares (2 acres) of cleared land and good water was listed for sale at $2,100. A 20-hectare (50-acre) waterfront place with a cabin was advertised at twenty-five dollars per 0.4 hectare (1 acre).

By this time, the island produced a large proportion of its own food. Milk, butter, honey, potatoes, cattle, sheep, hogs and poultry were the common products of about fifty farms of various sizes.[27] Eve (Willson) Eade recalled the farm routines of her childhood in her memoirs:

> Farm life was early to bed and early to rise. Dad would get up and light the wood heater and kitchen stove, we were all up in winter by 6 a.m.—there were chores to be done before school. Usually three cows to be milked, fed and the stable cleaned, chickens to feed and eggs gathered, wood from the woodshed to be wheeled up and the wood bin filled, change clothes, wash, breakfast and to school. We had an unheated room off the kitchen where the milk separator and butter churn were kept, also the water pails and a bench with a basin to wash. In the winter the water would freeze and we hated to wash so we would quickly dip our hands in the water, run into the kitchen where a roller towel hung on a roller behind the door, so we'd rub our hands and face vigorously and pretend we had a real good wash.
>
> After school there were more chores to be done, the cows to be brought in from pasture and the milking, cleaning, feeding the animals all over again. We had chickens and ducks, pigs, a

tame sheep we raised on a bottle, cats and a dog to be fed. In winter we cut up pails full of carrots, turnips, etc. to give them with the hay and oats.

In summer there was hay to be got in. A neighbor would cut the main fields but we raked it all by hand into windrows and then haycocks, then taken [to] the barn by wagon. After the oat field was cut and in Dad would make us go over the field and pick up every piece of oat stock that was missed. For bedding for the animals we would go out in the pasture with sickles, like big curved knives, and cut the ferns, stack it to dry then carry it in ropes on our backs to the barn.

We had a huge garden to weed and hoe and water. We picked the apples, pears, etc. and they were kept under the ferns we cut in the winter so they wouldn't freeze. Dad dug the potatoes and we sorted them to different sizes, little ones to be cooked for the pigs, ours to eat and the best to sell. Dad would sell what he could and trade what he could to the store for bread and flour and tea and coffee. The rest would be put into pits and covered with dirt, so they didn't freeze and we would take out what we needed for meals all winter.

We had three wells for water on our farm, one close to the back door, one down by the barn and one out in the pasture to water the animals. In summer the house well ran dry and we carried the water by pails from the creek. There was a good spring water hole that never ran dry about half a mile away and believe me not a drop of water was wasted after carrying it so far. Being the smallest and lightest of the family, Dad chose me to clean out the wells. This was done every summer and it was a chore I dreaded. In those days you didn't say "no" to your parents, in fact, you didn't dare think "no," so the preparations would start. Dad would tie a galvanized pail onto a heavy rope and this was my chore, to get into the pail and be lowered down the 30 feet or so to the bottom. He would tie a shovel to the rope also and I would have to clear out all the guck and he would pull it up a pail at a time. There were snakes—lots of snakes to be shoveled into the pail and they would squirm out on the way out and fall back down on me. How I dreaded the cleaning out of the wells! When it was done to my Dad's satisfaction, I stood in the pail, hung onto the rope and was pulled up into the beautiful sunshine, until next summer.[28]

Only a few of the island's farmers were successful on a commercial level and some began to give up on what amounted to subsistence living in the 1920s, including George and Mary Haskins. They had invested both of their inheritances in the place (now a favourite hiking trail and a tree farm) but after thirty years of toil it was evident their farm would never be productive. They had a last meal in their log house and walked away. Grace (Willson) McPherson checked the house later and found everything as they'd left it, complete with their dishes and teapot still on the kitchen table. Tom Bell also turned his back on over thirty years of hard work on his southern Gowlland Harbour homestead. He and his wife of the past decade moved to New Westminster, where her grown children lived.

If it was a wrench for the Haskins and Bells to turn their backs on their youthful dreams, it was the end of an era when the Pidcock brothers dissolved their partnership and left the island in the early 1920s. George and Eleanor were the first to leave. They went to Courtenay, which was a compromise between Eleanor's desire for urban life and George's need to live in the country. "Uncle Reg," the bachelor brother, built a place on the Campbell River, and was followed a few years later by Herbert and Dolly, who built what's now the Haig-Brown Heritage House. When Harry married Freda Hoff, the companion of his mother's final years, "The Big House" in Quathiaski Cove was rented out and then sold in 1922 to the Claytons, canners and merchants from Bella Coola.

That same year, on the anniversary of their father's death, George and Frederick Yeatman drowned off Rebecca Spit. No one witnessed the accident but it was presumed one of the men fell in as they worked with a boom of logs, and the other went to the rescue. Almost exactly a year later tragedy struck the family again when Tom Yeatman, the eldest son, was killed by a falling tree while logging.

Cape Mudge lighthouse in about 1939.
PHOTO COURTESY JOHN GLYNES, MCR 12786

The Bull family suffered too in the "hard times" recession. Helen Bull passed away from cancer in December 1924 and months later, just as the economy began to revive, Hosea's creditors, his Vancouver wholesalers, foreclosed and took everything he owned. Bull moved to Vancouver with his late wife's son and daughter-in-law, where he worked as a travelling salesman for a while. Eventually he moved in with his son Cecil's family near Vancouver. When he died about a decade later he was still plagued by debts and a string of disgruntled creditors showed up on the Bulls' doorstep to make claims on Hosea Arminius Bull's non-existent estate.

Those who remained on the island at the end of the recession regained their enthusiasm for dances at the Valdes Island Social Hall, where there was an unspoken law—if you came to dance then you stayed inside the hall; if you came to fight then you stepped outside to have at it. Other celebrations continued as well. May Day picnics at Rebecca Spit remained the highlight of the year, followed by "The Christmas Tree" at the social hall, where there was a gift for everyone.

Islanders of every culture and creed were proud of what they had accomplished through the hard times. They had proved their resilience and they were ready for good things to come—but unfortunately they would be tested once again before the decade was out.

CHAPTER ELEVEN

The Dirty Thirties

The summer of 1925 was exceptionally hot. There were only three days of light rain in July, followed by twenty-two days in August with just one shower to break the heat. Such conditions should have suggested extra caution to government surveyors at work near Stramberg Lake, in Granite Bay, but they didn't. When the surveyors' campfire got out of control it was whipped into a fury by strong winds. The crew fought the fire on their own, rather than getting help, and within hours the flames devoured the old Lucky Jim mine buildings, ripped past the miners' cabins along the Hastings railway tracks and fanned out to the east and to the south of Stramberg Lake.

To escape the fire, Vida Stramberg ran with her mother Irene down the tracks to Granite Bay, pulling her younger brother and a goat through the thick smoke. They spent the night with neighbours in the wharf house at the end of the Granite Bay dock, consumed by thoughts of the fire they were sure would engulf their new home below the mine. But the next morning, with the fire on a race to the south, they returned to find their farm untouched.

As the pace of the fire increased, every able-bodied male in the district was recruited to fight it. A firefighters' camp was set up at Hyacinthe Creek, near the Leask homestead, where they built a fire block in an attempt to stop the blaze from spreading south into the residential districts. It worked for a time, aided by a lull in the wind, but when the wind picked up again the fire jumped the block and continued south.

Lord Bacon dashed down to Gowlland Harbour to warn the Halls to flee. There was just time, he said, to pack a few things and climb aboard whatever boat was at hand. He described the scene a few kilometres to the north, where the fire had wiped out the Weeks and Ford farms on the shore of Hyacinthe Bay. Their homes, orchards, outbuildings and livestock—the products of years of hard work—were destroyed. To the south, at the top end of Heriot Bay, writer Francis Dickie was taken off guard by the fire. "A booming roar from the west aroused me," wrote Dickie. "May I never hear its like again. I ran up the nearest ridge and looked toward the fast approaching sound. I saw miles of heavily timbered slopes aflame. I was held there, awed by this vision of an earthly hell destroying in a minute what had required a thousand years to grow."

Francis and his wife Suzanne hauled all their favourite books and possessions to the beach but they were spared the loss of their house when the Columbia Coast Mission boat arrived on the scene. The crew had water pumps on board, salvaged from a disabled forestry ship, so they sprayed the Dickies' home until the fire passed.

With huge clouds of smoke on the horizon, Charles Brunt, the new owner of the Heriot Bay Hotel, served beer to friends and neighbours who soaked the hotel with water. He made sure one friend in particular, who happened to be his insurance agent, got lots to drink and then tried to sweet-talk him into upping his fire insurance coverage.[1] But none of this proved necessary. The fire dashed along Heriot Ridge (to the west of what's now Hyacinthe Bay Road) and headed into Gowlland Harbour, just as Lord Bacon had predicted.

Tommy Hall had a job on the island that summer so he was on hand to help his widowed mother and sisters evacuate their home at the head of Gowlland Harbour. He got the family aboard a boat and dashed back to the house to cover the roof with wet burlap sacks. He kept this up for three days and managed to save the place from flying sparks as the fire swept past their homestead.

Panic ruled for some of the Gowlland Harbour evacuees. Caroline Beech dragged her new treadle sewing machine from her house and stood in a daze until a neighbour told her to put it down and get aboard a waiting boat. The extended Vaughn family had been in the process of moving their floathouses onto property at the northern end of the harbour. One of their homes was still afloat so they loaded it with possessions from the houses on shore. At one point, in the fast-paced chaos of packing, they discovered the children were missing, until someone yanked open the outhouse door and found the toddlers crouched inside. The children had heard the calls of the adults but three-year-old Norma (Vaughn) Hughes clapped her hand over her cousin's mouth to keep him quiet in their safe haven from the fire.

Once everyone was aboard the floathouse the Vaughns cut it loose to drift with the tides until a tug rescued them. Later, when Clara Vaughn checked through what she'd saved from her house, she found one basket full of things like mismatched shoes.

Tourists in Campbell River trolling for salmon on that fine summer day watched in amazement as long stretches of flame danced at

Children often walked or boated over an hour to get to school. Seen here at the Heriot Bay School in about 1912–13 is Roy Bishop of Gowlland Harbour (tall boy, left), with Georgina Ford of Hyacinthe Bay to his left and teacher Mrs. Derbyshire in the centre. Georgina's sons George Ford and James Ford have matching coats and are in the front row. The tallest boy in the front row may be Tommy Hall and the boy and girl on the far left may be his siblings. This photo came to light almost a century later and united descendants Charles Ford of Ladysmith, BC, and Don Bishop of Edmonds, Washington, whose fathers are in the picture. PHOTO COURTESY CHARLES FORD

the water's edge in Gowlland Harbour. The Moss family of Stag Island thought they were safe until fire whooshed up a massive tree on the Gowlland Harbour shore, crowned, then shot a fireball onto their island.

As the fire continued to move south, preparations began at Quathiaski Cove to evacuate the cannery, store and houses. But before the fire passed mid–Gowlland Harbour the weather changed and several days of heavy rainfall extinguished the fire. Some families who'd lost their homes were put up by friends and others moved into abandoned homesteads, like the Vaughns, who took over an old place at the southern tip of Gowlland Island.

A fire marshal and a BC Forest Service crew came to inspect the blackened wasteland some days later. The fire had destroyed 2,200 hectares (50,000 acres) of prime timber and eleven families were homeless.

When news got out that government surveyors were to blame, fifteen residents banded together under spokesman Thomas Noble (who had an interest in the Lucky Jim mine) to press for restitution. The premier refused, saying only the destitute would be assisted, so disgruntled islanders hired a lawyer to sue the government. No one remembers whether this case ever went to court. If it did, Norma (Vaughn) Hughes thinks nothing came of it.

Skookum Tom Leask survived the fire of 1925 only to lose his life in his own bay the following year. Though he'd spent much of his life on the water, Tom had never learned to swim. His children, who lost their mother Maggie in 1919, waited up all night for Tom to return. The eldest walked the beach with a lantern in hand to light his father home but by morning there was still no sign of him so Henry went to their neighbours, the Laws, for help. Bill Law found Tom's body at the bottom of the ocean, not far from his own beach.

Reverend Greene suggested the two eldest Leask children should keep the family together and hang onto their farm. Henry, at eighteen, continued to log and sixteen-year-old Sarah took charge of the household and children, aged from seven to thirteen. Both had been left in charge before while their father worked but ultimately the teenagers were not suitable replacements for parents. Henry began to drink and couldn't manage his meagre finances. Tempers got out of hand and

Sarah stayed only because Henry threatened to have her and the other children committed to an orphanage.

As winter wore on there were times when there was nothing to eat in the house. One day little Mary came home to find her brother had left a bag of oats and brown sugar on the table. In her famished state she stuffed dry oats and sugar into her mouth and barely stopped to chew as she rammed yet more into her pockets. When Henry came in and caught her he gave the girl a stiff beating. It was not the first time one of Mary's older siblings lashed out at her, but this one still burned in her memory as she recounted the details of her difficult childhood to her granddaughter and biographer Lisa Chason many years later.[2]

No one seemed to recognize the depth of the family's privation and turmoil, from their teacher to the Women's Institute ladies who sometimes brought clothes and food, to the social worker who called on occasion. Finally, a year after Tom Leask's death, Henry went to Reverend Greene to say he couldn't manage. Arrangements were made for the rest of the children to go to a Catholic orphanage in Vancouver. Friends and neighbours stood at the dock to see the children off and pressed coins into their hands as they filed on board the Union Steamship boat with a police escort.

Everything about the journey terrified the children, who had never travelled beyond Quathiaski Cove. Frank Leask, the youngest, dated his earliest memories from this trip—anything earlier was a complete blank. He cried all the way down to Vancouver, and shortly after they arrived his brother George died of pneumonia.

Sarah wasn't in the orphanage for long before she was old enough to leave. Mary had to stay for a number of years, until she got a pass to work on Quadra, where she became engaged to Lewis Joyce of Francisco Point. After her marriage, Mary got custody of her younger brother Frank, as her husband's ward. But Frank had been institutionalized so long he couldn't adjust. "In the orphanage everything happened by order," recalled Frank years later. "Bells rang to say it was time for meals. I never did really learn to look after myself."

Henry Leask hung onto his place in Hyacinthe Bay for many years but he never married. People made sure he got work, though it was hard to get logging jobs on the island after the fire of 1925. As a consequence, lots of people left the island—and as Quadra's fortunes fell the new community at Campbell River jumped to the forefront.

It wasn't just the loss of jobs on the island that sparked this change. Motor vehicles had become the preferred means of travel by the mid-1920s and Campbell River was accessible to Nanaimo and Victoria by road. With this change both the police station/courthouse and the fisheries office were transferred to Campbell River. Fortunately the Quathiaski Cove cannery continued to thrive and offered well over one hundred jobs in season.

Skookum Tom and Maggie (Cross) Leask of Hyacinthe Bay died within a few years of each other, leaving a large family who ranged in age from about seven to eighteen. Henry, the eldest, tried to keep the family together with his logging camp earnings but couldn't manage so his younger siblings were sent to a Vancouver orphanage. PHOTO COURTESY LEWIS AND MARY JOYCE, MCR 6049

The wreck of the *Northwestern* in December 1927 was a boon for cash-strapped islanders. The ship was loaded deep with passengers and Christmas freight bound for the Yukon when she ran aground off the Cape Mudge reef in a whiteout blizzard. "You could hear this mournful whistle blowing and the women and kids screaming," recalled Albert Bigold, who lived on a farm that overlooked the reef. Everyone was safely evacuated to Campbell River but the ship lay broadside on the beach for weeks while salvage attempts were made.

"The beach was lined for half a mile with turkeys," said Bigold. "They threw them overboard. And flour. Dad and Mom would go out there in the rowboat and the [salvors] handed over flour, sugar, tea, coffee, cartons of chewing gum." Everyone on the island loaded up until local storekeepers complained about the loss of business and the police came in to make random checks for "stolen" goods. People hid their loot in haystacks and under floorboards or buried it in their gardens.

The Bigolds' place on the bluffs (east of what's now Terra Nova Farm) was one of a handful of productive farms on the island. They had a standing competition with the Strambergs of Granite Bay to see who could grow the largest vegetables. "[Stramberg would] bring onions that weighed two-and-a-half pounds," recalled Albert Bigold. "His cabbages were a foot in diameter and he grew eight-inch turnips!" It seemed there was no way to beat the Strambergs, who gardened in the soil of a shallow lake they drained below Lucky Jim mine.

As long as Hastings Company continued to log at Granite Bay, ranchers like the Strambergs, Luomas and Stenforses had local jobs and a market for their produce. But when the company finished logging in about 1920,[3] men had to find work elsewhere until truck logging outfits took up where Hastings left off.

Henry and Florence Bull moved their family to Granite Bay some-time before 1918,[4] where Henry Bull worked as a logger, a ship's carpenter and a farmer. They lived within sight of Henry and Agnes Twidle on the beach at Granite Bay and though both the Henrys were Englishmen of a similar age they were decided enemies. Henry Bull tethered a randy old goat on his property line, where its intense smell penetrated enemy territory. Some suggest Henry Twidle threatened Bull with a rifle and it cost him his job as postmaster. The Twidles continued to operate their store after this rumoured event but in 1926 the Bulls opened a rival store, where Florence Bull became the new postmistress.

The many mine claims at Granite Bay continued to glimmer in the ever-hopeful imaginations of prospectors. Lucky Jim was the only one that still had a hint of promise but after the mine buildings were destroyed in the fire of 1925 even surface work was discontinued. There was, however, great excitement over a radium discovery at Open Bay in 1914 and again in 1922, but a mine wasn't developed because of the projected cost to move huge volumes of rock to get at the flake-sized seams of radium. Talk of this claim resumed in the early 1930s, when carnotite, a bright greenish yellow mineral, was staked and then dropped, again due to the expense.[5] The Comox Logging & Railway

The wreck of the *Northwestern*, caught in a snowstorm on the shoals at Cape Mudge, brought a wealth of Christmas bounty to cash-strapped islanders in 1927. BCA C-02391

Company got a contract to log 1.8 million metres (20 million feet) of dead standing timber in Open Bay after the fire of 1925.[6] They built a few kilometres of track inland from what's now Open Bay Estates for a ninety-one-man crew, who worked on the island from 1927 to 1928.

A few loggers lived at Bold Point in the 1920s, though the little community of about seventy people worked mainly as ranchers and farmers. There were homesteads scattered along the dirt road from Village Bay Lakes to Bold Point.

The Bold Point Hotel and store were long gone when Loyde and Minnie Bell bought the Ireland-Ward ranch in the late 1920s. They ran 120 head of beef cattle on the ranch and grew all their own hay and grain for the stock. They ran the cattle free-range around Village Bay Lakes and Open Bay, where there were numerous grassy marshes, and in swamps at places like Vic's Meadow, on the edge of Main Lake.

The Bells hired Roland Woolsey, a jockey from Victoria, as a ranch hand in the late 1920s. "The only time the ranch made any money," recalled Woolsey, "was when old Bell got beef shipments going out once a week to the logging camps. It didn't pay to ship any further." The ranch also had the advantage of close proximity to the Bold Point dock, where Minnie Bell looked after the post office in a little shack on the hill.

Unloading Erro Luoma's new Chevrolet in about 1930 from the Union Steamship boat *Chelohsin* at the Granite Bay wharf. PHOTO COURTESY GEORGE PUTTONEN, MCR 6690

One snowy winter a bunch of cattle got stranded in Open Bay so Woolsey and the Bells cut some boards into skis to round up the herd and bring them back to feed. They followed the road, which skirted the east shore of the Village Bay Lakes in those days, to the southeast of the current bridge. From there they had to break snow through the bush down to Open Bay.

Though Bold Point was a small community it remained a stop for the Union Steamship freight and passenger boats that also called bi-weekly at Heriot Bay.

The old Heriot Bay Hotel was still in operation in 1927 when a globe-trotting Englishman and his red-headed wife bought it from the Brunt family. Charles and Beatrice Webster had searched the world for the ideal home. They thought they'd found it at Heriot Bay, with its big maples, sandy beach and ocean views of islands and mountains. They maintained the hotel, the rental cottages and the store until their irritation over the bar's fractious clientele made them decide to shut the whole operation down. Islanders watched in dismay as Webster demolished the east wing of the hotel and converted the remainder into a large private residence.

The Bold Point dock was built some time after the Ireland-Ward family opened their hotel, store, post office and ranch there in 1901 and was maintained until the Union Steamship Company discontinued its freight and passenger service in the 1950s.
PHOTO COURTESY ROLAND WOOLSEY, MCR 6760

Heriot Bay School was the only one on the island with a teacherage. Annie Fenton, the teacher in 1923, described this as a "grand improvement" over the usual boarding system.

In 1926, Ruby (Hovell) Wilson of the We Wai Kai Band was invited to go to Coqualeetza Methodist Residential School near Chilliwack in the lower mainland to accompany her young nephew. She was a student in the band's day school until then, where she got a very basic education from a teacher selected on the strength of her connections rather than credentials. As a result Ruby was set back a few grades at her new school but she quickly caught up. Unlike so many who were forced to go to residential school against their wishes, Ruby enjoyed the experience. She had a choice of academic subjects in the morning and practical training in the afternoon. Ruby also learned to play piano through the Toronto Conservatory of Music for twenty dollars per year and got involved in drama and sports.

Ruby's father Jimmy Hovell and other Native fishermen benefitted from a change in fishing regulations in 1922 that allowed them to work on commercial boats (though at the same time the regulations banned

Japanese Canadians from the fleet).[7] Jimmy Hovell and Billy Assu got jobs on seine and gillnet boats shortly thereafter. "It was pretty near all Scotch people on the seine boats—Bill Wiseman, Alex Souter and Jimmy McPherson," recalled Tommy Hall of Gowlland Harbour. "They brought out their friends too. A few of these Scotsmen were pretty old when they came out, but they were good fishermen. They used to smoke Jervis, strong-smelling stuff, in clay pipes with broken stems jammed in between the gaps in their teeth with this powerful smoke going straight up their noses." Under these men's guidance, Jimmy Hovell and Billy Assu soon became lead skippers.

The government also changed the regulation that gave exclusive rights to cannery operators to fish within their areas. The *Comox Argus* newspaper published a detailed report on the local fishery in 1927 and 1928. There were twelve seine boats in the general region of Quathiaski Cannery, compared to five when W.E. Anderson had exclusive fishing rights. Some, including Anderson, thought this was too many for a sustained fishery. Anderson still relied upon handliners for part of his catch, but the number of people who wanted to do this work declined as the

Waiting for the freight and passenger boat at Quathiaski Cove. The Cove was the commercial hub for the district, with its busy cannery complex, government wharf, church, courthouse/jail and store. "And such a store it is!" said an article in the *Comox Argus* newspaper of 1926. "It is post-office, grocery store, butcher shop, hardware, draper's, grain, service station and drug store all rolled into one. Besides being this, it is the common meeting ground for all [on] Tuesdays and Fridays when all the Island turns out to get its letters." PHOTO COURTESY ED MCALLISTER, MCR 20126-70

economy improved. There were only 110 handliners at Cape Mudge in 1928, compared to 300 the year prior. They received forty-five cents per fish and the cannery's annual pack for 1928 was 20,429 cases.

The handline fleet increased again when the stock market crashed in October 1929, but otherwise most Quadra Islanders weren't directly affected. Life went on as it had for years. Many lived without store-bought goods, but few went hungry in a place rich in fish, clams and deer. Farms expanded in the Depression and one farmer tried raising silver foxes on the former Bagot property, at what's now Quadra Loop. Manager Jock McDougall ran the farm for the Johnsons, with huge wire cages spread across the big field that sloped down the hillside. But foxes didn't pay, in the limited Depression-era fashion market, so Jock gave up on it a year or so later and the fields became a tangle of weeds and scrub alders.

The Bigolds of Sutil Road had a huge garden and raised sheep, pigs and cows. Their mainstay was two hectares (five acres) of Greymount and Early Rose potatoes. They were proud of the fact their potatoes were usually ready for the May 24th picnic.

Young Albert Bigold would slide down the sand bank of his parents' farm to sell potatoes, eggs and milk to the many men and women who lived in rustic handliners' shacks on the beach below, at Mudge City. The handliners who lived there, as Albert recalled, were an interesting mix of eccentrics and misfits.

The Treadcroft brothers left professional careers to live year-round in two little shacks at Mudge City. Arthur Treadcroft's cabin, lined with books, was made from driftwood. It was just big enough to fit a cot and a heater. Arthur ate next door in his brother Edward's slightly larger shack, where Edward painted scenes of Quadra in his spare time. The brothers built two rowboats every winter, fished in them in the summer and then sold them and built two more.

Old-timers say the snow was deeper than normal in the Depression years and the storms were relentless. During one severe storm part of the sand-and-clay bank in front of the Bigolds' farm slid down the hill and smashed apart one of the handliners' shacks. "It pushed him out," recalled Albert Bigold, "and there he was still lying in his bed on the beach—dead. We had to haul him up the bank in five feet of snow in a sleigh, my Dad and I. We hauled him up to the house and put him in the dump truck and phoned the police." The police couldn't come in the heavy weather so the Bigolds kept the dead man in a shed out back for two weeks. "Then we had to drag him back down to the beach and then over to Campbell River. You couldn't get down the road," said Bigold.

Young women could earn good money on the cannery line during the Depression. Eve (Willson) Eade's father's house was within range of the cannery whistle that called everyone to work, so she was able to live at home:

> When the cannery whistle blew we knew the fish boats were in, both day or night, and dropped everything and headed for work. One day Dad and I were papering the ceiling and I had to leave him alone with the bucket of paste and sticky mess as there was no pre-pasted paper in those days. You slapped the homemade paste on the dry paper and tried not to get tangled up in the gooey mess!
>
> We worked piecework. The Chinese would bring bins of fish, cut in slices to the packing tables where we filled half flat or one pound cans. For the half flats, we got 4 cents for a tray of 48 cans and for the tall one-pounds it was 6 cents for a tray of 24, so you had to work fast to make a day's pay.
>
> After two years I was promoted to forelady which was easier

The remains of the last of the handline fishermen's shacks at Francisco Point in 1976. PHOTO COURTESY *COURIER UPPER ISLANDER* NEWSPAPER, APRIL 1976, MCR 10511

work, just inspecting the cans for proper weight, testing lid seal and cleanliness.

Ping Sun Chew was a Vancouver labour contractor who hired the Chinese foreman and cannery crew for Quathiaski Cove and elsewhere. Chew's life had gone from adversity to success. He'd left China in 1912, after his father's estate failed, in search of a better life. His first job in BC was as a houseboy and later he worked as a cannery labourer. With his classical education and quick grasp of English, Chew was promoted to bookkeeper for the Chinese crew and then foreman, which led to his own business as a labour contractor.

Chew returned to China periodically during his early years and after the birth of his second child he brought his wife and family to Canada. Cannery owners like W.E. Anderson looked to Chew to recruit their canning crew and arrange for all their needs. Various members of Ping Sun Chew's family worked at Quathiaski Cannery. His brother Nan was the foreman and his eldest son Yhet worked there too, from his start moving cans as a boy, at fourteen cents per hour, to being the timekeeper.

Ping Sun Chew's eldest son Joe was at work on his Ph.D. at Stanford University when Ping Sun died unexpectedly in 1937, in the middle of the packing season. Joe returned to BC to assume his father's business commitments and paid a visit to Quathiaski Cannery. Margaret Anderson and her daughters entertained Joe's wife while W.E. showed Joe around the cannery. "She too was a Stanford student," recalled Mae (Anderson) McAllister, "and very accomplished, a wonderful pianist."

After Ping Sun Chew's death

Eve (Willson) Eade, left, and Lorraine Inrig pause in their work on the Quathiaski Cove Cannery line in 1938, where they trimmed fish to fit the cans. PHOTO COURTESY EVE (WILLSON) EADE, MCR 17409

his widow insisted the family return to China to live in the fine house she built in her home village with her Canadian money, though she only lived a few months to enjoy it. The rest of the family spent a number of years thereafter caught in the turmoil of war with Japan and the Chinese Revolution, but eventually some of the family returned to Canada.[8]

Another couple who arrived in the 1930s and had interesting cultural roots was Major Frederick and Ameenie Foort. They bought a strawberry farm with 0.4 kilometres (1 mile) of waterfront in northern Gowlland Harbour for four hundred dollars.

The Foorts had wandered the globe in Fred's restless search for a place where his eccentric political and religious views could take root. British Columbia seemed as good a home as any. Ameenie and Fred were an unlikely pair. They met in Ameenie's native Lebanon when Fred was there on war service. She was a shy young woman, who acted as an interpreter for the army while studying at college. The couple's first home in the region was on Read Island, after which they rented a few different places until they bought their Gowlland Harbour property.

Ping Sun Chew immigrated to Canada from China after his family's fortunes fell. He started out as a houseboy and ended as a successful cannery recruiter. His company hired and managed the employees for many canneries, including Quathiaski Cove, where his brother and sons worked. Ping Sun is seen here with his wife Chan She who, after Ping Sun died suddenly, returned to China with her grown children to live in the house she and Ping Sun built in their home village.
PHOTO COURTESY PATRICIA CHEW

Running a farm on Quadra Island suited Ameenie perfectly. The Foorts hired a carpenter at three dollars and twenty cents per day to help build their house and Ameenie developed a productive garden and orchard. Fred, however, was not cut out to be a farmer so he stayed in a house they owned in Vancouver for increasing lengths of time, enjoying the fellowship of like-minded people in the British Israel Movement (white supremacists who thought Britons and Europeans were the Lost Tribes of Israel).

The Foort kids spent as much time as possible on the water

fishing, to add to the family income and, as Jim Foort recalls, to day-dream to the slow rhythm of water time. Jim knew all the boats that passed by or anchored in the harbour to wait out the weather:

> I remember the sounds from their horns on foggy days. I would be sitting with my lines out begging for fish, surrounded by fog, the lapping sounds of water against the rocks to tell me where I was. These ships, seeming great in size, would sound their whistles at intervals to locate their positions from the shores by echo time counts.
>
> What I remember with feelings of loneliness or nostalgia, was the sound of the "Chelohsin's" whistle, one long, two shorts and one long. [That] was the signal to get into the "Merrybelle" if we expected freight, or, otherwise, to bum a ride or walk to Quathiaski Cove from our place in Gowlland Harbour to get the mail and small supplies.[9]

The Native people at Cape Mudge made enough money from fishing to build a new church in 1931. The church was built under John Dick Jr.'s direction and every-thing from the pulpit to the pews was made by the parishioners. It was opened on Easter Sunday in April 1932[10] and was named for missionary R.J. Walker, who was on hand to enjoy the inaugural service in the church.

The village of Quathiaski

Ameenie and Fred Foort with their son David in 1934. Ameenie, a native of Lebanon, lived out her days on Quadra Island, where some of her descendants continue to live, including the BC Ferries' first female captain Esther Allen.
PHOTO COURTESY JIM FOORT, MCR 19480

Fred and Ameenie Foort built a home on their property in northern Gowlland Harbour and developed a farm that Ameenie managed on her own after she and Fred separated. PHOTO COURTESY GRACE (WILLSON) MCPHERSON, MCR 20285-66

Cove had an estimated population of 270 people in 1931. The hub was the busy cannery complex, with its store and wharf on Pidcock Road, and on the hill at the junction of what are now Heriot Bay and Green Roads. The latter road was added in the 1930s, and was where the grown children of some of the island's early non-Native families built bungalows. (Green Road petered out at what's now Harper Road, which was not added until some years later.) The Hopkins family had a little ranch near what's now the Petro-Canada Station at the intersection of Heriot Bay and Harper Roads. West Road was added in the late 1920s to connect Cove residents to the community hall and over time it was extended to Heriot Bay to link up with Hosea Bull's old trail from the beach at Gowlland Harbour.

Because most people let their livestock browse free range, cows and sheep ambled down these country lanes and lazed in the sun at the Cove. In the late fall farmers herded their cows and sheep to winter pastures. The Bigolds' cows sometimes wandered as far as Rebecca Spit. "We'd have to chase them home," reminisced Albert Bigold. "You'd get them half way there and some guy would come along in a car and blow the horn and the cows would head for the bushes!"

The school on Heriot Bay Road, south of the cemetery, became a topic of debate again in the 1930s. The people who lived at the southern tip of the island, like the Joyces and Bigolds, wanted a school closer to their homes and the people in Quathiaski Cove wanted the school in their village hub so children could go home for lunch. School board meetings were a hotbed of dissent until the school went up in flames in 1936, in a fire some suspected was arson.

After the fire the Anderson family donated a piece of land for a new school on Anderson Road, across from the current school parking lot. And another school was promised for the residents of the Joyce and Lighthouse Roads area.

The donation of land for the new school in the Cove was one of W.E. Anderson's last gifts. After nearly thirty years on the island, his health began to fail and he decided to sell his cannery. True to the man's strong ethics, he called together his four top fishermen, all of them from Cape Mudge Village. Harry Assu and his father Billy, Johnny Dick and

The We Wai Kai people built a church at their own expense and labour in 1931, named in honour of Methodist missionary Robert Walker. John Dick Jr., a self-taught carpenter, took a lead role in its construction and served on the church board. Seen here are Reverend Knox and an unidentified group of children, with the church on the left and the school on the right. The church has been carefully maintained and is now in use for multi-denominational services. PHOTO COURTESY MRS. DES MARAIS, MCR 8714

Jimmy Hovell trooped into Anderson's office, as Harry later recalled, to hear the news. "Three companies want to buy my cannery," Anderson told them, "and we would like you to choose which company you want to fish for." The men were split at first on who to go with but eventually they decided on BC Packers and Anderson followed their wishes.

"The news that Mr. W.E. Anderson has sold the Quathiaski Canning Company to the BC Packers had, of course, been whispered for some time," reported the *Comox Argus* in November 1937. "We have not bought the plant with a view to expansion," said the new owner, H.R. MacMillan, "but rather to round out our interests in an important area. It is a going concern and will strengthen BC Packers."

True to his word, not much was changed at the cannery, though BC Packers did add a machine shop to repair fishing boats and barged in some bungalows that ran along the waterfront and on the brow of the hill for their employees. (Most of these are now private residences.)

The Cove became the transport hub for the island during these years, as more islanders went to Campbell River by water taxi for sports, shopping and entertainment. Frank Gagne ran a series of boats, including the *Blue Goose* and the *Blue Heron*, and Jimmy McPherson took people across on the *Connie Mac*.

Heriot Bay had about ninety residents through the Depression. It was a sleepy little community with a few homesteads dotted along the bay to the north. Inland from the bay, at what's now the community garden[11] at the south end of Hyacinthe Bay Road, was a farm pre-empted by Ed Callow, a logging engineer, and his We Wai Kai wife Sadie Assu. John Berg and his family were the next owners of this farm, followed by the Dahlnases. To the east, toward Drew Harbour, was the large Buker ranch where Annie lived on her own after her husband Fred cranked the flywheel of his car and it pushed him off the dock in Quathiaski Cove.

The Heriot Bay Hotel remained a private residence, though a man named Tom Hundley bought it from Charles and Beatrice Webster in 1935. Down the beach from the hotel, at the foot of Antler Road, was a small store and post office. Joseph Calwell bought the store in 1930[12] and moved his family into the upstairs suite. In 1936 he hired sixteen-year-old Midge Smith from Cortes Island (who later married his son

The first non-Native schools on the island were located on Heriot Bay Road but a new school was opened in 1936 on Anderson Road, across from the current entrance to the school parking lot. Instruction was provided up to grade eight, after which children whose parents could afford it sent them to the city for high school.
PHOTO COURTESY JOY (WALKER) HUNTLEY, MCR HUNTLEY-05

Cliff) to help with the store and his invalid wife. Midge was paid ten dollars per month, including board, and got two hours off per week. "The store was open as soon as Mr. Calwell got up at 6:00 a.m.," recalled Midge, "and stayed open until he went to bed."

It was during Midge's years at the store that Joseph bought the Heriot Bay Hotel from Hundley, though he had to have a Vancouver friend stand in as the buyer because he and Hundley weren't on friendly terms. Midge walked through the old building soon after her father-in-law took possession. Among the remaining effects were a massive hall-stand with an inset mirror and coat hooks and piles of mattresses stacked in disused rooms. Most of the furniture, crystal, dishes and bar spittoons were dumped off the end of the wharf as the Calwells transformed the place into a family home and boarding house.

It was fitting that Joseph Calwell should have the old Heriot Bay Hotel. He had the same energetic entrepreneurial zeal as his predecessor, Hosea Bull—though perhaps more refined ethics. Besides running the store and the boarding house and managing a garden and chickens, Joseph and his sons ran a taxi and trucking service, charging one dollar per trip to Quathiaski Cove. They also salvaged what was left of Bull's sawmill and revived it, and built a dock in front of their store for fishing boats.

Francis and Suzanne Dickie returned to Heriot Bay in 1931. They had left their property after the fire of 1925 to work as foreign correspondents in Paris, where Francis wrote for the *Daily Province* and Suzanne covered Paris fashions for Canadian magazines. They settled back into their rustic house, built from the remnants of an old fish saltery, at the end of what's now Dickie Road.

The Dickies hired a secretary to type their manuscripts in exchange for room and board, and the meals consisted almost exclusively of fish, clams and oysters. True to writers of the Dickies' generation, they had numerous eccentricities, but they were quietly accepted on the island. Their neighbours knew, for instance, to yank hard on the bell pull at the top of the Dickies' trail to give Francis time to get his clothes on because he liked to garden in the nude.

Heriot Bay School, 1928. There were so many Swedish farmers and fishermen in Heriot Bay that it was dubbed "Little Sweden." There were between sixteen to thirty-five children in attendance at Heriot Bay School through the Depression years. Seen in the back row from the left: Lillian (Carlson) Meredith, Dorothy Kilgour, unidentified, Elmer Krooks, John Johnson. Middle row: Marie (Vaughn) Wakefield, Phyllis (Walker) King, Dorothea (Cramer) Creelman. Front row: Elmer Oswald, Hillive (Carlson) Quocksister, Joy (Walker) Huntley, John Oswald and George Hovell. PHOTO COURTESY H.M. FERGUSON, MCR 7021

The Bigold family on their farm on southern Quadra Island. PHOTO COURTESY VIRGINIA MCPHEE, MCR 19670

Granite Bay sometimes froze over and as there was no road connection to southern Quadra until 1951, it left residents stranded. During the Depression out-of-work men cleared a road around the northeast side of the bay to an alternate boat dock near Shell (or Green) Island. PHOTO BY HENRY TWIDLE AND COURTESY J.H. DALTON, MCR 9107

In the Dickies' day a fairly well-developed one-lane track skirted around the curve of Heriot Bay to about what's now Endersby Road. From there a trail ran down to the beach at the Dickies' property and along the rocky headlands to Hyacinthe Bay. From Hyacinthe Bay there was a trail to Bold Point and Granite Bay.

By the 1930s, with cars and trucks becoming more common on the island, residents of northern Quadra wanted a road connection to the south island. The island's road foreman Charlie Bigold was hired for the job in 1931,[13] and used relief workers from off-island. Until then Bigold had worked on his own to maintain the island's dirt roads, tossing rocks off the roads and resurfacing the potholes with mud from the roadsides. For heavier work Bigold used an old hard-rubber-tired road grader pulled by a team of horses, and later by a Model A Ford.

In 1944 Les and Agnes Bestwick moved their truck logging camp to Granite Bay. The couple were married when they were both seventeen and worked as logging camp cooks until they started their own truck logging outfit in 1934. Agnes Bestwick couldn't imagine why anyone would want to live in the city, as she told a *Vancouver Sun* columnist. She liked her "pretty white painted house" on its 17 X 21-metre (55 X 70-foot) float, with no grass to cut and a garden of gladiolas and geraniums in boxes on the deck. "I don't know why more young couples don't move up to camps," said Agnes. "It's a life free from worry, and there are lots of activities for youngsters." PHOTO COURTESY BILL BESTWICK

Bigold's forty-man road crew wasn't motivated to work very hard. They got ten dollars a month, worked by hand and slept on the beach. Their project was to connect Granite Bay's logging roads together to reach Heriot Bay, but they didn't make much progress, as Bigold's son recalled. "One fella fell asleep," said Albert Bigold, "so Dad slipped his boots off him. When Dad come back three or four hours later he says, 'What happened to your boots? You must have worked awful hard to walk right out of those boots.'" Under such conditions it wasn't until much later, in 1951, that a road was built to Granite Bay.

A relief crew also built a public road along the eastern shore of Granite Bay, across the farm owned by Matti Hill (yet another of Granite Bay's Finns) to a headland opposite Shell Island at the entrance of Granite Bay. Before the road was built residents were cut off when the bay froze over in winter—with no boat or road access to the outside world. One winter a pregnant woman at term had to be dragged across the frozen ocean on a makeshift sleigh to the thin edge of the ice and then over the rocks to a dock. This road, now called Hill Trail, remains

Granite Bay School 1929–30. The children are identified, but not in order, as Alice Strooce, Edith Stenfors, teacher, Teddy Stenfors and Henry Luoma. PHOTO COURTESY GEORGE PUTTONEN, MCR 66833

open, though it has been blocked by a gate at the entrance so hikers must walk the beach to reconnect with it.

Granite Bay had an estimated population of fifty-eight people in 1931, as noted in the provincial directory. Archrivals Henry Twidle and Henry Bull kept their nearby stores in operation through the Depression, more out of stubborn tenacity than for economic gain.

Clay Anderson's Granite Bay Timber Company brought new employment to the bay in 1934 when he opened a seventy-man camp to cut an estimated 8.36 million metres (90 million feet) of timber.[14] Anderson converted the old Hastings railway grades into truck logging "fore-and-aft" wooden roads on a track above the slash. It was a tough time to be in the logging industry. When Clay and his partners ran into difficulty his father, veteran logger P.B. Anderson, and his brother Dewey bought his partners out. The family's well-established reputation was their saving grace through the Depression. At one point, as Dewey recalled in an interview, the family owed $28,000 in credit at Marshall-Wells, for their various operations. "They had faith in us, and later of course, they received every cent," said Anderson. As Granite Bay people had feared, when Anderson finished logging in 1937 the population dropped and the school was forced to close. It was another decade before it opened again.

Granite Bay's residents hung onto their community with a tenacious will, in spite of the constant roller coaster of their logging-dependent economy. And while southern Quadra Islanders may have been more smug about their stable situation during these years they too were about to learn what happens to a village when it loses its major industry.

CHAPTER TWELVE

Adapting to a New Era

In 1903, the island's name was officially changed from Valdes to Quadra, but islanders didn't like the "new" name. "At the risk of displeasing our many friends on Valdes Island," wrote the editor of the *Comox Argus* in 1932, "we are going to ask them why they call the very beautiful island they live on Valdes and not Quadra?" He posed the question again in 1937 and someone wrote back to say Valdes was the name of their first school, their social club and hall, and the first non-Native boy born on the island. They had no intention of dropping the island's original name, which they pronounced "Valdeeze." But in spite of such feelings, the new name was slowly adopted in the 1930s.

The Quadra Legion selected a spot at the apex of Quathiaski Cove's village hub at Pidcock and Green Roads to plant a coronation oak tree, sprouted from a Royal Windsor Forest acorn. One hundred children and their families observed a few moments of silence on November 13, 1938, in memory of the fallen of World War I. The sapling (now a grand tree) was surrounded by a triangle of benches to create a place of reflection—and to keep the stray cows away. BC Packers passed out candies and young Ayako Atagi, whose father maintained the cannery boats, sold poppies for the Legion.

If islanders were united about anything it was their strong support for unions and the socialist movement. The national Co-operative Commonwealth Federation (CCF), the forerunner to the New Democratic Party, got many island votes. In this spirit, islanders decided to open a credit union. Matthew Gerrard was the founding president of the bank in 1941, which he ran from his home on West Road, across from the current fire hall in Heriot Bay. Gerrard was a staunch socialist. Before he moved his family to Quadra Island he had a fish-buying station on Stuart Island, where he only bought from fishermen who had joined the union. Sepp Bayer, a well-educated Austrian who had a large family and a farm in southern Gowlland Harbour, took over from Gerrard as manager of the credit union. The first office people remember was a portion of what's now the public library, built by Sam Hooley on Cramer Road. The building was later expanded to its current size.

Ruby (Hovell) Wilson of the We Wai Kai Band has the year 1941 emblazoned on her memory. She was approaching term with her first pregnancy that August and living in one of the cannery shacks that followed the curve of the beach. Her husband was away on one of the cannery boats when she awoke to the incessant scream of the cannery whistle. She thought at first it was just the usual call to work, though it was not yet daylight. When she looked out the window she saw the cannery was in flames. By 5:00 a.m. it was fully engulfed. Very few locals joined the firefighters, assuming, like Ruby, that the whistle was just another call to work. The few people on hand managed to keep the blaze away from the store and bunkhouses, but the cannery itself was gone within what seemed like minutes. Charred cans that drifted as far as Seymour Narrows gave fishermen like Bill Law their first hint something had gone terribly wrong.

The loss of the cannery (and 4,500 cases of salmon) was an annoyance for BC Packers, but not much more than that as the company was well insured. But they chose not to rebuild the cannery, which was a huge loss to Quathiaski Cove. With the advent of fast boats BC Packers had begun to consolidate all their canneries into central locations like Steveston. Fishermen could continue to work in their favourite fishing grounds and unload their catch into packer boats headed for distant canneries. Women who worked on the line were the ones most affected. Some became cooks on fishing boats, but that wasn't the same as having a job close to home and family. With the closure, the little village at the Cove lost all the spinoff business the cannery generated—and its reason

Eve (Willson) and Jack Eade moved to Vancouver for work during World War II but returned to Eve's childhood home on Quadra to take up commercial fishing. PHOTO COURTESY GRACE (WILLSON) MCPHERSON, MCR 20285-42

for being. The store continued, along with a small café, and the fishermen's net lofts remained in use, but they were minor businesses. And they too were razed in various fires that occurred over the coming decades.

When war was declared in Europe in 1939 a few islanders responded, but most were exempt because they performed essential services like fishing, logging and farming. Eve Willson and her "young man" got married when he decided to enlist but Jack Eade failed the physical examination, as Eve later wrote, so he got a job as a machinist for Boeing Aircraft. Eve

Prior to World War II, the Matsunagas lived below what's now Whiskey Point Resort in Quathiaski Cove. They were among thousands of Japanese Canadians whose possessions were sold cheaply when they were interned in camps during World War II. The Matsungas returned to the coast after the war. They found and bought back their cod boat *Soyakazi* (*Fair Winds*) and worked with it until fish stocks gave out. The family maintained the boat for decades after and it's now on display at the Museum at Campbell River. PHOTO COURTESY MATSUNAGA FAMILY, MCR 20395-1

got a city job too, where she ran a trip saw making boxes to be sent to China to fill with tea for the troops.

When Eve and Jack Eade returned to Quadra for a visit Jack decided to go into commercial fishing with Eve's family. "The Japanese had been interned to the Interior of BC by this time," wrote Eve, "and all their fishing boats were for sale by the government so we bought a twenty-eight-foot boat [and] loaded our belongings in the stern."

Young Ayako Atagi, who sold poppies at the Legion's armistice service in 1938, was among the hundreds of Japanese Canadians interned. Her family and several others on Quadra got only a few hours' notice to pack their belongings before they were taken to prison-style camps in the interior of BC. All they could take were their grip bags; everything else was sold for a song. It was many years after the war ended before Japanese Canadians were allowed to return to the coast. Many opted not to come back.

Islanders experienced a tremendous earthquake just after the war ended. The quake, measuring 7.2 on the Richter scale, broke the stillness of a warm Sunday morning on June 26, 1946. Eve (Willson) Eade had just started to give her infant son his 10:00 a.m. bottle when the ground began to shake:

> I thought a cyclone had struck us, then the house started bouncing up and down and things started falling off the stove and shelves. We realized it was a serious earthquake and we ran outside. My father-in-law's house was next door and we watched it rock back and forth and I thought surely nothing could lean that far and not fall over. The trees beside our fence were leaning over almost touching the ground and a huge boulder in our front yard was bouncing up and down like a rubber ball. It felt as if the earth would open up and swallow us all. It only lasted a few minutes, but what a terrible sensation it was.

Herbert Joyce (son of pioneers Anna and Alfred Joyce) was headed across his farm field on his tractor at what's now Terra Nova Farm at the southern tip of Quadra when the field began to undulate like a rolling sea. He threw himself off the tractor and let it carry on without him.

An earthquake in 1946 that measured 7.2 on the Richter scale slashed open trenches at Rebecca Spit and caused the end to slump into the sea. Seen here, surveying the damage, are Cliff Lacey, Mina Stanley and Ed Clandening. PHOTO COURTESY ROB CLANDENING, MCR 19436

Some people watched in awe from their yards as their chimneys swayed back and forth and then snapped off at the roofline or cascaded into their homes. The Heriot Bay Hotel, licensed once again as a hotel and bar, also lost its chimneys. Down the beach at Calwell's store everything fell off the shelves, leaving a mess of smashed goods and broken glass that cost them one thousand dollars to replace. The greatest damage took place at Rebecca Spit, where trenches were gashed open and the end of the Spit slumped down.

There was a push by government after the war to modernize the province's rural areas with better schools and electricity. In 1946 School District 72 was formed to manage all the schools in Campbell River as well as on Quadra, Cortes and Read Islands. The plan was to consolidate as many of these schools as possible into centralized facilities, and bus pupils to them where necessary. Johnny Blenkin brought the first school bus to Quadra Island when the old teacher's residence at Heriot Bay School was converted into a high school. St. John's Church in the Cove became a classroom for primary grades and the nearby school on Anderson Road continued to offer the elementary grades.

Children in the We Wai Kai Village at Cape Mudge, seen here in 1941, had their own school from as early as 1893. According to elected chief Ralph Dick, the fact that children weren't forced to go to residential schools has contributed to the band's success. PHOTO COURTESY ELSIE (JOYCE) WARGO, MCR 9279

A new "consolidated" school, which brought all the island schools together, was opened in 1950 on the current site of Quadra Elementary School on Heriot Bay Road, east of the Anderson Road intersection. PHOTO COURTESY ESTELLE ROSE, MCR 18368

School District 72 was one of the first to integrate First Nations and non-Native children into the same schools, thanks in part to Peggy Yeatman of Gowlland Harbour. She taught on the Campbell River Reserve in the late 1940s and 1950s and demanded that her high school students be accepted into the mainstream system.

A few years after School District 72 was formed a new school was built in Quathiaski Cove on its current site, to accommodate the primary and elementary grades. It was the fifth incarnation of the school in just over half a century, from the 1895 log cabin on Heriot Bay Road to the ultra-modern school opened with pride in 1950. Anna Joyce, as a pioneer who fought hard for better school facilities, gave a speech on opening day. "My fondest hopes have been realized as we have the consolidated school in a central place, accessible to all the children of the district. This is a far cry from our first log school, to this very modern building." Shortly after the new school was opened the We Wai Kai children from Cape Mudge began to attend.

High school kids continued to go to Heriot Bay until a subsidized foot-passenger ferry service to Campbell River began in 1949, after which teens went to school there. Scheduled passenger ferry service was

With no car ferry service on the island prior to 1960, the Heriot Bay School teacher had to use a barge to move to the island in 1941. PHOTO COURTESY JOY (WALKER) HUNTLEY, MCR 5349

Bill Nutting and skipper John Oswald on the *Victory II* foot passenger ferry, 1950.
PHOTO BY AND COURTESY GODFREY BALDWIN, MCR 1377

a boon for other islanders too, at a time when the old Union Steamship Service began to curtail its business. Islanders could now plan trips to town for medical care, to shop or to go to movies at the new Van Isle Theatre (now the Tidemark).

Tommy Hall, Bill Hall and John Oswald served as captains on the 11.5-metre (38-foot) *Victory II* ferry. There was room for twelve passengers in its cabin, where people sat on benches on either side of the Vivian diesel engine. The ferry's capacity was later increased to twenty-five.

While Cape Mudge Village had its own power plant as early as the 1930s, most islanders didn't have electricity until the province hooked them up to the grid in 1952. Emily Breitenbach opted not to get her house wired. She was used to living without electricity and couldn't afford the cost of wiring. But when she won an electric iron at a BC Power Commission cooking class, the Quadra Island Women's Institute raised over one hundred dollars to pay for her house to be wired.

In the ebullient times of the postwar years the Peterson family of Vancouver turned a passion for fishing into their living. It was an exceptional camping and fishing trip to Discovery Passage in 1948 that gave Phil Peterson the idea to open a lodge. He met with George Pidcock in Courtenay to enquire about his land at Poverty Point, at the southern entrance to Gowlland Harbour. George had retained the property over the years, loaded as it was with fond memories of his youthful hopes and dreams, and he wasn't eager to sell. Though Phil just wanted to buy 4 hectares (10 acres) Pidcock refused his offer until Phil agreed to buy the full 60 hectares (150 acres). The Petersons got the down payment from Phyllis's mother and a deal was struck. Over the next five years the family spent summers at the place they renamed April Point, where they built a lodge and renovated some of the existing cabins for guests.

"In those early years," wrote their granddaughter Heidi Peterson, "Phil handled the day-to-day operations of the lodge while Phyllis did the cooking and baking, laundry and cleaning." Everything had to be absolutely perfect, from the polished silver to the cinnamon buns

April Point Lodge was started by Phil and Phyllis Peterson after a fishing trip to the Quadra Island area in 1949. They bought Poverty Point, where there were handline fishermen's shacks, and renamed it April Point. The Petersons built a lodge on site and the business flourished from its humble beginnings to become a prestigious lodge. PHOTO COURTESY HELEN MITCHELL, MCR 8300

and pies. Phil and his sons Thor, Eric and Warren—all enthusiastic fishermen—served as guides. As Thor Peterson recalls, his mother was the backbone of what became a prestigious resort. She was the business's brains, the one who made everything tick and kept people wanting more. "She should be remembered for that," says Thor.

A resort of a very different kind opened on the island in the late 1940s when the Pacific Coast Children's Mission Society purchased the Walker family's Homewood Farm in Gowlland Harbour. Alf and Margaret Bayne had operated the mission from aboard their eleven-metre (thirty-six-foot) boat for several years until in 1948 they opened a camp at Homewood that offered a blend of bible study and outdoor activity for children.

It was during these postwar years that Native people were finally given the right to vote in provincial elections in 1949, and in 1951 the federal government quietly dropped the anti-potlatching law. Only vestiges of the old tradition had survived in the hinterlands of

Maypole dancers at the annual May Day festivities at Rebecca Spit in 1955. PHOTO BY GEORGE ROSE AND COURTESY ESTELLE ROSE, MCR 6788

Kwakwa̱ka'wakw territory, where potlatches were secretly carried on in remote places.

Quadra Island remained a conglomerate of little communities in those years, with lots of tolerance for eccentrics like Maria Carlotta Boond. Maria and fisheries officer Sam Boond came to the island with Maria's mother in about 1931 and moved into the old cannery bunkhouse at the intersection of Pidcock and Heriot Bay Roads in the Cove.

Of the handful of islanders said to have aristocratic blood—from Lord Bacon to Eleanor Bagot—Carlotta was the real thing. Her mother was born in Calcutta in 1848, the youngest daughter of Major-General Richardson. At sixteen she married Captain Chevalier de Portugal. They lived in Paris for a time and frequented the court of Napoleon III until they moved to Brazil, where the captain made a name for himself in his exploration of the Amazon River. After his death, Countess de Portugal served as a lady-in-waiting to Queen Victoria.

The countess lived in quiet retirement on Quadra but her daughter Carlotta served on the Women's Institute executive and ran a taxi. She didn't get a lot of business though, because a ride with Carlotta was a death-defying experience. Carlotta's oddities escalated when her mother passed away in 1937. At the funeral she snatched up all the flowers at the graveside and tossed them into the casket—and thereafter she walked the streets alone in animated conversation with her late mother. Her manner of shopping at the cannery store was also odd. She roamed the aisles, picked out what she needed and left, without the fussy bother of paying for it. However, the storekeeper noted her "purchases" and added them to her monthly bill, which she always paid.

After Carlotta's husband Sam died in 1950 she took up with a popular Fisheries officer named William Rockey. When she discovered Rockey was seeing other women Carlotta mixed a lethal concoction of paint solvents for them both to drink. Dudley and Howard Richards returned late from town that snowy night and needed a ride home so they went to Carlotta's to get the taxi. When there was no answer at her door and no sign of tire tracks in the snow of the past few days they went next door and phoned the police in Campbell River. The police

By 1955 both Native and non-Native residents participated in the island's annual May Day celebrations. Young Vicki Assu on the right was a princess in 1958. Next to her are Christine (Ogren) Thompson, Carolyn (Grafton) Peers, and Shirley (Bassett) Palmorly. Their attendants were not identified. PHOTO BY GEORGE ROSE AND COURTESY ESTELLE ROSE, MCR 6790

instructed the young men to force their way inside, where they found Carlotta and William dead. When their deaths were announced no less than two women stepped forward to claim William Rockey's remains.

Islanders—both Native and non-Native—had a wealth of stories to share for BC's centennial year in 1958. Joy (Walker) Huntley (daughter of Methodist missionary R.J. Walker and his second wife Theodora) and schoolteacher May Hendrickson wrote numerous articles for local papers about pioneer and First Nations men and women whose old way of life was fast disappearing.

It was also in 1958 that the twin peaks of Ripple Rock in Seymour Narrows were blasted asunder. The constricted passage in the main shipping lane for the inside coast took many lives over the years. Turbulent whirlpools formed around the peaks, which lay directly in the path of ships. They were only covered by about 2.7 metres (9 feet) of water at low tide.

In 1945 a Vancouver company got the contract to drill the surface of Ripple Rock to set dynamite charges. They asked Frank Gagne to anchor their scow as a work platform in the middle of the passage. He told them their plan wouldn't work because there were no cables strong enough to hold a barge in place against the tidal currents in Seymour Narrows. The Vancouverites insisted, however, so Gagne anchored their barge with steel cables five centimetres (two inches) thick that were tied to either shore. As predicted, when the tides changed the cables snapped like threads. They were replaced by even heavier lines, but they still had to be replaced often.

Seymour Narrows is the main shipping lane through the inner coast but the fast tides and the twin peaks of Ripple Rock just below the surface at low tide caused many shipwrecks. After a failed attempt to remove the peaks through surface explosions, mine shafts were tunnelled under the seabed from Maude Island and up into the twin peaks. The project took two years, during which time the crew was housed on the Quadra shore (in the background here), with a causeway across Canoe Pass to Maude. The peaks of Ripple Rock were removed in the largest non-nuclear explosion to date in April 1958.
PHOTO BY GEORGE ROSE AND COURTESY ESTELLE ROSE, MCR 18735

The drilling crew could only work from the platform at low tide, when they could reach the peaks of Ripple Rock. They were headed back from one of their shifts in their chartered fishing boat when it got caught in one of Seymour Narrows' infamous whirlpools and sucked down. Two of the eleven-man crew miraculously survived because their hands locked onto the guy wires of the boat as it went down and resurfaced.

"The only way to remove that rock," said Gagne a few years later, "is to go into the ground and go at it from below." And he was right. It was an expensive proposition, but advanced mining technology was used to drill two tunnels from Maude Island to below seabed and up into each peak of Ripple Rock.

The drilling took two years, under the direction of Vancouver scientists Victor Dolmage and E.E. Mason. They set 1,237 tonnes (1,375 tons) of explosives into "coyote drifts," narrow lateral tunnels that fanned out from each of the main shafts. The whole operation was experimental and there were no guarantees the largest non-nuclear explosion to date wouldn't trigger a tidal wave or perhaps even an earthquake.

The Discovery Passage region was evacuated on April 5, 1958, when a volcano of water and rock erupted at Seymour Narrows. It cascaded in layers that displaced 330,000 tonnes (370,000 tons) of rock far to each side of the base of Ripple Rock. It was a perfectly executed operation and not even a hint of the explosion was picked up beyond Seymour Narrows.

Even with the hazard of Ripple Rock removed, the fast tides of the narrows demand attention and skill. The waters to the south in Discovery Passage are also difficult to navigate. By the late 1940s parents were no longer willing to send their kids to school in Campbell River aboard the little *Victory II*. It was too small for the frequent southeast storms.

In 1953 a delegation from the Quadra Island Ratepayers' Association went to Victoria to meet with provincial transportation minister "Flying" Phil Gaglardi to ask for a car ferry. He didn't say no, but he didn't say yes either. Gaglardi said he would subsidize a car run if the federal government would build the terminuses. "And since the federal government," wrote a local newspaper editor, "moves with all the ponderosity of a hippopotamus climbing a Christmas tree, it hardly seems likely that Mr. Gaglardi will be called upon to make good his promise for many years to come. But we've been watching the Quadra battle on this question, and from this corner it doesn't look like they're going to give up too easily."

The island's population was over six hundred people[1] by the 1950s and, as islanders reiterated in a barrage of letters to the government and to newspaper editors, they were ready for better service. Taking the lead in the campaign were members of the Quadra Island Ratepayers' Association—president Bill Law, Estelle Rose, Lloyd McIlwain and Don Huntley.

A disgruntled delegation again visited Gaglardi in 1958. They'd had enough. If he didn't take action, they warned, they were going to boy-cott the ferry and keep their kids home from school. Shortly thereafter the Social Credit government assigned the *Uchuk I*, a leased boat with a one-hundred-person capacity, "as a stopgap measure." The problem, said Gaglardi, was a new shopping plaza being planned for downtown Campbell River. The developers had offered to build a breakwater to protect a ferry terminal at the proposed Tyee Plaza Mall but the project was in limbo because Campbell Riverites didn't want Willow Bay (at what's now the plaza) to be filled.

There were other objections for Riverites as well. Frank Gagne, who had envisioned the project and proposed to fill the bay with his pile-driving rig, was a likeable fellow but his business partner William Mullett, an accountant with a tarnished past, rubbed townsfolk the wrong way. Mullett took matters into his own hands and went over the heads of Campbell River's village council to get provincial government sanction. One of his levers was the promised dock for the Quadra Island ferry.

Tommy Hall, who'd come to Quadra Island as an infant in 1901, was appointed as senior skipper of the new ferry built for the Campbell River to Quadra Island run. It was launched in Vancouver in March 1960. Tommy was on hand as Estelle Rose of Quadra Island broke a bottle of champagne across the *Quadra Queen*'s ample bow. Once she was afloat, Captain Hall took over the wheel and brought the ship up coast for her inaugural run.

A strong southeast wind snapped through the bunting and flags that bedecked the *Quadra Queen* on the morning of April 15 when government dignitaries cut the ribbon at the Campbell River ferry dock. A cavalcade of fifteen cars drove aboard the shiny new boat, led by the Beech family's 1914 Model T Ford, and the ferry was accompanied across the passage by a fleet of seine boats, led by Ivan Dick of the Cape Mudge Band, who claimed descent from We-Kai and Sewis. The ferry was cheered into the dock in Quathiaski Cove at the foot of what's now Old Ferry Road.

With car ferry service, the island's new Rebecca Spit Park became a key attraction. The park was dedicated at a picnic on June 20, 1959, and well over one thousand people turned out for the day of festivities, from foot races to a picnic and dance at the old community hall. It was a perfect day. There were a few showers in the morning to settle the dust on the island's dirt roads, but the sun came out in time for a plaque to be unveiled. It acknowledges the foresight of the Clandening family, who wanted to see their exceptional property become a park. Lloyd McIlwain of the parks committee, fiery Don Huntley of the ratepayers' association, Chief Billy Assu and his son Harry Assu, then the elected chief, joined Social Credit MLA Dan Campbell on the dais for speeches.

Mary Clandening represented her extended family and the memory of her late husband at the opening. After her husband James passed away in 1952, Mary consulted with her children who agreed the Spit should be sold to the province for a park. A deal was struck that included a land swap and some cash.

Many residents already felt as if Rebecca Spit belonged to them, thanks to the generosity of the Clandenings over the years. They had honoured the fact that islanders had celebrated May Day picnics at the Spit from the settlement's earliest years and welcomed them to continue.

It was Mary's father-in-law James Clandening Sr. who bought Rebecca Spit from sawyer W.P. Sayward in the 1890s, when there was a second proposal for a transcontinental railway to cross from Bute Inlet to Vancouver Island. Clandening was a Vancouver railway man, alderman and road builder credited for some of that city's earliest roads, including Granville Street and Stanley Park Road. He was on a hunting trip on Quadra when he decided to buy Rebecca Spit—as a gravel source for the Bute Inlet railway. The railway didn't come to pass, ruled out in favour of Prince Rupert on the northern coast, but James kept the property and allowed Winfield and Louise Maxwell to run their chicken ranch there.

Eventually James Clandening gave Rebecca Spit to his son James Jr., who moved to the island with his wife Mary in about 1924.[2] They lived for a time in Quathiaski Cove, where James worked as a cannery machinist. It wasn't until the Depression years that they moved to the Spit, where they raised turkeys to help put their sons through school in Vancouver. Later the family opened Clandening and Sons Machine

Shop at the Spit for boat repairs, near their home to the south of the current boat ramp.

By 1959 there were multiple generations of the Clandening family on hand to enjoy the tremendous pleasure the newly dedicated park brought to both residents and visitors. Word of the beauty of the place soon spread among coastal cruisers and with car ferry service the park became a favourite summer retreat for car campers too. Poet and novelist Brian Brett spent many boyhood summers at Rebecca Spit:

> We just drove up and camped, and felt welcome, both by the community and the landscape. The beach was still littered with oysters, and there were more butter clams than you could dig. One year the northern coho were so thick their finning awoke me. It was like a giant rustling whisper and I got up to watch the dawn reflect on their black-shadowed fins surrounding the Spit like an army of spirit fish. At first, the fishing was so easy we never bothered with Tom Macks or other lures. We just

Mary Clandening being presented with a gift by Lloyd McIlwain (right), park committee chairperson, at the dedication of Rebecca Spit Park on June 20, 1959, as provincial minister Earle Westwood looks on. PHOTO COURTESY JOY (WALKER) HUNTLEY, MCR HUNTLEY-02

used a white rag on a hook. The killer whales used to surface suddenly, and spy-hop our dory, scaring us before they rolled over and disappeared.[3]

In 1965, when park officials realized Rebecca Spit was too fragile an ecosystem to sustain random camping, the province offered to buy part of the Cape Mudge Band's Drew Harbour Reserve for a campground. The band, who felt all of the Spit was their rightful property, rejected an offer they considered parsimonious. Shortly thereafter they opened their own campsite, which continues to be a popular vacation spot today.

Billy Assu, whose life spanned massive change, became an oracle in his senior years, sought by anthropologists and historians to reflect upon a past few could now imagine. Musicologist Ida Halpern recorded many of his songs, allowing us into the heart of his culture and the days of the potlatch.[4]

Assu was nearly one hundred years old when he passed away in February 1965. Three BC Air Lines and Island Airlines planes flew in

A group assembled at the We Wai Kai Village to celebrate when Billy Assu was awarded a King George medal in 1937. Seen here from top left are Mrs. Peters holding a child, Mary Naknakim, Adalee Assu and Lottie Price. To the far left is Louise Hovell, Ethel Assu with Emma Wallace just behind her, the schoolteacher beside unknown children and Emma Dick (in front row), next to Ida Assu, Bessie Seaweed (later King) with an unknown child and Mrs. Johnny Chickite (far right). PHOTO COURTESY JOY (WALKER) HUNTLEY, MCR 20389-68

formation over the Cape Mudge Village cemetery to pay last respects at his funeral. The crowd below, laden with flowers, formed a massive cortège that went from the community hall to the cemetery, where Billy Assu was laid to rest near his eldest son's grave. Newspapers across the province sang Assu's praises. He had been twice decorated by the British monarchy, in 1937 and 1958, for meritorious service as an exemplary leader. "The old chief ran hard up against the white man, and refused to back down or knuckle under," said the editor of Campbell River's *Upper Islander*. "Today, the men and women who are now leading the Indians must adopt the same attitude. They must fight for what is right, and refuse to sell themselves short for the easy way out."

A driven young visionary was the elected chief for several terms during the 1960s. Lawrence Lewis embraced an idea floated by the provincial government to make Cape Mudge Village the test case as an incorporated Native-run municipality. Under this plan, the band would operate through a mayor and council, and would be eligible for provincial cost-sharing for infrastructure. "Indian people would be able to vote on school bylaws, run for school boards and be members of regional districts," said North Island MLA Dan Campbell. The controversial aspect of the plan was that occupied reserve lands would be divided into individually owned lots, with a proviso that they could never be sold into non-Native hands. The concept, however, did not find favour with the Department of Indian Affairs. When they did finally agree to it years later, the plan was narrowly defeated by the band.

It was the start of a new era for the band, and for all island residents, when car ferry service started in 1960. Many islanders envisioned a bright new future, with an influx of new residents and development. They did not, however, anticipate that among those newcomers would be long-haired young men and women, with flowing robes, beads and guitars.

CHAPTER THIRTEEN

Going Back to the Land

Tourists crossed Discovery Passage to Quadra Island on the car ferry to fish and camp for a tranquil getaway. Some, with their long hair and beads, decided to stay. Among them were well-educated youths with high ideals and a burning desire to create a new and simpler life. Still others, like Courtenay surveyor Gordon Wagner, recognized that easier access to the island brought an opportunity for profit.

When Wagner surveyed the Noble brothers' land at what's now Quadra Loop it struck him the place was perfect for recreational lots. By the 1960s the Nobles owned land all over the island, which they purchased for logging as the first generation of homesteaders passed away or moved on. Many left large properties their descendants considered worthless. As Wagner recalled in his memoirs, when he suggested the idea of a subdivision to the Nobles they weren't interested. "We're loggers," they told him. Wagner then approached Wallace, Harper and Jack Baikie, Campbell River loggers and developers. The brothers, with Wagner as a working partner, bought the land from the Nobles and phased in a subdivision they called Wa-Wa-Kie, in an exotic-sounding blend of their names. Their first twenty-seven beach lots went up for sale at $2,500 each, but initially they were slow to sell. Pete Craddock and others who grew up on the island thought Wa-Wa-Kie Beach was a ridiculous place to buy land, with its boulder-strewn beach and direct exposure to southeast storms.

As if to prove this point, a southeaster battered against Wagner's Campbell River office window the day Tom and Audrey Dorset came to see him. "They were from the mainland and somehow heard we had beach lots for sale on Quadra Island," wrote Wagner. "I gave them a map of the subdivision and told them how to get to Wa-Wa-Kie Beach. I did not expect to see them again. Two days later we made our first sale."

More lots sold thereafter and islanders began to pay attention. Land was abundant and relatively cheap. You could buy an old homestead at Granite Bay for $1,000 per 0.4 hectare (1 acre), or get two 0.2-hectare (half-acre) lots in Drew Harbour with views of Rebecca Spit and the mainland mountains for $5,000.

It wasn't just speculators who bought land on the island. Janet Jones, an American ceramic artist, bought Walter and Mary Joyce's old farm at Francisco Point and opened it as an artists' commune. In Granite

Dennis and Ellen Humes, seen here, started an "experimental college" in Granite Bay to teach young people log building, gardening and handcrafts.
PHOTO COURTESY *COURIER-ISLANDER* NEWS-PAPER, MCR

Bay Dennis and Ellen Humes bought the old Henry and Agnes Twidle property to open a "unique experimental college"—a plastic and canvas campus, as the island's first newspaper, *Discovery Passage*, described it in July 1973. The program, loosely affiliated with the University of Washington, attracted people from as far away as Maine and Hawaii to learn crafts like weaving, spinning, stonework, organic gardening and astrology. On the southern end of the island, anyone was welcome to move into a stump or an old Volkswagen van at Home Free on Cape Mudge Road, where there were ample supplies of pot and used car parts.

Some of these folks had lofty ideals but minimal experience in rural seacoast life. They had to learn it all from scratch, just as the first wave of non-Native settlers did. Many gave up and left, but others stayed to make the island their permanent home. Among them were artists and artisans, and a few started businesses. The disused church in Quathiaski Cove became a craft shop and the restaurant of the old Heriot Bay Inn (formerly the Heriot Bay Hotel) was transformed into the Inn Between, where Jim Moats made hamburgers served on whole-wheat buns that bulged with sprouts. The Inn Between became a hangout for women in flowing robes and young men with hair that cascaded down their shoulders. At the hotel's bar, with a convivial table that ran its length, joints circulated freely after the last ferry run of the night ensured the Campbell River–based police were gone. Morgan, the father of Heriot Bay Inn co-owner Dorothy Hayward, lived in a room upstairs. At midnight he would stamp through the bar with the broken pool cue he used for a cane. "Time to go!" he'd bellow.

By the 1970s the long-time residents had begun to wonder what hit them. The "hippie invasion" felt like a hostile takeover by a foreign race. But the young people had a simple goal for a new kind of life that was "better and different from all that terrible scramble out there," as writer Alan Fry put it. He was part of a diverse mix of people who came from across Canada and the US, including young men who resisted the draft for the Vietnam War.

The newcomers started a variety of community projects in 1972, funded by youth employment grants. These included a recycling centre, fish habitat enhancement and *Discovery Passage*, a bimonthly newspaper that offered back-to-the-land lifestyle tips, horoscopes and local news.

Discovery Passage editor Lorne Mallin wrote in defence of criticism lobbed at him and other youths who appeared to be taking over the island. "So what are a bunch of newcomers and Americans doing publishing a community newspaper on Quadra Island? Good question. The answer, in part, is that all of us believe that we belong here."

Conflicting views over land development issues were a regular topic in the newspaper. As Mallin noted, rapid growth on the island and subdivisions like the one at Wa-Wa-Kie Beach called for a community plan

Larry Rousseau, right, was hired on a youth grant to manage a recycling project based in Heriot Bay. He's seen here with his friend David VanDerEst in July 1972.
PHOTO COURTESY *COURIER-ISLANDER* NEWSPAPER, MCR

and bylaws. Some islands to the south sprinkled with small-lot subdivisions had become vacation retreats.

A new level of government, the Comox-Strathcona Regional District, provided basic services for Quadra in the 1970s. The island's elected representative was World War II veteran Sam Hooley, who operated through an advisory planning commission. He also had to respond to the Quadra Island Ratepayers' Association, led by Don Huntley, a passionate man with a plan for a resort and a subdivision in Gowlland Harbour. Don's complex, on land he and his wife Joy (Walker) Huntley owned on a corner of her parents' Homewood Farm, was called Villa don Quadra. They started with Captain's Cove Resort (now Seascape Marina), a cluster of "Gothic arch" cedar buildings terraced up a bluff. Don wanted to add two ten-unit condominiums, a lodge and a subdivision of 0.2- and 0.4-hectare (1/2- and 1-acre) lots on the land above the bluffs.[1] And there were others with high density schemes in mind. Calgary developer Bill Fudikuf had a plan for an apartment complex at the corner of Green and New Ferry Roads.[2]

With these housing and subdivision plans under discussion an action committee was formed to devise a set of bylaws for the island. A four-hectare (ten-acre) minimum lot freeze[3] was put in place in 1971[4] to maintain the status quo as the committee set to work. Their meetings were rife with debate. "Four members . . . walked out of Tuesday's committee meeting," reported the *Discovery Passage*, "after heated exchanges broke out between Don Huntley and Alan Fry over the subdivision control bylaw."

In spite of ongoing tension, by mid-May 1973 the action committee had a draft proposal ready for consideration. It included provisions to encourage private tree farms, protect wilderness parkland (especially around wetlands), restrict small lots to high density areas like Quathiaski Cove and Heriot Bay, protect the rural atmosphere and aesthetic qualities, define planned growth and bar mobile home parks.[5] Regional District planners tried to assist in the process of debate and implementation but their involvement was deemed an intrusion by the feisty islanders. "Regional District Rejected by Quadra Island Residents," ran a headline that followed a ratepayers' association meeting. The Social Credit provincial government also weighed in. They were involved in

Remains of the cannery complex in Quathiaski Cove in 1968. The Anderson's large home and store are on the left at the former steamship dock, and there are two boat ways on the former cannery site. To the right are net lofts brought in from another cannery and set up on the spot where the "China House" once stood on its pilings. PHOTO COURTESY *COURIER-UPPER ISLANDER* NEWSPAPER, MCR 11765

community plans for the Gulf Islands and assumed what was good for the southern islands was good for Quadra too.

"The recurring theme I hear on Quadra," said Alan Fry at a large public meeting, "is—'why do they not leave us alone?'" But, he hastened to add, there was no turning back. "The island needs planned development," said Fry. "What happens here is not for us alone, but for those who come after us." He urged islanders to take time for reflection and come up with a global vision for how the island should be developed—and then launch into the specifics of bylaw development. The controversial process continued for nearly a decade of neighbourhood meetings and questionnaires and ultimately resulted in an adopted plan that confirmed a four-hectare (ten-acre) freeze for much of the island.

Some of the opposition Regional District representatives experienced on Quadra was the result of their push to have the building code introduced in 1973. If there was one thing the majority of islanders agreed upon it was their opposition to the building code. (With no code on the island they were able to build their homes to their own particular taste and style, without the interference of bureaucratic rules or structural inspections.)

The island's population was about one thousand people in the 1970s. The two principal roads were called the Back Road (Heriot Bay Road) and the Main Road (West Road). A local man known as "The Old Prospector" could often be found in one or another of the roadside ditches sleeping off a hangover. He was not to be disturbed, even when his thin frame was covered in a dusting of snow. He claimed to be a retired RCMP officer and wielded a handgun to prove his point.

Addresses were unheard of and most people lived down anonymous-looking driveways that led into the forest. Details on how to reach a new friend's home required a convoluted description, as was the case for the *Discovery Passage* office. The paper's masthead directed people to drop by the office. "It's an old farm house on Hyacinthe Bay Road, about a mile past the pavement."

The animosity between "the hippies" and "the rednecks" hit a boiling point in the early 1970s. "Hippie is merely a word," said Phil Thompson, a lifelong fisherman and logger who was more liberal-minded than some, "a name people use when they are mad at someone." Phil started to grow his hair in the early 1970s and said he'd cut it when his wife stopped swearing. With every passing year his hair grew longer, until he needed a headband to hold back his white locks.

Everyone followed the progress of Phil Thompson's hair. There were few secrets in such a small community. And everyone knew each other's vehicles, so as tension mounted between newcomers and rednecks the cars of the former became targets. If one of the island's long-haired youths ran out of gas or had a breakdown on the roadside they were likely to find their windshield smashed by morning. Sixteen-year-old Kim Mann, whose father taught at the island's school, fell somewhere between these two factions. But when she ran out of gas one night and was forced to park her red Volvo, a recent gift from her parents, she found it a battered hulk the next morning. Others had rocks thrown at them, as was the case with the island's first openly gay couple, who were forced to leave.

Al McLaughlin crossed the line when he took up residence as a squatter on the old Haskins property at the Smith Road and Heriot Bay Road junction, a place some islanders used as a rifle range. In an attempt to scare him off, young men on motorcycles fired shots over McLaughlin's head as they drove past him on the roadside. One day in 1975 he returned to his makeshift home with a flutist and a photographer who also lived on the Haskins property and they found one of their flimsy shacks on fire.[6] They put it out but the next morning the fire flared up in a log. McLaughlin and his friends were just about to douse the log when a crowd of about thirty people, including a woman with a baby, emerged into the clearing with rakes and shovels in hand. McLaughlin's two friends ran off but Al stood his ground. Comox-Strathcona Regional Director Sam Hooley and his friends put the fire out and gave McLaughlin thirty minutes to remove his things from his shack before they pushed it over.

When Al returned to the meadow a few days later he found three nooses hung in a tree, which got the attention of *Courier* editor Ron Percival. From there the story hit national news. "What the hell are you up to?" Sam Hooley's sister quipped when she called him from Winnipeg. She heard the news on television and it sounded like Sam was part of a lynch mob. As Hooley explained years later, it was the fire in the log near the squatter's shack that had them concerned. They were worried the fire would get out of control and thought the squatters were living in an irresponsible manner. The nooses, he admitted, were over the top—the work of some of the "young bucks" who got carried away. "You might expect this kind of thing down in Alabama or Mississippi," a young man with a mass of curls told a *Vancouver Sun* reporter.

In the maelstrom of debate and public outcry that followed, some speculated the fires at the Haskins property were arson, set by people who wanted it designated as an official rifle range.

A *Vancouver Sun* reporter interviewed islanders to get at the root of the divisions in the community. Richard Sumner told the journalist he was fed up with hitchhikers asking for rides on the ferry. Sam Hooley said the island's young people had started to take drugs, thanks to the new residents. "A common complaint," said the *Sun* reporter, "is that

Heriot Bay Store in about 1964. "Doogie" and Pauline Dowler bought the Heriot Bay Store at the foot of Antler Road in 1953 and moved their young family into the suite upstairs. The storekeeper picked out the customer's purchases from behind the counter and most things were bought on credit, to be paid for at the end of the fishing season. A big cheese cutter dating back to the early 1900s dominated one end of the counter. PHOTO COURTESY SUSAN (ENNS) DOWLER

transients have 'taken over' the Heriot Bay Inn pub, a popular drinking spot among island residents until a few years ago. The Heriot Bay 'take-over' is symbolic of the changes on Quadra Island."

Several decades later Ted Mathers, a new resident in the 1970s, recalled the incident at the Haskins property and said the story was blown out of proportion, but the dramatic media coverage that likened Hooley and the others to vigilantes made them rethink their actions. "Suddenly all the rednecks were really nice to me, going out of their way to show they weren't like they were portrayed on television," said Mathers.

There were other, less controversial developments on the island during these years. The Lucky Jim mine attracted attention again in 1972 when Captain Bill Hall, born in Gowlland Harbour in 1904, found the old workings. Like his father, Bill Hall had the prospecting bug. He had just revived a copper mine at the head of Gowlland Harbour, in his father's old workings, when he made a claim at Lucky Jim mine. "I saw the gold sticking right out of the rock," Hall told a *Courier* reporter.

Hall had the ore assayed and the results were so good Prince Stewart Mines optioned his claim and began tests. The company reported the yield was a "phenomenal" twenty-seven ounces of gold per ton, along with high yields of copper and silver. But further tests demonstrated the expense of drilling in the mine's water-filled shafts would outweigh the gold's value so the mine was dropped—until a similar scenario (with the same ending) unfolded again when gold prices skyrocketed in 1984.

The opening of the Kwakiutl Museum (now the Nuyumbalees Cultural Centre) at Cape Mudge Village on June 29, 1979, was another good-news story. The museum was built to house potlatch regalia seized by the federal government in 1922 and returned to this and a sister museum in Alert Bay. The return of what artifacts remained unsold to museums and collectors was the result of decades of lobbying by Native leaders. "One of the primary functions of the museum," stated the opening day program, "is to form a link between the past, the present and the future." The building was constructed in the form of a sea snail, to denote the "vital importance of the sea to the Kwakiutl people." The museum was an instant success, drawing tourists from around the globe.

A few years later the band opened Tsa-Kwa-Luten Lodge, with accommodation and a restaurant, on the bluffs at Cape Mudge next to the spot where Captain Vancouver visited in 1792.

The number of children at Cape Mudge rose through the 1970s, as was the case on Quadra as a whole. The school was expanded to meet this rapid growth and a few years later a committee was formed to build a community centre for dances, classes, meetings and indoor sports. The old Valdes Island Social Hall next to Blenkin Park was long gone by this time, buckled by a heavy snowfall in the early 1970s. The recreation society, under president Carol Harling-Bleeks, started construction at Blenkin Park while they were still in the midst of fundraising. It was a familiar process for many islanders, who lived in their unfinished houses and worked on them as time and money allowed.

As was the case with the opening of the island's first hall, the new centre was launched with a dance on Valentine's Day in 1985, though one wall still gaped open and the floor was dusty concrete. The facility was the product of hundreds of hours of donated labour and expertise—accomplished in spite of a deep recession. Danny Niedziejko made a handsome set of exterior doors for the building and Gretchen Peters led a volunteer team who peeled the massive beams in the central structure.

The daily operation of the centre was managed by a volunteer board for the first few years, until Sandy Spearing was hired as co-ordinator. She continued the original board's approach of user-driven management, which kept staff costs at a minimum and fostered pride and ownership in the centre. Sandy encouraged groups like the cultural committee, who brought performers to the island, and Friday Flicks, the bimonthly film club, to manage their own programs. "We give them the keys and expect them to look after the place," said Sandy in an interview for the facility's twentieth anniversary in 2005. The centre, she added, has been a marvel to recreation groups elsewhere, for its low vandalism rate and busy schedule.

A major addition to the community centre was opened in 2001, following years of work by volunteer committees led by Discovery Islands realtor David Smith and gardener Val Barr. Committee member Hilary Stewart, a writer who retired to the island, was joined by long-time

In 1978 Jeanette Taylor of the Campbell River Museum, with assistance from Madge
Nutting and others, organized a reunion for Quadra Islanders at the Heriot Bay
Inn. Katie (Walker) Clarke, top right, poses with her Heriot Bay School class of 1914.
Below Katie is Tommy Hall, far right, beside Chester Haas. Across from him may be
Bill Hall. Bill Law is on the far left and above him is Bob Hall. James Law is on the
top left, next to Linnea (Johnson) Leverett. MCR

regional director Jim Abram in cutting the ribbon to open the addition.
The three new meeting rooms and renovated stage and kitchen went
into instant use. "There's at least one activity in the centre every night in
peak season," said Sandy Spearing. "And some nights there's something
going on in all four rental spaces."

Where it was people with young families who built the community centre in the 1980s, many of those involved in its expansion
were middle-aged or older, a sign of the island's ageing population.
New residents came to the island during these years, attracted by an
engaged rural lifestyle, but they tended to be retired. There were a few
noteworthy exceptions, like John Waibel and Christine Portmann, who
started Spirit of the West Adventures, offering kayak trips. (The company later branched out into Quadra Kayaks, owned by Jane West and
Tracy Sinclair.) Writer Philip Stone bought the *Discovery Islander,* a

commercial venture that succeeded the *Discovery Passage*, and pharmacist Colleen Hogg opened a drugstore with her husband Shane in a row of shops and offices adjacent to the Quathiaski Cove shopping centre and credit union.

Quathiaski Cove and Heriot Bay both had shopping malls by the 1990s. Bill and Freda O'Connor's shopping plaza in the Cove changed hands when all but the grocery store was purchased by a consortium of islanders. Among the partners were some who came to the island with the back-to-the-land movement in the 1970s. And in the Cove itself, the last few buildings from the cannery were pulled down in a massive cleanup as the foreshore, contaminated by a century of industrial activity, was dug up and filtered. Blood Alley, the trail behind the net lofts, was blocked by a chain-link fence and a no-trespassing sign barred access as the property was left to settle in anticipation of a new phase of development.

There were only a few commercial fishing boats tied up at the

The steering committee for the construction of the Quadra Island Community Centre. Seen here with their golden keys when the centre opened in June 1985 are Rod Clark, Mich Hirano, Carol Harling-Bleeks, the late John Fell and Jim Mathias. Missing from this photo is Barry Hodgson, who also served on the committee.
PHOTO COURTESY SAM FELL

Quadra Island Regional Director Jim Abram, Hilary Stewart, MLA Glenn Robertson and Val Barr at the sod turning for the expansion of the Quadra Island Community Centre, which was completed in 2001. PHOTO COURTESY QUADRA ISLAND RECREATION SOCIETY

government dock by the start of the twenty-first century. Les Pidcock, who lives with his wife and family on the Cape Mudge Reserve, participated in talks about ways to remedy the loss of fish stocks—but the halcyon days of big money being made in herring and salmon fishing were gone. W.E. Anderson of Quathiaski Cannery foresaw this end nearly a century earlier, when he sent his seine crews to clean logging debris from the salmon streams in fall and joined a vocal few in a plea for tighter regulation of fish habitat and stocks. Many people dependent upon the fishing industry had to find other work, leaving behind an independent profession passed to them through generations, as in the case of the We Wai Kai people. And the problem was not confined just to a loss of income. Commercial fishing carried on cultural traditions and brought a sense of self-worth to those working in a skilled industry filled with risk and occasional windfall rewards. Yet a few found related work. Billy Assu's grandson "Bear" Scow became a guide for sport fishing groups and cultural tours and encouraged young people to find independent work, not government-sponsored jobs. Rick Assu, another of the old chief's many grandchildren, skippers his father's seiner to transport fish-farm product.

The We Wai Kai Band, once considered a "vanishing race," reached a population of nine hundred people in 2009, including five hundred who lived off-reserve. Some members of the younger generation have built houses on the Quinsam River in Campbell River, where there were eighty residences and a subdivision of forty-two new sites under way in 2009.

Ralph Dick, who traces his lineage to both We-Kai and Sewis on his paternal side and Wamish on his maternal side, was in his twenty-fourth year as elected chief of the We Wai Kai Band in 2009. He took pride in his band's many accomplishments. There was no social housing on their reserves, or the associated debt. "Everyone builds their own houses," said Dick in an interview that year. Tsa-Kwa-Luten, their award-winning resort on the bluffs at Cape Mudge, had a high occupancy rate and the band was developing plans for shellfish farms.

Fish farms and mariculture in general have played a role in the evolving economy of Quadra Island. Walcan Seafoods, a fish and shellfish processor, was the island's largest employer by 2009, with 150 people at work year-round and a six-million-dollar payroll. Bill Pirie started the cannery in 1974, processing herring and later salmon for sport fishermen at a plant near April Point Resort. Pirie was joined by partner Jim Lornie and in 1979 they moved their cannery to a large new facility at the end of Morte Lake Road on northwestern Quadra Island. At the company's peak in the mid-1980s they processed 180,000 cans of fish for an international clientele.

Walcan Seafoods has had to be adaptable in the volatile fishing industry. The company converted to "retort pouches" and was the first in Canada to register a thermal process for smoked salmon sold in the light plastic packaging. They stopped canning sport-caught fish in 1991, when production dropped, and switched to processing farmed fish, herring, prawns, spawn-on kelp and wild salmon. A primary market for their products became Japan, where Walcan maintained an office.

Bill Pirie's company took flack from some quarters for its involvement in the farmed-fish industry, but he told a Sustainable Aquaculture

Commission in 2006 he has confidence in the tight regulations of the Federal Fisheries Act. "I think the current industry is sustainable, and I think it's safe."

The island's longest-standing business came under threat in 2006 when Heriot Bay Inn owner Lorraine Wright overextended herself with a massive makeover of the old landmark and decided to sell. The inn's staff, and islanders in general, watched with dismay as off-island investors toured the site and talked about tearing down the hotel. That's when bookkeeper Lois Taylor and carpenter Paul Mortimer, two of the lead partners in the Quathiaski Cove Shopping Plaza, stepped forward to form a co-op to buy the hotel. They were joined by ten others. Many of them, like Vic Nacci, Blake Dixie, Juanita Maclean, Neil Maffin and Noelle Maffin, were employees at the hotel. Others had different connections to the place, like musician Mo Davenport, a regular entertainer at the hotel's bar. Nick Lawrence, Christi Edwards and Yuri Delisle felt a strong connection to the hotel. And Tina (Hayward) Oswald's involvement continued a family tradition that dated back to the days when her parents owned the inn in the 1970s. Lorraine Wright also remained as a partner. With so much investment of island funds and talent, the Heriot Bay Inn snapped with revitalized energy by 2009—in spite of a global recession.

It was difficult for young people to buy into the island's high-priced real estate market by the new century, with land prices driven up by urban wealth and out-of-province investors in search of a holiday retreat or retirement home. Impassioned debate ensued when an idea was floated to adjust the community plan to make smaller lots available. There were those who wanted to cash in on the booming real estate market. Others hoped smaller lots would decrease land values and bring more young families to the island—but their detractors claimed land values would remain high no matter how many lots were made available. The demand was too high to fill. While islanders took different sides on this debate, most agreed the island's rural character was precious. They were also unified, once again, in their opposition to the Regional District's suggestion to adopt the BC Building Code.

In classic, outspoken islander fashion a spate of neighbourhood study sessions culminated in a series of fractious public meetings in 2007. And as in the bylaw debates of the 1970s, Regional District staff were criticized by impassioned residents who wanted their say about the future of their community. In the end a fragile compromise was struck, with higher-density development to be confined to the two old rivals, Quathiaski Cove and Heriot Bay.

While you could tell a person was from Heriot Bay or the Cove in the 1950s simply by the way they held their cigarette, there were only whispered differences by the new millennia. People from around the island pitched in to develop a community garden on Fay and Milton Wong's farm in Heriot Bay, just in time for a bumper crop in the hot summer of 2009. The Cove has the farmer's market, credit union and drug store and Heriot Bay is the social hub, with the Legion, Heriot Bay Inn and Rebecca Spit Park.

Contentious issues can still rock this island of staunch individualists. The mention of small lot subdivisions, fish farms, the eradication of wolves, or raising funds for feral cats is sure to spark a debate. But there are also shared values among the island's 3,500 residents. They're proud to live in a small community where people care about each other and they cherish their traditions, whether it's cheering on the maypole dancers or raising a pint at the Heriot Bay Inn pub. Above all else, they're in love with the wild landscape of their island home. Their options are limitless, from a climb up China Mountain to survey their domain, or to gaze far to sea from the bluffs at Cape Mudge, where the First Nations people welcomed Captain Vancouver over two centuries ago.

Notes

Chapter One: A Man's World

1. It's not known what disease took George Vancouver's life. He died at the age of forty, a few years after his return to Britain following his Pacific Northwest Coast expedition. Sir James Watt, a former surgeon with the British navy, analyzed Vancouver's journals for clues to his illness and believes Vancouver contracted malaria on a previous voyage, which damaged his thyroid and adrenal glands. Some of the symptoms match Addison's disease, which could have been brought on by his compromised condition. See "The Voyage of Captain George Vancouver 1791–95: The Interplay of Physical and Psychological Pressures," *Canadian Bulletin of Medical History* 4, no. 1 (1987), pp. 44–45.

2. Archibald Menzies, *Menzies' Journal of Vancouver's Voyage, April to October, 1792, edited and with Botanical and Ethnological Notes by C.F. Newcombe, M.D.* (Victoria: King's Printer, 1923).

3. Report from Heritage Conservation Branch, Borden No. EaSh 3, by Mark Skinner, courtesy of Joy Inglis.

4. Donald H. Mitchell, "Excavations at two trench embankments in the Gulf of Georgia region," University of Victoria, 1968. Mitchell dates the last occupation of the site to between 1600 and 1760.

5. An archaeological site at Bear Cove, near Port Hardy, has been dated at eight thousand years. According to Grant Keddie, an archaeologist with the Royal British Columbia Museum, a 2008 dig on the Fraser River, near Pitt River, was dated at ten thousand years (personal communication, 2009).

6. In Reginald Pidcock's report to the Department of Indian Affairs on October 11, 1894, he said a logging company had dammed Village

Bay Creek, which stopped the fish from spawning and hampered the Native people "who sometimes manufacture canoes on the lake."

7. Homer Barnett, *The Coast Salish of British Columbia* (Eugene, OR: University of Oregon, 1955), p. 167.

8. Homer Barnett, *The Coast Salish of British Columbia* (Eugene, OR: University of Oregon, 1955).

9. Barnett, in *The Coast Salish of British Columbia*, goes on to say this name resembles that of a sea monster of great power and wealth in the Kwakwaka'wakw tradition (p. 26). The similarity, suggests Barnett, is evidence of one of a number of ways the Island Comox and Laich-Kwil-Tach traditions were entwined. Barnett also ascribes a different version of the "komakwe" story to the Island Comox (p. 148). "The Comox conceived the sea dweller, komakwe, to be the custodian of wealth . . . The Comox got their name from this being, it is said."

10. Mary Clifton provided the name of George Mitchell's mother in a taped interview with Jean Barman in 1993. A transcript is held in the Courtenay and District Museum.

11. Cole Harris, *The Resettlement of British Columbia: Essays on Colonialism and Geographic Change* (Vancouver: UBC Press, 1997).

12. Archibald Menzies, *Menzies' Journal of Vancouver's Voyage, April to October, 1792, edited and with Botanical and Ethnological Notes by C.F. Newcombe, M.D.*, p. 35. The British traded with a group near Carr Inlet and "two of them were much pitted with the small pox & each destitute of a right eye."

Chapter Two: The Laich-Kwil-Tach

1. James R. Gibson, *Otter Skins, Boston Ships and China Goods: The Maritime Fur Trade of the Northwest Coast, 1785–1841.* (Montreal: McGill-Queen's University Press, 1992).

2. Cole Harris, *The Resettlement of British Columbia* (Vancouver: UBC Press, 1997), p. 60, and Marie Mauzé, *Les fils de Wakai, Une histoire des Indiens Lekwiltoq* (Paris: Editions Recherche sur les Civilisations, 1992).

3. Edward Curtis, *The Kwakiutl*, vol. 10 of *The North American Indian, being a series of volumes picturing and describing the Indians of the*

United States and Alaska. Published 1907–1930 by Edward S. Curtis. Edited by Frederick Webb Hodge. Foreword by Theodore Roosevelt. Field Research conducted under the patronage of J. Pierpont Morgan, p. 114.

4. Marie Mauzé, *Les fils de Wakai, Une histoire des Indiens Lekwiltoq* (Paris: Editions Recherche sur les Civilisations, 1992).

5. Morag Maclachlan, ed., *The Fort Langley Journals, 1827–30* (Vancouver: UBC Press, 1998), pp. 103–111.

6. Marie Mauzé, *Les fils de Wakai, Une histoire des Indiens Lekwiltoq* (Paris: Editions Recherche sur les Civilisations, 1992), p. 68.

7. *Victoria Colonist*, May 24, 1895.

8. Jack McQuarrie, "Few Indians Can Build Dugout Canoe," *Victoria Colonist*, November 3, 1968.

9. See Robert Galois, *Kwakwaka'wakw Settlements, 1775–1920: A Geographical Analysis and Gazetteer* (Vancouver: UBC Press, 1994), p. 256. John McLoughlin was supplying information for a report by James Douglas.

10. As befits people of the Nimpkish River, We-Kai is said to have had a right to fish for oolichan on the Kingcome River.

11. The fact that it was a copper being recovered suggests this oral account dates from after contact with Europeans, in the 1770s, when Native people acquired large sheets of copper.

12. Billy Assu to Philip Drucker, as recorded in Drucker's field notes. See Marie Mauzé, *Les fils de Wakai, Une histoire des Indiens Lekwiltoq* (Paris: Editions Recherche sur les Civilisations, 1992), p. 29.

13. Harry Assu with Joy Inglis, *Assu of Cape Mudge: Recollections of a Coastal Indian Chief* (Vancouver: UBC Press, 1989), p. 10.

14. In Wilson Duff's notes made in conversation with Mungo Martin he indicates he wasn't sure if Mungo meant it was We-Kai's father-in-law's village that he attacked.

15. Mungo Martin, n̓əmǧis elder, to Wilson Duff. See BC Archives, GR 2809, Laich-Kwil-Tach/Comox files.

16. Wilson Duff, BC Archives, GR 2809, Laich-Kwil-Tach/Comox files.

17. "Chief Tells Story Behind Murals In Indian Hall," *Campbell River Courier*, February 22, 1961.

18. Harry Assu with Joy Inglis, *Assu of Cape Mudge*, pp. 5–6. Anthropologist Marie Mauzé suggests the Laich-Kwil-Tach people carried the legend of the flood with them as they moved southward, reshaping it to different locations.

19. James Martin Smith corresponded with anthropologist Wilson Duff, whose papers are in the BC Archives, GR 2809, Laich-Kwil-Tach/ Comox files. Both Harry Assu's and James Smith's accounts agree the canoes were tied to a massive rock on a mountain behind the village. Smith says the mountain was called hay'-waek-ta-ba-too and that it grew, as was the case in a flood myth attached to Estero Peak near the mouth of Bute Inlet. Anthropologist Joy Inglis recorded the name of the mountain at Tekya as Tlakustan. Harry Assu also provided details that support the veracity of these legends. Assu said the bowl-like basin at the top of the mountain has salt water in it. Smith said his father climbed the mountain and found the marble anchor rock with its distinctive quartz veins. "He said it would take ten men to move it," wrote Smith.

20. Robert Galois, *Kwakwaka'wakw Settlements, 1775–1920: A Geographical Analysis and Gazetteer* (Vancouver: UBC Press, 1994), pp. 244 and 256.

21. HBC Chief Factor James Douglas, in his 1843 journal (BC Archives, A/B/40/D75.4A), said there were six Laich-Kwil-Tach groups with a total of 1,060 men. This number multiplied by four gives a total population estimate of just over four thousand. Anthropologist Wilson Duff tabulated approximate census figures taken by John Work of the HBC from 1836 to 1841 (BC Archives, GR 2809, Laich-Kwil-Tach/ Comox files) and arrived at a population estimate of 10,060 people among the Laich-Kwil-Tach, comprising six distinct groups.

22. Edward Curtis, *The Kwakiutl*, vol. 10 of *The North American Indian*, p. 308.

23. The figure on the top of this totem was identified by the *Campbell River Courier* as an eagle but it appears to be Kolus, younger brother to Thunderbird.

24. When William Hills visited Cape Mudge in 1853, aboard the

Virago, he gave a similar description of the location of the We Wai Kai village. He said there were a few huts and a "war village" belonging to the "Ucultah tribe, which is scattered along many miles of this part of the Island." See Robert Galois, *Kwakwaka'wakw Settlements, 1775–1920: A Geographical Analysis and Gazetteer* (Vancouver: UBC Press, 1994), p. 269.

25. Billy Assu of Cape Mudge got a similar sounding name, Nugedzi, from his uncle Wamish, the great war chief. A lake and a hiking trail on the north end of Quadra Island have been given this name in Billy Assu's honour.

26. Transcript of James Douglas's diary, BC Archives, A/B/40/ D75.4A, pp. 9–10.

27. The approximate year of birth for both men was estimated as 1829, in the 1881 Dominion Census. In a later census Wamish's birth was noted as being some years later, but on his headstone in Cape Mudge Village it is recorded as 1831.

28. Interview with elected We Wai Kai chief Ralph Dick, February 2009.

29. Herbert C. Taylor Jr. and Wilson Duff, "A Post-Contact Southward Movement of the Kwakiutl," *Research Studies* vol. 24, (State College of Washington, 1956), p. 63. It's possible their move happened in overlapping stages that started much earlier by intermixing with the Island Comox. The Hudson's Bay Company's Fort Langley journal of 1829 said the Laich-Kwil-Tach lived "on both Sides of the Channel, not far beyond Marshall Point on north Texada Island, near Powell River."

30. Marie Mauzé, *Les fils de Wakai, Une histoire des Indiens Lekwiltoq* (Paris: Editions Recherche sur les Civilisations, 1992).

31. Information provided by anthropologist Joy Inglis to the author, April 2009.

32. Seymour Narrows was called Yuculta Rapids, a variant spelling for Laich-Kwil-Tach, until 1846, when that name was switched to the equally tricky set of rapids that separates the mainland from Maurelle Island. See Captain John T. Walbran's *British Columbia Coast Names: Their Origin and History* (Vancouver: Douglas & McIntyre, 1971), p. 455.

33. *Comox Valley Weekly News*, December 28, 1892.

34. Edward Curtis, in *The North American Indian*, vol. 10, *The Kwakiutl*, pp. 110–111, says the final defeat of the Island Comox took place in about 1850, after a major battle with another Salish group near Duncan. Salish accounts of what may be the same battle, at Maple Bay, suggest it took place around 1840. See Chris Arnett, *The Terror of the Coast: Land Alienation and Colonial War on Vancouver Island and the Gulf Islands, 1849–1863* (Burnaby, BC: Talonbooks, 1999).

35. This name was applied to Gowlland Harbour as a whole and sounds similar to a family name claimed by Wamish, the Laich-Kwil-Tach chief, who had a seasonal site in Gowlland Harbour. In *Kwakwaka'wakw Settlements*, p. 270, Robert Galois says the fortified site was called hemxwema?as. The site may have been on Steep Island, which is a registered archaeological site at the north entrance to the harbour.

36. Other sub-tribes of the Island Comox must have escaped this attack, as the group who took over the village on the Courtenay River, which belonged to Puntledge people (who were depopulated by war with the Nuu-Chah-Nulth of the west coast of Vancouver Island) had a population of about seventy-three people in 1864. See a quote from Robert Brown's exploration in D.E. Isenor et al., *Land of Plenty: A History of the Comox District* (Campbell River, BC: Ptarmigan Press, 1987), p. 27.

37. The Island Comox who lived at the Qualicum River were depopulated by disease and war with the Nuu-Chah-Nulth people. In 1864, in a census compiled by Robert Brown, there were only three Qualicum people left.

38. Edward Curtis, in *The North American Indian*, vol. 10, *The Kwakiutl*, pp.110–111, linked this defeat at Maple Bay with the final takeover of Discovery Passage. The surviving warriors went to the Island Comox village on the Campbell River to seek refuge with Hekwutun, a man of mixed Laich-Kwil-Tach and Island Comox descent, but some were tricked and beheaded by an Island Comox man. Hekwutun then sent for the Laich-Kwil-Tach at Tekya, which precipitated the attack on the Island Comox, who fled to their fortified retreat at ǧʷiǧʷakulis.

39. The name is spelled "Claylick" in a naval report on this same incident. He may have been the same man listed in the 1879 census as

the head chief for the We Wai Kai, spelled "Tlay-leet-ul." Nothing further seems to be known about this chief.

40. The *Victoria Colonist* newspaper of December 17, 1898 reviewed a report on the First Nations and said the Cape Mudge people "emigrated to Nanaimo in large numbers to work in the mines, and lived there, not on a reservation, but as squatters on the Newcastle townsite." The Cape Mudge people's camp was also frequently mentioned in the *Nanaimo Free Press*.

41. Bill Merilees, *Newcastle Island: A Place of Discovery* (Surrey, BC: Heritage House, 1998), pp. 32–34.

42. *Nanaimo Free Press*, October 24, 1889, and July 15, 1890.

43. This population figure was noted by I.W. Powell of the Department of Indian Affairs, and cited in the papers of Wilson Duff, BC Archives, GR 2809, Laich-Kwil-Tach/Comox files.

Chapter Three: A New Wave of Settlement

1. Robert Brown, *Robert Brown and the Vancouver Island Exploring Expedition*, ed. John Hayman (Vancouver: UBC Press, 1989), p. 124.

2. The islands were initially called Langevin (for Sonora), Tache (Maurelle) and Valdes but the names didn't stick. An additional problem was the existence of another Valdes Island to the south, off Nanaimo.

3. Another interpretation of the name is that it means chamber pot, for a bowl-like dip in the rocks on the south shore.

4. Information provided by anthropologist Joy Inglis.

5. The name Nugedzi Lake was assigned in honour of the late Billy Assu in the 1980s. The translation, "big mountain," refers to the immense social stature of the holder of this name.

6. Wamish's headstone at the Cape Mudge cemetery also says: "Sacred to the Memory of Wawmish, Qua-quock-Gilles, Chief of the Wi-wai-ai-kai Tribe, Died January 5, 1903, aged 72 years." See *Quadra Island Cemetery Listings: Cape Mudge, Quadra Island* (Campbell River: Campbell River Genealogy Club, 2000), p. 15.

7. There are many spellings of the name Chickite in written records. In the 1879 census the name was spelled "Tsah-kayt" (a married man with no children). It was "Tsuk-hait" in the 1881 census (born in 1846,

with a wife Lass-toal-sel-lass, born in 1855), and "Tsuk-e-ti" in the 1901 census (born in 1851, with a wife named Mum-yi-u-kwa, born in 1871, and a son E-wha-kas, born in 1894). Current We Wai Kai elder "Ole" Chickite says his ancestor Jim Chickite was descended from Sewis and was given this name and position when a We Wai Kai man named "Tsuk-hait" (also called Wilson) died without a male heir.

8. W.W. Walkem, *Stories of Early British Columbia* (Vancouver: News-Advertiser, 1914), pp. 95–104.

9. W.W. Walkem, *Stories of Early British Columbia* (Vancouver: News-Advertiser, 1914).

10. On September 19, 1995, the Federal Court of Canada dismissed the claims of the We Wai Kai and the We Wai Kum, who claimed the government made errors and misrepresentations in their allocation of land on the Campbell River and that both bands should be compensated.

11. There is some confusion about who Sewis's birth children were. The current We Wai Kai Dick family claim descent from Sewis. This is supported by Harry Assu, in his book *Assu of Cape Mudge*, and Eleanor (Dick) Clifton, in an interview with Jean Barman (see Courtenay & District Museum), who said Sewis's sons later took the names Jim Chickite and John Dick Sr. A Department of Indian Affairs letter dated March 1, 1913, also says the two were related and that Major Dick (John Dick Sr.'s son) inherited Chief Jim Chickite's potlatch rank when he died in a boating accident in December 1912. Ole Chickite of the We Wai Kai, however, claims John Dick Sr. and Jim Chickite were not brothers.

12. George Dawson's diary, cited in Robert Galois's *Kwakwaka'wakw Settlements*, p. 275, estimates sixteen houses at Cape Mudge in 1878.

13. The names used here are those that appear in later census records. In the 1881 census Wamish had two children in his household, a daughter named Ya-Kowek and son O-Kwe-La. Both were young adults. His youngest, Tom, was born at Cape Mudge in about 1853, according to vital statistics.

14. Anthropologist Joy Inglis says this tradition may have been carried to the Quadra Island area by the We Wai Kai from when they lived near the Nimpkish River. It would have arrived there from the West Coast, where people had a ceremony with similar elements.

15. As recalled by James Henderson, a descendant of shipwreck survivor Kenneth Henderson. For more details on the wreck of the *Grappler*, see Jeanette Taylor, *River City: A History of Campbell River and the Discovery Islands* (Madeira Park, BC: Harbour Publishing, 1999), pp. 36–37.

16. *Victoria Colonist*, June 8, 1884.

17. Rebecca Spit would not have been prime logging land. Sayward may have wanted it for a campsite or to secure booming rights in the bay next to the reserve. He may have also bought it, as later owner James Clandening Sr. did, for gravel for railway and road building.

18. Bill Assu, grandson of Billy Assu, provided this information. See also Robert Galois, *Kwakwaka'wakw Settlements, 1775–1920: A Geographical Analysis and Gazetteer* (Vancouver: UBC Press, 1994), p. 274.

19. Reginald Pidcock, *Adventures on Vancouver Island, 1862–1868*, unpublished manuscript, BC Archives, MS-0728, Pidcock family collection.

20. *Victoria Colonist*, September 4, 1886.

21. Notes made in conversation with George Hugh Pidcock by Ruth Barnett, in her collection given to the author in trust to later deposit in the Museum at Campbell River Archives.

22. Reginald Pidcock took a keen interest in a sawmill operated in Alert Bay by the Anglican Church, with Native labour. He also made careful notes on the operation of a cannery and a sawmill he toured in 1884. He could see the potential of industrial development, based upon the rich resources of the province, and though he didn't raise the capital needed during his lifetime his sons fulfilled his vision.

23. An anonymous Quadra Islander wrote to the *Nanaimo Free Press* on August 19, 1890: "The pioneer settler is an American Mr. Chas Dallis [*sic*] from Missouri. Charley has been here four or five years and has quite a stock of cattle and hogs . . ."

24. Heriot Bay was alternately called Dallasville in the 1890s. The last time it was referred to as Dallasville was in the 1901 directory.

25. "The centre of the island," wrote Anna (Walsh) Joyce in her memoirs, "was settled by some miners after the explosion in Nanaimo

in 1887." She names the three she recalled, who "remained to improve their holdings": Jack Smith, Jack Bryant and Bryant's partner John Dauton Dixon. The other Nanimo miners who came to the island were Thomas Bell, William Hughes and Bob Hall.

Chapter Four: The Rancher Takes a Wife

1. *Comox Argus*, January 23, 1924.

2. Eric Duncan, *Fifty-Seven Years in the Comox Valley* (Courtenay: Comox Argus, 1934; reprinted by the Comox Books Division of Eric Duncan Literary Properties, 1979), p. 35.

3. *Nanaimo Free Press*, October 30, 1886: "Taken Up Land—Messrs. R. Hall and J. Williams returned yesterday having staked off a section of land apiece near Cape Mudge. They will return to their locations in a few weeks."

4. Thomas Leask may have been in the region as early as 1886, when someone of that name appears in Comox Valley records and as a labourer for surveyor George Drabble.

5. Rene Harding, "The Gift Canoe," *Victoria Colonist*, Museum at Campbell River Archives, vertical file, clipping with no date.

6. Billy Assu is quoted in several biographical sketches as saying he wasn't sure of his exact birth date, but in the 1911 census he estimated the year as 1869. Yet when birth certificates were issued for Native people in 1940 he estimated the year as 1873. In a letter to the *Campbell River Courier* in 1956 he said he was born in 1870, and his family listed the year as 1869 on his death certificate. His son Harry Assu gives 1867 as the year in his autobiography.

7. There are various spellings for her Native name. An alternative is Klabenaka. This spelling comes from the 1901 census.

8. Not much was recorded about Annie's family. When Billy Assu gave a model pole to Premier Byron Johnson in 1951, he was quoted in the *Campbell River Courier* of March 14, 1951, to have said the whale figure on the bottom came from his maternal grandfather, Na-Na-Chugusch, who was from "Qui-sua-quiiliis at the north end of Vancouver Island." His mother Annie, however, appears to have been raised at Cape Mudge, where she had three sisters. Annie's sister Lottie

Price said on her marriage certificate that her father's name was Thelhit and her mother's name was Quataquast. Harry Assu, in his autobiography, said Billy's Village Island relatives included Emma Cranmer.

9. James Martin Smith of the We Wai Kai Band in Campbell River wrote a letter to the Rotary Club, dated July 21, 1956, saying Assu was the son of an Italian. See Museum at Campbell River Archives, manuscript collection, 87-29.

10. Mildred Valley Thornton, *Vancouver Sun*, January 12, 1952.

11. This attendance estimate is probably exaggerated as the Native population was probably too low to support such a number.

12. "They soon spotted the dusky warriors they were after, with the exception of Gin'eral Arso, the chief offender and his son," said the *Weekly News-Advertiser* of Vancouver, November 17, 1892.

13. *Nanaimo Free Press*, April 14, 1893: "Six Months. Bill Assu, one of the Indians arrested at Cape Mudge, on the charge of participating in the Valdez Island whiskey trouble, was tried yesterday on the S.S. Joan by Magistrate Pedcock, and sentenced to six months imprisonment. He was brought down on the Joan this afternoon and locked up in the Provincial jail. Constables Maitland, Dougall and McLeod came down with him." As this report appeared many months after the arrest at his father's potlatch it's not clear if Billy's jail sentence was the result of that charge or a new offence.

14. In the 1901 census English names were not given, but the Assus' eldest daughter, Na gi li tsum Ka, was said to have been born in 1898 and his second daughter, Num pan Kwa a Kwa, was born in 1900. In the 1911 census Lucy's birth year was listed as 1894. Her headstone in the Cape Mudge Cemetery says she was born in 1895.

15. The exact date of death for Wamish's eldest son was not recorded. Billy Assu recalled in later years that he became a chief when he was twenty-four, which would be around 1893, the same year he held the very large potlach reported in the *Colonist*. There is a note in Indian Agent Pidcock's 1897 report saying the son of a We Wai Kai chief died, but he does not provide the man's name. Agnes Walker, the Methodist missionary, wrote in her memoirs that a chief's son and his friend died in 1897, as the result of alcohol abuse.

16. "Chief Billy Assu Tells of Early Days," *Campbell River Courier*, October 31, 1956.

17. Bill Quocksister changed his surname to Roberts when he enlisted to serve in World War I. He was born in 1899, some years after the estimated date of Frank Nagaghu's death. Bill Roberts's nephew, long-standing elected band chief Ralph Dick, says Bill's mother held a potlatch following the death of Wamish to give her son her father's positions and names.

18. As early as 1898 the Department of Indian Affairs puzzled over the fact that the Cape Mudge people chose the Methodist faith, in spite of the fact that the Kwakwa̱ka̱'wakw people to the north were mainly Anglican. A DIA report cited in the *Victoria Colonist* on December 17, 1898 said: "He supposes they may have come under the influence of Canon Good, who at the time was doing work among the Nanaimo Indians." Billy Assu recalled, in an interview later in life, that he attended a Methodist convention in "the city," and though he didn't say where, it may have been in Nanaimo.

19. Methodist missionary Agnes Walker noted in her memoirs that Wamish was a devout Christian.

20. This information comes from notes made in conversation with Billy Assu by the Walkers, who were Methodist missionaries. See the Joy (Walker) Huntley collection and the Billy Assu vertical file, Museum at Campbell River Archives. Billy Assu's obituary in the *Vancouver Sun* of February 20, 1965 (p. 24) says Assu boarded a mission boat anchored in Duncan Bay and asked for a missionary and a teacher at Cape Mudge.

21. R.H. Pidcock's diary, April 20, 1888.

22. Letter to the editor, *Campbell River Courier*, December 9, 1953.

23. Agnes Walker did not specifically name Billy Assu in her memoirs as the man who built the first Euro-Canadian-style house, but the details suggest it was Assu: "One young man, who is an intelligent half-breed . . . built a neat cottage. By the tribe, it was a white-man's house, and so the owner had to pay the penalty of departure from the ways and traditions of his people . . ."

Chapter Five: Quathiaski Cove—The Hub for Quadra Island and the Discovery Passage

1. Fred Nunns mentioned in his diary on March 13, 1892, that one thousand dollars was allocated for a wharf in Quathiaski Cove. See Museum at Campbell River Archives, Helen Mitchell typescript, p. 54.

2. Anna (Walsh) Joyce's memoirs, Museum at Campbell River Archives, manuscript collection, 77–79.

3. Taped interview with Katie (Walker) Clarke in May 1978, Museum at Campbell River Archives, Tape A133-1.

4. Though Tom Bell is not listed in postal records as a postmaster, he filled the position, with or without the meagre government stipend. He's referred to as the island's first postmaster in Fred Nunns's diary (Museum at Campbell River Archives, 77-1), in the 1892 directory listing for Valdes Island and by contemporaries such as Katie (Walker) Clarke (Museum at Campbell River Archives, Katie Clarke vertical files).

5. In the 1891 provincial directory, there were two Quadra Island residents in the Comox listings: John Bryant and Charlie Dallas. In 1892 Quadra Island was described as a community for the first time, but no names were given. In 1893, when the directory finally included names for Quadra, Tom Bell was listed as the postmaster.

6. Eliza and William Hughes did not legally marry until 1910 in Vancouver, just two years before William died.

7. *Comox Argus*, November 17, 1927.

8. Katie (Walker) Clarke's memoirs, Museum at Campbell River Archives, 87-66.

9. Vital statistics, death certificate for Mary Hilton, June 24, 1896, BC Archives, says she died in Vancouver. The Quadra Island columnist for Vancouver's *Weekly News-Advertiser* on July 8, 1896 reports that her death occurred on the island.

10. Anna once wrote an article for the *Comox Argus* newspaper on practical nursing tips, and her descendants wonder if she went to New York to study nursing. Very little is known about her Swiss childhood or her years in New York, where at least one of her cousins lived, but various family members were doctors. Her cousin Dr. Alexis Carrel was a Nobel Prize–winning surgeon based in the US.

11. William Pidcock's obituary says he moved to Quadra Island in 1890. He pre-empted land in Quathiaski Cove in his own name in 1892.

12. *Comox Valley Weekly News*, January 3, 1894.

13. Agnes Walker's diary, BC Archives, F/7/W15 and F/7/W15A1. See also the *Vancouver Weekly News-Advertiser*, October 9, 1895, and the *Victoria Colonist*, September 26, 1895.

14. The anonymous Quadra Island columnist for the *Vancouver Weekly News-Advertiser* sometimes mentioned the school. An October 30, 1895, article listed how many students were in attendance.

15. Katie (Walker) Clarke collection, Museum at Campbell River Archives, 87-66.

16. The wharf at Quathiaski Cove was still in place on May 6, 1896, when the *Vancouver Weekly News-Advertiser* columnist wrote: "There is a wharf now on the west side at Quathiaski Cove, which is neither useful nor ornamental. Anything that is landed on it has to be taken off again by either raft or boat, and there is a rumor that the government intends repairing it this Summer . . ."

17. In one of Reginald Pidcock's letters to Indian Affairs, however, he said his sons took over the store in April 1898.

Chapter Six: A Tale of Two Villages

1. According to the 1891 census Dallas had two one-room "shanties" on his property.

2. Journeyman carpenter Robert Willson worked with Hosea Bull in Steveston and met him again at Heriot Bay, where he helped Bull build his store in about 1894.

3. In the 1911 census Hosea Bull was reported to have come to Canada in 1887. The first directory listing for him is in Steveston in 1889, where he worked as a bookkeeper.

4. Sheila Bull telephone interview with the author, May 5, 2001.

5. Samuel Bull West was sometimes mentioned in the Quadra Island column in Vancouver's *Weekly News-Advertiser*. Though he lived with the Bulls, Cordelia did not name him in her will, as she did for the son she adopted a few years after they arrived on Quadra. Samuel was

listed as a Bull in the directories for Heriot Bay through the 1890s but as an adult he made a permanent switch to West. He never married and at the time of the 1911 census he was a logger in Rock Bay, where he later committed suicide.

6. Cecil Bull's death certificate, completed by his wife, says he was born November 5, 1895, in Vancouver, BC. His adoptive mother, Cordelia Bull, listed Cecil's birth date in her will as December 5, 1897. See probate records, BC Archives.

7. Aleen appears to have been the only one of the Hughes children with a Salish name.

8. Katie (Walker) Clarke's memoirs, Museum at Campbell River Archives, 87-66.

9. Ruth (Pidcock) Barnett found Pidcock Brothers papers dated June 5, 1900, that listed the members of the firm as Alice Pidcock, W.T. Pidcock, Harry Pidcock, Reginald Pidcock and George Hugh Pidcock.

10. For more details on this story see Jeanette Taylor's *Tidal Passages: A History of the Discovery Islands* (Madeira Park, BC: Harbour Publishing, 2008), p. 256.

11. The death of a Native woman in 1907 involved the purchase of liquor at the Heriot Bay Hotel, which by then was licensed. No other information has come to light to establish when Hosea finally secured a licence.

Chapter Seven: New Settlements on Northern Quadra Island

1. There was a Hugh Grant who was prominent in the Comox Valley, but he does not appear to have been related to the Hugh Grant of Discovery Passage. A Hugh Grant married a Kispiox (Prince Rupert area) woman in 1885 and had two children. The children were born between 1887 and 1889 near Prince Rupert, when Hugh Grant lived on the Discovery Islands.

2. Department of Indian Affairs records, BC Archives, Kwawkewlth Agency, GR 2043.

3. Notes from A.F. Lloyd's diaries provided by his daughter Gwynedd Bartram, Museum at Campbell River Archives.

4. Donnie Haas lived on a floathouse on Village Bay Lake prior to

1920, as he told historian Richard Mackie, when his father logged for the Moffats. In the middle of the night they found themselves on dry land after the Native group blew up the dam on Village Bay Creek.

5. Irene (Stenfors) Stramberg recalled in Helen Mitchell's "Remember When?" column in the *Campbell River Courier*, undated clipping, that the Hastings Company started work in Granite Bay in 1894.

6. Ken Drushka, *Working in the Woods: A History of Logging on the West Coast* (Madeira Park, BC: Harbour Publishing, 1992), p. 69. In the 1903 voters' list for Granite Bay "Michael Green, locomotive engineer" is listed among the loggers, woodsmen, blacksmiths and teamsters.

7. The 1906 voters' list has forty names for Granite Bay, most of them loggers, and there are about the same number again on the 1907 list. Not all of the crew would have registered to vote so it's likely there were many more loggers on the payroll. In 1910, when Granite Bay was first listed in the provincial directory, there are twenty-nine people, most of them loggers.

8. Robert D. Turner, *Logging by Rail: The British Columbia Story* (Victoria: Sono Nis Press, 1990), p. 21.

9. *The Log*, Columbia Coast Mission, December 1908, p. 12.

10. Yeatman Collection, Museum at Campbell River Archives, 77-25.

11. John Antle's memoirs, copy, Museum at Campbell River Archives, pp. 92–93. A.W. Vowell turned a blind eye to both prostitution and potlatching, so little changed during his tenure. See *Chiefly Feasts: The Enduring Kwakiutl Potlatch*, ed. Aldona Jonaitis (Vancouver: Douglas & McIntyre, 1991).

12. *The Log*, Columbia Coast Mission, April 1906.

13. Irene (Stenfors) Stramberg recalled in an interview with Helen Mitchell that it was the Yukon Gold Rush that attracted her father. Her daughter Vida said it was a combination of that and Sointula—plus the fact that Canada was heavily promoted in Finland as the land of plenty.

14. The Larsens (an older couple with no children) registered for their neighbouring pre-emption on the same day as Wilho and Maria Stenfors, on January 19, 1903.

15. Land registry records, BC Archives, as reported to Helen Mitchell in 1968, Museum at Campbell River Archives 77-1.

16. Interview notes with Reino Luoma, March 1975, Museum at Campbell River Archives. A *Campbell River Courier* article of April 11, 1953 about Emil and Amanda Luoma's anniversary says they were married in Finland in 1902 and came to Granite Bay in 1907.

17. There is no death certificate for Konstantin Wilhelm Stenfors registered in vital statistics at the BC Archives, but by the 1911 census Maria was listed on her own, as the head of her household at Granite Bay, with three children to care for, aged eight to twelve. Arthur was back at work again by 1911, in one of the Hastings camps. Vida (Stramberg) Carlson thinks Konstantin Stenfors died when she was about one (in 1911) but research notes compiled by Campbell River historian Helen Mitchell from an interview with Irene (Stenfors) Stramberg suggest he died in the 1920s at the age of sixty.

18. In the 1901 census William Stramberg was working in a large logging camp on Thurlow Island, but he seems to have moved to Granite Bay later that year. In an interview conducted by Helen Mitchell, Irene (Stenfors) Stramberg recalled that William arrived in Granite Bay in 1901. See Museum at Campbell River Archives, 77-1 (f).

19. Hosea Bull may have thought of entering a partnership with his friend and sometime employee Frank Gagne, who wrote to the superintendent of police in 1909 to discuss the possibility of getting a liquor licence for a hotel in Granite Bay. See BC Archives, GR0093, liquor-licensing records.

20. *The Log*, Columbia Coast Mission, July 1908, p. 6, and October 1908, p. 9.

21. Moses Ireland purchased the property in 1889 and held it until he finally moved his family there in 1901.

22. *Victoria Colonist*, May 9, 1905.

23. For more on Lilly Joy Ward and the Ireland family see the Cortes Island and Read Island chapters of Jeanette Taylor's *Tidal Passages: A History of the Discovery Islands* (Madeira Park, BC: Harbour Publishing, 2008).

24. In the 1912 voters' list John O'Neil is listed as the hotelkeeper and Hugh Smalley as the bartender.

Chapter Eight: The Slippery Quadra Island Postmaster

1. A July 5, 1892, ad in New Zealand's *Inangahua Herald* says, "Mrs. Dick begs to notify the public of Reefton and surrounding districts that she has taken the above centrally situated premises. The Hotel has been newly renovated, and offers every comfort to visitors. Wines, Ales, spirits etc, of selected and superior brands only in stock." Helen's mother and stepfather ran a hotel when she was in her late teens.

2. *New Zealand Mail*, November 3, 1898.

3. The exact date of Helen's arrival in the Pacific Northwest has not yet been determined. She may have lived in Seattle for the first few years, where Hosea's granddaughter, Sheila Bull, said Helen ran a brothel. In the 1911 census Helen said she came to Canada in 1903, just a few years prior to her marriage to Hosea. The fact that her nephew Albert Ross came to Canada earlier may have been another reason for her move to this particular part of the world.

4. The photograph MCR 4356, Yeatman collection, is dated 1902 and Katie (Walker) Clarke recalled that the wharf was built in 1902–1903, in a letter to her sister Joy (Walker) Huntley in 1958. See Museum at Campbell River Archives.

5. *Victoria Colonist*, May 6, 1904, p. 3.

6. For more on the murder of Annie Assu see the Sonora and Maurelle Islands chapter of Jeanette Taylor's *Tidal Passages: A History of the Discovery Islands* (Madeira Park, BC: Harbour Publishing, 2008).

7. There is a John Hannacher, logger, in provincial directory listings for Heriot Bay from 1899 to 1910. An Irish logger named "Henigar" fathered several children with a We Wai Kai partner.

Chapter Nine: The Finest Salmon-Fishing Waters in the World

1. John Antle wrote in his memoirs that the Pidcocks had just started work on building their cannery in Quathiaski Cove the first time he visited there in June 1904. See John Antle, unpublished memoirs, copy, Museum at Campbell River Archives, p. 37.

2. T.W. Lambert, *Fishing in British Columbia, with a Chapter on Tuna Fishing at Santa Carolina* (London: H. Cox, 1907), p.103. The number of fish caught likely applied to the whole handline fleet. The Pidcock family member wasn't named by Lambert, but it may have been George (Hugh) Pidcock, whom the *Colonist* of August 12, 1905, said was the top fisherman in Quathiaski Cove. "Mr. Pidcock studies the streams, tide rips and winds like a book and understands better than all competitors where the fish are . . ."

3. Wamish's estimated birth year is a few years off from what was in the 1881 census, when he was said to have been born in 1829, but census spellings and dates were approximate and Native people did not calculate their ages using the European calendar.

4. In the June 1908 issue of the Columbia Coast Mission's newsletter, *The Log*, Reverend Antle wrote that the cannery was sold to Anderson and Comeau. "They have already begun operations, under the experienced supervision of Mr. Fritz Rathgerber." Management of the post office was not, however, transferred from Atkins to Anderson until May 1, 1909, which suggests he stayed on for some time after the cannery sale.

5. *The Log*, Columbia Coat Mission, June 1908, p. 12.

6. Harry Assu interview with the author, May 6, 1988.

7. John Antle, *The Log*, Columbia Coast Mission, 1910.

8. Harry Assu, in his autobiography, said Bill Nye was manager of the cannery. He was married to Harry's maternal aunt Pauline. However, in the 1911 census the man's name is Albert Nye.

9. George Pidcock wrote "Anderson wanting to buy mill site" in his diary on October 17, 1911.

10. Obituary for George Hugh Pidcock, BC Archives.

11. Sir John Rogers, *Sport in Vancouver and Newfoundland* (London: Bell, 1912).

12. George Pidcock interview, Ruth Barnett collection.

Chapter Ten: The Land of Milk, Honey, Canned Fish, Giant Firs and Precious Spuds

1. Harry Assu with Joy Inglis, *Assu of Cape Mudge: Recollections of a Coastal Indian Chief* (Vancouver: UBC Press, 1989), p. 57.

2. Francis Dickie, "Great Chieftain of Wee-Wai-Kis," *Colonist*, March 21, 1965.

3. Department of Indian Affairs, Kwakiutl Agency report, 1911.

4. A system of electing chiefs was not instituted until 1951.

5. *Victoria Colonist*, November 8, 1914, p. 6.

6. Archie Walker, *A Moment in Time as it was on Quadra Island when it was Called Valdez Island*, unpublished manuscript, Museum at Campbell River Archives, 87-34.

7. Mrs. Walker, "St. John's Church at Quathiaski, Story of its Building," *Comox Argus*, October 24, 1929, and "The Forgotten Church at Quathiaski Cove, Mrs. R.J. Walker Tells the Story of St. John's," *Comox Argus*, May 23, 1951.

8. *Comox Argus*, July 25, 1918.

9. Doreen Ursula Walker Lewis, "The Walker Heritage, a family history," Calgary, AB, 1997, p. 53.

10. Mrs. R.J. Walker, "St. John's Church at Quathiaski," *Comox Argus*, October 24, 1929.

11. Mrs. A. Joyce, "Valdez Island Community Club," *Comox Argus*, October 31, 1929.

12. *Campbell River Courier*, "Personality of the Week," February 7, 1951.

13. *Victoria Colonist*, November 4, 1903.

14. These figures come from a report of the fishing season published in the *Comox Argus* on July 21, 1927.

15. Reverend Robert C. Scott, *My Captain Oliver: A Story of Two Missionaries on the BC Coast* (Toronto: United Church of Canada, 1947).

16. "Tea Cup Stories, Episodes in the Social History of Valdez Island," *Comox Argus*, April 19, 1928, and "Quadra Island W.I. Birthday, 50th Anniversary Celebrated," *Comox Argus*, March 6, 1947.

17. Reverend Robert C. Scott, *My Captain Oliver: A Story of Two*

Missionaries on the BC Coast (Toronto: United Church of Canada, 1947).

18. Notes made for Billy Assu's "A Recollection of the Life of Johnny Dick," Museum at Campbell River Archives, 87-82.

19. *Campbell River Upper Islander*, January 17, 1970.

20. Candy-Lea (Ridley) Chickite, "Here Come the Brides!, Mass Marriage at the Cape Mudge Indian Village," *Musings* vol. 21, no. 1 (January 2002). The couples married in unison were Daniel Assu and Lilly Quatell, John Dick Jr. and Maggie Frank, John Ferry and Jenny Charles, Samuel Lewis and Jennie Naknakim, Thomas Price and Lottie Thelhit, John Quocksister and Susan Assu, and Charles Seward and Emily Britchard.

21. Helen Codere, *Fighting with Property: A Study of Kwakiutl Potlatching and Warfare 1792–1930* (Seattle: University of Washington Press, 1950).

22. *Victoria Colonist*, January 18, 1922, p. 2.

23. Marie Mauzé, *Le fils de Wakai, Une histoire des Indiens Lekwiltoq* (Paris: Editions Recherche sur les Civilisations, 1992), pp. 199–201.

24. "New School for Quathiaski Cove," *Comox Argus*, August 9, 1923.

25. Grace (Willson) McPherson, in an interview with Margo McLoughlin.

26. Margaret (Hall) Corbett interview with Jean Barman, July 29, 1992.

27. "Comely Daughters of Comox, Valdez Island is Largest of 28 Lying Between Mainland and Vancouver Island," *Comox Argus*, July 1, 1920.

28. Eve (Willson) Eade's memoirs, Museum at Campbell River Archives, 88-22.

Chapter Eleven: The Dirty Thirties

1. Donald Capon School reunion notes, 1993.

2. Lisa Chason, unpublished biography of Mary (Leask) Joyce.

3. "Comely Daughters of Comox, Valdez Island is Largest of 28

Lying Between Mainland and Vancouver Island," *Comox Argus*, July 1, 1920.

4. Henry Bull was listed in the 1918 directory for Granite Bay; as there is a gap in directory listings from 1910 to 1918 it's not possible to determine exactly when he arrived.

5. *Comox Argus*, February 23, 1922, March 30, 1922, August 4, 1932, and December 8, 1932.

6. Information provided by historian Richard Mackie, author of *Island Timber: A Social History of the Comox Logging Company, Vancouver Island* (Victoria: Sono Nis Press, 2000) and *Mountain Timber: The Comox Logging Company in the Vancouver Island Mountains* (Vancouver: Sono Nis Press, forthcoming).

7. Dianne Newell, *Tangled Webs of History: Indians and the Law in Canada's Pacific Coast Fisheries* (Toronto: University of Toronto Press, 1993), p. 98, and Cicely Lyons, *Salmon Our Heritage: The Story of a Province and an Industry* (Vancouver: BC Packers, 1969), p. 354.

8. Information from Peter Chew, 2008. His fascinating life in China during the Japanese occupation is being documented on film by his daughter Patricia Chew.

9. Jim Foort, *Family Matters One* (1991) and *Family Matters Two* (2000), published by and available from the author.

10. *Comox Argus*, April 27, 1933.

11. Fay and Milton Wong owned this property in 2009, when they allocated a large area for use as a community garden.

12. *Comox Argus*, July 15, 1943.

13. *Comox Argus*, October 22, 1931.

14. *Comox Argus*, March 8, 1934.

Chapter Twelve: Adapting to a New Era

1. In a letter to the editor published in the *Campbell River Courier* December 5, 1956, Estelle Rose estimated the population at one thousand, as did a few others during the ferry campaign. On May 25, 1955, a writer for the *Courier* gave the population as approximately six hundred.

2. J.D. Clandening was listed under Quathiaski Cove in the provincial directory of 1923.

3. Brian Brett, in an e-mail to the author.

4. See Various Artists, *Indian Music of the Pacific Northwest Coast*, Folkways Records, Smithsonian Center for Folklife and Cultural Heritage. To purchase or sample the album, which features many songs by Billy Assu and one that includes Mary Wamish, visit www.smithsonianglobalsound.org.

Chapter Thirteen: Going Back to the Land

1. *Discovery Passage*, August 18, 1972.

2. *Discovery Passage*, August 17–30, 1973.

3. The ten-acre freeze was in place when Don Huntley wrote to the Regional District with a request to review the policy and other regional government controls. *Victoria Colonist*, October 24, 1970.

4. Minutes of the Quadra Island Residents Action Committee meeting of April 12, 1971, with Lloyd McIlwain in the chair.

5. *Discovery Passage*, February 2, 1973.

6. While newspaper articles of the day say one shack was razed prior to the confrontation, resident Bill Nutting said it was only a log on fire.

Index